SPURS'
UNSUNG
HERO

OF THE GLORY GLORY YEARS

SPURS' UNSUNG HERO

OF THE GLORY GLORY YEARS

My Autobiography
Terry Dyson
with Mike Donovan

Foreword by Cliff Jones

First published by Pitch Publishing, 2015

Pitch Publishing
A2 Yeoman Gate
Yeoman Way
Durrington
BN13 3QZ
www.pitchpublishing.co.uk

© Terry Dyson and Mike Donovan, 2015

A CIP catalogue record is available for this book
from the British Library.

ISBN 978-178531-012-6

Typesetting and origination by Pitch Publishing

Printed and bound by
CPI Group (UK) Ltd, Croydon, CR0 4YY

Contents

*To all Tottenham
Hotspur supporters —
the most important
people at the club.*

Acknowledgements

THERE ARE a lot of people I would like to thank for helping me through my 80 years on this planet. They go way back to my mum and dad for giving me such a wonderful upbringing; my brother John for always being there for me; and schoolteacher Bruce Rolls who helped me so much. Of course, there is my wife Kay, who does not like such attention, and my sons Neil, Barry and Mark and all my wonderful grandchildren who deserve credit. I'd also like to thank my friends down the years for some marvellous times.

Professionally there are many I owe a debt of gratitude, namely the mystery scout who spotted me and launched my professional football career. Besides the supporters, all those massive influences at Tottenham Hotspur, such as Bill Nicholson, Eddie Baily, Danny Blanchflower, Dave Mackay and so many more I'd fill up my allotted space listing them.

To those at Fulham, like Vic Buckingham and Bobby Robson. To Colchester United manager Dick Graham, who had his ways but helped me extend my professional career. And those in non-league like Eddie Presland.

Thank you Jackie Price and John Page for being huge parts of my career in education. I'm also grateful to all at Pitch Publishing.

Lastly, I must mention Mike Donovan for believing my life story was worth telling and working so hard to help me put it together and making the process so enjoyable.

Mike has acknowledgements of his own. He writes, 'I'd first like to dedicate my role in this book to – as well as acknowledge – Andy Porter, the kind, helpful, selfless and knowledgeable Tottenham Hotspur historian who passed away in October 2014 aged 54. He had thoughtfully agreed to check the manuscript like he had done when I ghost-wrote Darren Anderton's autobiography and *Spurs' Greatest Games*. His input always gave my work credence.

'I wish to thank Terry Dyson and his wife Kay for their unsurpassable hospitality, lovely company and unending co-operation in getting the job done, along with supplying photographs, memorabilia, contacts, tea, sandwiches and lots of laughs. And to Cliff Jones, Terry's Spurs team-mate in the glory days, for his foreword.

'I am grateful to Terry and Kay's sons Neil, Barry and Mark, plus Terry's brother John for providing personal insights which shone the light on the real Terry Dyson; the warm, affable individual who deserves to be recognised as a Tottenham Hotspur legend.

'Bill Pierce for supplying stats on Terry's professional playing career. Mike McNamara for his sterling work on the illustrations.

'I would like to thank the Bruce Castle Museum (Haringey Culture Library and Learning) close to White Hart Lane for supplying *Tottenham Herald* newspapers and other sources of reference to aid the search for detail, from Spurs' first to reserves to A team, in particular Valerie Crosby who also informed me how her grandfather was part of the 115,000 crowd which saw Spurs take on Sheffield United in the 1901 FA Cup Final at Crystal Palace. And how Henry VIII used to visit a friend in Tottenham!

'I am also beholden to Bob Goodwin's excellent *Tottenham Hotspur The Complete Record* (DB Publishing), *Fulham The Complete Record* (also DB) by Dennis Turner, who sadly passed on in 2014, and Jeff Whitehead's *Colchester United: From Graham to Whitton: A Complete Record* (Desert Island).

'Thanks to John Fennelly and Victoria Howarth at Tottenham Hotspur for their support. Rob White and Julie Welch for *The Ghost: Search for my Father* (Yellow Jersey); Brian Scovell for *Football's Perfectionist*, his biography on Bill Nicholson (John Blake); *The Double and Before* by Danny Blanchflower (Nicholas Kaye); *And The Spurs Go Marching On* by Phil Soar (Hamlyn); Colin Gibson and Harry Harris's *Spurs Glory Glory Nights* (Cockerel Books); *The Double* by Ken Ferris (Mainstream); *61 Spurs Double* (Vision Sports); *Football My Life* by Ron Burgess (Souvenir); *Lilywhite*, *Team* and *Backpass* magazines.

'Paul and Jane Camillin and all at Pitch Publishing for believing in the project. Mentor Kevin Brennan for his invaluable advice.

'Thanks to *The Sun* for helping me keep the wolf from the door with their match orders. My beautiful Rosie, lovely son Matthew, Mark Friedlander, Tony Harris, David and Sue Harley, Kevin and Pauline Rogers, Nick and Jan Saloman, Glen and Lynn Bowen-Ward, Kate and Keith Howells, Mims, brother Sean, sister Christine, Charlie, Daniel and Rebecca (congrats on baby Louisa Ann), the rest of the family, Adrian Shaw, Paul and Eliza, Marc and Louise, Graham, Mark Burgess, the Loughton five-a-siders, Jean and Chris and the rest of the Bexhill Mob, The Beatles and 6 Music BBC Radio.'

Foreword

I KEEP in touch with Terry.

It might be either to play a game of golf or when Tottenham ask both of us to do a club tour for fans.

Or get together at reunions of surviving members of our glory team. It is always great to see him.

He's a lively character, Terry. Great company.

He was a great team member.

Very popular with the boys and quite a lad. Pretty much an ever-present in the Double-winning team, he had great technical control and a terrific left foot.

He was a very important member of the side.

Terry got his fair share of goals, reaching double figures in the history-making season of 1960/61.

In 244 games for Spurs, Terry scored 68 goals which is a very good return for a winger from any era.

In addition he scored a hat-trick against our big London rivals Arsenal, a feat that has not been achieved by any other Spurs player before or since.

It is always important for a player, a winger in particular, to hit the back of the net.

You don't see many wingers in today's game getting double figures for a season.

He popped up with important goals.

One came in the 1961 FA Cup Final against Leicester City and two in the 1963 European Cup Winners' Cup Final against Atletico Madrid, in which he was the man of the match.

It was a very special night and he was outstanding, giving 100 per cent and showing us he had all the skills. It was his night, no doubt about that.

After that, when we'd be saying, 'Come on Dyson, pull your finger out' during a match, he'd go, 'Oi, remember Rotterdam!' That's his punch line.

He was and is easy to get along with. Terry was a special player and is a special character.

His contribution to our great side will never be forgotten.

As far as the team was concerned, they realised the importance of the skills of Terry, Ron Henry and Peter Baker.

Also, you had other important players who came into the side like Tony Marchi, Mel Hopkins and Terry Medwin.

They don't get the credit they deserve either. Unsung heroes, if you like, of the Double team.

We were just a great squad of players.

The year we did the Double I think we only used 17 players, which is amazing compared with what they do now.

There were no subs in those days. If you got an injury you just had to make a nuisance of yourself.

It was a totally different period.

One of the strengths of our team was that although we all had different temperaments, different personalities and different skills, we were all good pals off the pitch and we took that on to it.

It really worked for us. Fans talk about the Glory Days – they certainly were.

Compared to what Terry and I earned, today's players don't realise how fortunate they are with the amount of money they can earn.

It is money for doing something that they love doing – playing football isn't work.

Our lifestyles were modest in comparison.

We earned more money than the average worker and most of us had modest cars.

But nothing like the top-of-the-range models they drive around in today.

Yet we were fortunate to be a part of those Glory Glory Years.

Our manager Bill Nicholson always used to remind us that the most important people at the club weren't the players, they weren't the management. They were the supporters.

Socially back then, Terry's life and mine were different. While I was married with children, Terry was a single lad. He had a great time. It was the Swinging Sixties, a great time to be young.

We both did National Service, and I'm sure Terry would agree, that National Service was a good thing.

Most of the lads who went in came out a little bit better for it.

It gave us a bit of respect for authority, made us more disciplined and we learned to look after ourselves.

After our professional playing careers were over we worked together in the PE department at Highbury Grove School in Islington surrounded by Gooners!

Blimey, we were only a corner kick away from the Emirates!

FOREWORD

Terry and I have both been fortunate to be a part of those Glory Days at Tottenham under a great manager in Bill Nicholson, 'Sir' Bill.

But you don't know what's around the corner.

You've just got to get on with life and make the best of it and see what happens.

I'm sure Terry thinks the same way.

Let's hope the book goes well for him.

He's a terrific bloke, with a lovely wife and a very nice family.

Cliff Jones
Goffs Oak
Hertfordshire
February 2015

Prologue

I HAVE HAD a full and charmed life. A lovely family, a wife, three children and grandchildren aplenty, wonderful friends and neighbours, a comfortable home, health good enough to get me to my 80th birthday.

And two fulfilling careers. One as a professional footballer with Tottenham Hotspur, Fulham and Colchester United before playing and managing in non-league. And the other in education, partly trying to give disadvantaged children a future.

I have shed a tear for those close, professionally or personally, who have either passed or are struggling with their health and know I've been more fortunate than most.

Also, I can look back on my life without regret because I've tried my best in all areas; as a husband, father, grandfather, teacher and sportsman.

My name, of course, has been made by playing football for a team rated as the best ever club side in Britain and, perhaps, for a season, the world.

And for producing goals crucial to that team fulfilling its potential for glory on the biggest stages for the biggest trophies. Glory achieved in glorious fashion in a time riches and the highest of profiles afforded the leading modern-day footballers were absent.

I had the good fortune to escape serious injury and a manager, Bill Nicholson, who appreciated what I could do for that team. He once said in Ken Ferris's book *The Double*, 'If I had to nominate a player who had the attitude I wanted it was Terry. He needed no motivation.' That comment in itself makes me swell with pride.

I appreciated the opinion of Eddie Baily, who I played with and who returned to assist Bill in October 1963, on my role in the Glory Glory Days. He said, 'I'm telling you, Terry, that you were a key player in that side.'

To the wider public, though, I feel, much of what I achieved in Tottenham Hotspur's Double-winning team of 1961 and, indeed, the tweaked version which became the first in Britain to lift a major European trophy, has largely been buried by time.

The legend of Spurs team-mates such as Dave Mackay, my pal, Danny Blanchflower and tragic John White and the greatest goalscorer of them all, Jimmy Greaves, deservedly grows through audible, visual, posted and printed plaudits.

But, if I am honest, any legendary status I have had has been pretty much limited to Spurs aficionados of a certain age and footballing stattos. In most modern households I am guessing my heroics are largely unsung.

I do not have a problem with that. It is something I do not lose sleep over, and something I don't either expect or dream of having. I'm content that what I achieved has provided me with unforgettable memories no one can take away. I came to my footballing peak – squeezing every last bit of my potential – at the perfect time.

Football might be a team game but you have to accept each side has its high- and low-profile members. That's just the way it is.

Yet I thought it might be interesting to educate those unaware of the part I played in the achievements of the greatest side Spurs, or, arguably, any British club, has ever had (and I make no excuse for recalling my memories of every game that Double season, particularly as so little film of it seems to be about). How I came to be part of the last team from White Hart Lane to lift the premier title. How I came to score in the final to seal the first English First Division championship and FA Cup Double of the 20th century. How I scored two, made two and had the game of my life in the club's biggest Glory Glory Night of all in the 1963 European Cup Winners' Cup Final. And what led up to it all and, indeed, followed – on and off the field. And just what it was like to be in the centre of a football maelstrom that blew everyone away and which continues to blow until this very day. Just ask every member of every Spurs team which succeeded my one.

I enjoyed all my years in the game but nothing to touch my experiences in Spurs' Glory Glory Years.

Terry Dyson
Stevenage
Hertfordshire
February 2015

1

Inner Sanctum

THE SOUND of our studded, muddied boots clattered down the concrete steps and echoed along the indoor corridor as we made our way into the bowels of the stadium away from the hubbub subsiding on the foreign, floodlit field of dreams where glory had just been achieved. All amid banter and backslapping. We reached our dressing room, stumbled inside, switched the light on and closed the door behind us.

The changing area was a fair size and reminded me of my school cloakroom. It had slatted wooden benches and individual pegs screwed into the wall on which we'd hung our outdoor clothes. Steam began to cloud the room, having risen from sweating bodies and dirtied kit and giving off a smell all footballers recognise in their nostrils. Pungent.

No one but the players, manager and staff of Tottenham Hotspur Football Club were allowed in. We were in our inner sanctum sharing privacy after a public celebration. Alone together for a precious 30 minutes before becoming public property once more.

I sat down lost in reverie for a minute or two. Glowing. It was just beautiful. Moments of reminiscence on what had got me into this state of ecstacy. Moments I cherish more than anything else from the experience as I took in what we had done and the part I had played in it.

Not many footballers get the opportunity to play the game of their lives on one of the biggest of stages. I just had – to ensure Spurs became the first British team to lift a major European trophy.

I had scored two, made two and been inspired by the injured Dave Mackay to defend as if my life depended on it to help Spurs seal the 1963 European Cup Winners' Cup by crushing Atletico Madrid 5-1 in the final at the Feyenoord Stadium in Rotterdam.

It was a great feeling as I conjured up the magical highlights of an unforgettable 90 minutes. One of the greatest feelings of my life. Hard to put into words. One of pride and contentment in equal measure. That I'd stood up to the challenge and achieved glory. That'd I'd helped my mates achieve glory. That we'd done it all together for a club we all loved. For its wonderful supporters. I was on a high.

Bill Nicholson, our manager, broke my perfect daydream with a 'well done'. That was more than unusual coming from someone who rarely praised. I gathered myself from the shock and politely told him, 'Thanks very much, Bill.'

I know I got the headlines the following morning, but I was just part of a great team performance. And everyone had played their part.

We had defended very well. Maurice Norman and our full-backs Peter Baker and Ron Henry were outstanding in front of Bill Brown. Jimmy Greaves had grabbed a couple himself. Cliff Jones had been outstanding, while our captain Danny Blanchflower, John White, Tony Marchi, Dave's stand-in, and Bobby Smith were superb.

And Bill Nick recognised that as he went around each and every member of the side offering the same words of praise he'd uttered to me. We had beaten Atletico Madrid in style. That is what had pleased Bill the most. He loved that because he knew that was how our supporters would have wanted us to write our name in British football history.

Our boss had the reputation for being a serious-minded perfectionist – and he was – but in that room that night he was all smiles as he handed out his compliments.

Bobby Smith, our centre-forward and my pal, also decided to dish one out to me, if in rather tongue-in-cheek fashion, laughing, 'You'd better retire now.' I asked, 'What are you talking about?' He replied, 'Well, you'll never play like that again.' And I joked, 'I'm just coming into my prime Bob.'

Another good friend, Dave Mackay, who had done so much to get us to the final but missed it through injury, was in there in his 'civvies'. He might have been devastated at not being out there – and it was such a shame he couldn't play – but he couldn't have been more pleased for us. He wore his heart on his sleeve in private as well as on the field and gave me a massive hug with tears in his eyes. We enjoyed our embrace. It was one of many touching moments. We knew we were experiencing something that didn't happen every day; something wonderful in our lives, something we would always remember.

But there were no high jinks, no people bouncing around the walls, chanting and cheering loudly. The sort of scene you often see on your television today after a cup or title-clinching win, the mystique of the dressing room exposed by outsiders holding cameras.

Yes, we were happy. So happy. We were buzzing with excitement and certainly hadn't calmed down on the inside. There was a lovely atmosphere around the room. But we all sat side by side along the benches having normal conversations about the game we had just taken part in at a normal volume. Nothing serious, just light-hearted chat about this incident or that. We took it in turns to sip the champagne bottle being passed around the room while admiring the huge famous silver trophy Danny had brought in to the room.

People might have assumed some of the players would be noisy and boisterous but they would have largely had the wrong impression of our group. Jimmy has always been portrayed as a chirpy character but in that dressing room the greatest goalscorer the game has ever known was subdued as we nattered within our own four walls. He was a quiet lad, Jim. He had just got on with his game in the final, aware of his role as scorer-in-chief. Danny usually had something to say but he had said his piece before the match – reminding us how good we were in the wake of Bill praising our opponents to the skies. So he too was relatively quiet, certainly not his normal voluble self.

Gradually we stripped down, leaving our grubby, sweat-soaked white shirts, white shorts and white socks to the kit man and padded off barefoot across the muddied floor for a shower to clear off clinging turf and sweat beads while shampooing our matted hair.

Once dressed in our club blazers and ties we were out the door and walked into a restaurant area to grab a sandwich and something to drink. My team-mates' wives were in there – I was still single at the time – and they seemed as pleased as anyone.

I remember Isobel Mackay, Dave's wife, came up to me, and planted a big kiss on my cheek then said 'well done'.

I also bumped into the referee. He shook my hand and said to me, 'Well done. England next for you.' I said, 'Thank you, but it is not up to me.' And he replied, 'You should play.' That was nice of him. He was a highly respected figure in the game. He must have been impressed with how I played.

The celebrations between the players and our supporters continued into the evening at a small club bar next to our hotel. We knew a lot of them because they travelled to away league game around the country and over to the continent for our European ties. We all let our hair down, together as one. It was how it should have been. It was an unbelievable night. And a late one.

I managed a chat with Bill in the bar and he told me again 'well done'. And I replied again, 'Thanks, Bill.' He was made up. People saw him as a dour Yorkshireman but he was forever the romantic when it came to how the game should be played.

The public celebration had well and truly resumed but the main thing I remember are those private moments over the few minutes we spent in the inner sanctum before the hinge of the dressing room door swung back open. I had been caught up in what Danny called 'the rapture of the game'; totally consumed, body and soul. And the emotions stay with me.

There had been a similar scenario two years earlier. My Spurs team had just kicked off the Glory Glory Days at the club by completing the first English First Division and FA Cup Double of the 20th century.

Our history boys had defeated Leicester City 2-0 in the most famous domestic knockout final of them all in front of 100,000 at Wembley Stadium and millions on television with the match broadcast across Europe and the United States. And I had laid on the first goal and scored the second. I was buzzing. We all were. The champagne flowed. We all dived in the communal baths they had at the iconic national stadium, THE home of football. Our laughter rang out, our joy palpable. Having a splashing time. The bath was huge. I nearly went for a swim in it. In fact I did a couple of 'lengths' for a bit of fun.

Bill wasn't as chipper as he would be in Rotterdam. Comments of 'well done' were in short supply. Although we had completed the Double, he was far from satisfied with what we had produced in front of the six-figure crowd and the global televised audience. He had wanted to show the world how good we could be.

If I had expected praise for my goal and assist I had another thing coming. I'd missed a great chance, hadn't I? So the first thing Bill said to me was, 'What about that goal you missed?' I said, 'What about the one I scored?' He said, underlining his point, 'Never mind about that, what about the one you missed.' He was right. I thought at the time, 'Flipping hell, I should have put that in' and admitted, 'I got under it, Bill. I should have scored.' And he said, 'All right, but fancy missing it.'

He was just disappointed about the way we'd played. He was a perfectionist and it hadn't been a great final. Ron Henry didn't get a better reaction when he went up to him afterwards and said, 'We did it, Bill.' And he replied 'Yeah, but it wasn't good, was it?'

But overall there was no question we proved overall that season to be a sensation. We were rated by many best ever British club team because we succeeded by lifting silverware, smashing records and banging in goals with a style the fans loved.

After lifting the European Cup Winners' Cup, we planned to savour all the euphoria, store away the memories and then look forward to next season. We thought we could achieve it all again and have more private dressing room moments of ecstacy.

But Rotterdam proved the last hurrah for the greatest side in Spurs' history. Our last great moment. Danny retired, Dave broke his leg and John was killed. But I will always be grateful to have been a part of it.

2
Great Escapes

ALL THE Glory Glory Days with Spurs – or any days for that matter – would not have happened but for two great escapes in the Second World War. My home town of Malton in Yorkshire remained relatively safe with the enemy targeting other cities with strategic sites. Sirens did used to go off to warn of an air raid. They had an up and down tone. You heard the planes and we used to go down the shelters before they went off again to tell us it was all clear.

We might not have used any of them anyway, opting to stay under a table or whatever in the house. The sirens didn't go off too often, thankfully, because we weren't near shipyards or any other potential targets. And the raids close by remained close by and not on top of us – apart from one incident I remember. It gave me the experience of the realities of war first hand. And it could have cost me my life.

The Doodlebugs – the V-1 bombs with auto-pilots – came over when I was about ten. One crashed literally next door to us. It destroyed the attic of our neighbours' house. It was used as a bedroom, but fortunately no one was home. A few feet over and it could have been us.

Also during the war, I had an illness which could have ended any thoughts I might have had of playing any kind of sport again, let alone of earning my living from football. I was around eight. I'd got quite thin and it was diagnosed that I had contracted rheumatic fever. Something that was supposed to affect your heart. There was a genuine concern I had heart problems. I spent three months in bed. I wasn't allowed to go out; not even allowed to move. For someone who loved to be active it was a nightmare.

But I found consolation listening to the series *Dick Barton – Special Agent* on the radio at 6.45pm every Saturday. It was a godsend. Also, I used to look forward to getting my comics every Friday; *Beano*, *Dandy*, *Wizard* or *Tiger*.

I started to be allowed to get up but could still not go out. Then I was told I would no longer be able to play sport because my problem had affected my heart. I was absolutely distraught.

My mum wanted a second opinion and took me to a doctor's surgery where they tested my heart and everything else. They gave me the news I so desperately wanted to hear; that everything was fine and that I could resume playing sport. I was ecstatic but it had been a bit of a moment to say the least. I had been shocked. Any sporting career – for fun or for a living – being over for a sport-loving youngster before it properly began would have been heartbreaking.

I had no idea how I developed the fever. I don't remember any explanation. There wasn't the available knowledge that there is now. I recall my mum and dad being worried about me. And it seems they had every right to be judging from what I read recently on an NHS website. It posted, 'Rheumatic fever can cause permanent damage to the valves of the heart; this is known as rheumatic heart disease which can lead to serious complications, including heart failure and strokes.'

Also, during the war my mum and dad – who was considered too light to go to war and worked in a munitions factory – took in a couple of evacuees from one of the factories in Middlesbrough, on Teesside, into our home. The town was about 60 miles away and the first big one to be bombed in Britain. The German Luftwaffe came over in May 1940 and one of their bombers dropped 13 in and around the town's steel plant on just one raid. And Middlesbrough's railway station was bombed two years later. In all 200 buildings were destroyed by the end of the hostilities. The girls who stayed with us were certainly better off in the family home in Wentworth Street in our small market town!

ENGLAND WAS distracted by a Royal Wedding on the day I was born, Thursday 29 November 1934. Prince George, the Duke of Kent, the fourth son of King George V, married Princess Marina of Greece and Denmark at Westminster Abbey. And it led to me being called Terence Kent Dyson, the first child of John and Jessie Dyson. Dad was a jockey and mum a waitress. I sported the same coloured hair which earned my father his nickname: Ginger.

Malton was a bit residential and a bit country. Everybody knew everybody. You didn't lock your doors. No one would take advantage. A police officer used to stroll around each night and meet up with his sergeant at midnight to report that nothing untoward had happened. There was a burglary once – and there were murders, as in major ructions rather than actual homicides! It was big news. They got him. I knew the lad – and won't name him – but he was a silly sod.

Generally, it was a lovely, safe, stable environment and the best thing my parents could have given me – and my brother John when he came along eight years later. Wentworth Street was the middle of a row of five terraced houses among similar rows divided by alleyways. We were working-class but owned our own home. I don't think that was unusual. Some could afford to, some couldn't.

I developed a routine when I was old enough for school and attended Malton Primary and then Malton Grammar. I'd come home from a day of study, do my homework, have tea and go out and play until it was dark. You could do that in those days. You were never in danger. As I said, we felt safe.

My friends – there was not one special mate – and I enjoyed a variety of fun activities in those pre-computer times. There was Whips and Tops, in which you wound the 'whip' around a 'top' and pulled it to cause it to spin. We often got out the marbles. Hide and seek was popular. A few of us built a little 'den' in the woods just up the road.

If the season was right it was conkers, using the town's horse chestnut trees for supplies. You know the game. You'd tunnel out a small hole through a conker which had fallen to the ground off a tree and feed a piece of string through it, knotting it at one end and holding it out in front of yourself at chin level. Your opponent, with his or her conker similarly accessorised, whipped their offering through the air in an attempt to smash yours into bits.

If yours survived and, on your turn, you succeeded in reducing your opponent's conker to such a condition, it made your own a 'one-er', then a two-er and so on with each subsequent 'victory' until it – as it always did – got shattered. Some were rumoured to soak their conkers in vinegar to harden them up. But that would be cheating in my book!

There was also sport. It had already started to dominate my life. We played cricket against the walls in the alleyways between the terraces in the summer. Yorkshire was big on the sport – still is. It has produced a lot of top cricketers down the years with the likes of Freddie Truman, Geoff Boycott and Darren Gough coming out of the county, along with Malton Grammar old boy Vic Wilson. When I was growing up the big name was Len Hutton.

We'd either use the walls as chalked goals for football in the winter or go over to a big field to play my favourite sport. I think a farmer owned it, although I never noticed any sheep, cows or crops on the field. We could have got turfed off but we never were. There were loads of us, often enough to make up a 14-a-side game. We picked the teams and off we went – after the ball! All 28 of us! Or however many there were. I know Cliff Jones, my Spurs team-mate and pal, did something similar when he was growing up, but his games were on the beach at Swansea.

WE WERE a close-knit family – but there were no professional footballers in it. The closest was my uncle Maurice. He played a bit locally and ended up cleaning my boots. And he pumped and laced up the balls I played with.

My parents were sporty, though. My mum – who was lovely, by the way – was a runner. She told me how she beat the Yorkshire champion over 100m. Quite a few times. Maybe that was where I got the pace I had as a footballer from.

My dad developed his career as a jockey, becoming a stable lads' boxing champion on the way. Malton was very much a racing as well as market town (and the place Charles Dickens wrote *A Christmas Carol*, incidentally).

Horse race meetings were advertised in Malton as early as 1692 and it now has nearly 20 stables. A link with horses dates back to Roman times. The town stands on the site of a Roman settlement a few miles east of York, one which had a cavalry fort at the hub of road networks all over north and east Yorkshire. Thus the occupying garrison – which could have been originally raised by Julius Caesar himself – kept and bred the horses needed to go into battle on.

Dad rode for trainer Bill Dutton in the town. The handler won the 1928 Grand National on Tipperary Tim as a jockey and saddled Limber Hill to the 1956 Cheltenham Gold Cup.

My dad was a good jockey and used to take me to the races to see him in action. I saw him ride a few winners. I was there trackside going 'come on, dad'. One I remember was at Doncaster because he beat Edgar Britt who was a top jockey then. Dad was on a horse called Ovandel. He came through at the post. I ran to where they came in after they'd pulled up. He didn't know whether he'd won or not because it was a photo finish and I told him, 'You did it dad, you did it.' I was excited. He was delighted. He had that competitive streak and passed it on to me.

He got injured getting caught in starting straps once. There were no starting stalls in those days. Just these four horizontal straps which sprung up. This one time dad's horse smashed into them and he was knocked off and thudded against the ground. Dad didn't do too much damage but was fortunate as there were no skull protection helmets for jockeys to wear in those days. He rode some good horses and won a lot of races – but he was also on some flipping bad ones!

I rode out for Mr Dutton during the school holidays at his Grove Cottage Stables. I started when I was about 13 or 14. I ended up grounded early on, falling off a horse which had taken off on the gallops. It certainly didn't put me off and I used to love going up there.

My ambition was to follow in my dad's footsteps and I was small. But I was also stocky and too heavy. I didn't fancy the wasting I'd have to do such as spending half of my life in a Turkish bath to keep my weight down or watching what I ate all the time because I needed to be on a constant diet. My dad was fortunate in that respect because he was a natural seven stone.

Dad had no interest in football but mine had been growing in either those big multi-sided games over the field or kicking a ball against the wall in the alleyways – and when I got to grammar school, a teacher called Bruce Rolls gave me a lot of encouragement, not just with football.

I remember being pleased I had made it to grammar school after passing an examination at Malton Primary called the 11-plus because places were limited. I was even more pleased to have got a teacher like Mr Rolls. He taught English Language, English Literature – and sports. It was thanks to him I got my English O Levels. He'd given me a big part in a play we put on in the fifth form at an open-air theatre. It was Shakespeare's *A Midsummer Night's Dream*. I was Bottom the Weaver. It was a big part. I had to wear an ass's head! And, of course, learn my lines. Like, 'I will get Peter Quince to write a ballad of this dream: it shall be called Bottom's Dream, because it hath no bottom'. It's on instant recall!

The local paper, the *Malton Gazette and Herald*, was interested enough in our production to send a photographer around to our open-air theatre, where we were performing it, to take pictures. In fact, I've still got a clipping of me acting my part. It has a little write-up underneath it.

When I prepared for my English Lit exam I was unsure whether I'd pass or fail. We'd studied John Bunyan's *Pilgrim's Progress* and Milton's *Samson Agonistes*, based on the Bible tale of Samson and Delilah, as well as *A Midsummer Night's Dream*. Then I looked at the main question and it asked, 'Who said this?' It was quoting Bottom the Weaver! I knew I'd be all right then.

It was the influence Mr Rolls had on me in sport which was to be of most significance for me. He got me playing basketball. I know it is a sport you associate with seven-foot giants but, even though I was close to two feet shorter than the perception, I did okay, although I didn't manage any slam dunks from memory! I enjoyed gymnastics and found I could do all the acrobatics. I also played cricket in the summer and thought myself half-decent as a batter, wicketkeeper and spinner. I enjoyed it. The school had good facilities for the sport and produced Vic Wilson not long before I arrived and he went on to captain Yorkshire and play for the MCC under Len Hutton in the mid-1950s while I was joining Spurs.

But it was Mr Rolls's support of my football which – as you would guess – has proved the most beneficial influence on my life. With a couple of mates, I used to have a kickabout every day after school. Malton Grammar had two pitches – one without nets and a bigger one with them. We weren't allowed on the big one but still enjoyed our sessions.

Mr Rolls ensured all of us interested in playing had a structured development in the game. Part of that came through him running the school football teams. I did not win any competitions representing the school. That was because we stuck to friendlies, playing local rivals like Pickering. Even as a junior, he put me in the senior side.

I used to like playing inside-left because you got more of the ball and were therefore more involved in the game. I was quick and could score goals. I recall scoring some good ones. But I remember Mr Rolls telling me that if I made it then it would be as an outside-left. I believe he was referring to the fact I had good speed. And he was a good judge, because that is exactly what happened.

After I won the Double with Spurs, I went back to the grammar school to present the trophies at the school sports. Mr Rolls was still there and in my speech I mentioned how much he had done for me. I said that without his help and encouragement I would not have achieved what I did.

I meant every word. He gave up his Saturday mornings for free in order for me and my team-mates to get a game of football – for all the time I was there. And that he still had time to get me through my English O Levels. What Mr Rolls did for me is why I would never forget my time at the school. I had a chat with him and he was grateful for my kind words and hopeful what I'd done would inspire the current crop of pupils at the school. I was only too glad to have said what I said.

AS A junior, I played for a grown-up local team in Norton United for a bit but my first senior non-league club was Scarborough, just 18 miles up the road from Malton and the birthplace of Bill Nicholson, my Spurs manager. They were managed by a chap called Reg Horton, a nice man. The facilities weren't good but we trained every Thursday night and looked forward to a game on a Saturday. It was brilliant.

I started to play for their reserves when I was about 16 or 17 before getting in the first team. They were in the Midland League, which was quite decent, and I turned out at inside-left for them on an expenses-only basis, scoring a few goals. I remember one I got one Boxing Day. I hit one from about 25 yards. A bit of a screamer. The local paper, the *Scarborough Evening News*, gave me a write-up because of it. My first one!

A team-mate of mine was Colin Appleton, who captained the Leicester City side Spurs beat in the FA Cup Final to complete the Double. What's the odds of that happening? Fate perhaps. He was a good lad too.

I'd left school aged nearly 17 for a job in an estate agent after staying on for another year in the sixth form to successfully re-sit my Maths O Level. I did a shorthand and typing course at night school to help me tap out the blurbs advertising the houses being bought and sold.

It wasn't my first paid employment, mind. I had got five shillings a month for being an angelic choirboy! I might have even got myself on the recent television programme *The Choir* hosted by Gareth Malone if I'd been a primary school kid today. It was the local St Michael's Church choir. I even performed with it at York Minster, the largest Gothic cathedral in Europe which dates back to 627. Quite a big stage for this little boy.

The truth was, though, I'd have rather gone to watch the town's cricket team play, but my mum insisted I exercised my vocal chords. I was considered to have a good voice. Maybe I missed my vocation and could have become a recording star like Aled Jones.

In the meantime, my dad's riding days were finishing and him and my mum took over a pub in Malton called The Fleece, which was full-on. They had no spare time to come and watch me play but that wasn't a problem for me. It was perfectly understandable and, besides, I was enjoying the football, the playing and the banter, with my team-mates. It was a standard which gave me a good grounding for football at a higher level.

I was becoming more and more interested in football and first became aware of the professional game when I heard the results on a Saturday night on the radio – in the days before television, of course.

And I used to go with friends to York City, which was our nearest Football League club. I'd play for the school in the morning and travel across by bus to Bootham Crescent in the afternoon when they played at home. We even got in to see derby matches against Hull City. Even though they were always all-ticket, we always got one.

We used to stand close to where the players came out. It was brilliant and gave me a real buzz, especially when I saw my first footballing hero come out, Alf Bottom. I saw his 100th goal for York. He was a prolific goalscorer.

3
Life Changer

ONE MATCH changed my life. I had been called up for National Service and my date with destiny came when I played for the Army Amateur XI against the Grenadier Guards at their place in London.

Fortunately for me the Guards played a big part in making me look good. They largely stood like statues and I was able to run around them. The freedom allowed me to use my pace against their lack of it and I was able to score FIVE goals.

Unbeknown to me, Spurs had a scout at the game. And I don't know who he was until this day. The next thing I know is that my battalion sergeant major was bellowing at me, 'Bombardier Dyson please report to my office.' I wondered what I'd done. Whatever it was had got me in trouble. I couldn't guess what is might be.

I walked into his office and saluted the BSM who was sat behind his desk. His voice was quieter and lower than it had been in front of my colleagues back in the barracks. He looked up and told me how Spurs had watched my performance against the Guards and wanted me to go for a trial and would I like to go for it.

It was right out of the blue. A club like Spurs interested in little me? Little being the operative word, of course, in many eyes who had witnessed my football playing career, such as it had been, as I stood 5ft 4in without my boots on. I was chuffed. I didn't need asking twice.

I'd no idea where the Spurs ground was, so I had to ask strangers the way from Woolwich. I was told, 'Get a bus to here, get a train to there and get off at Manor House, then get the 149 bus.'

I was panicking as I came up from the London Underground station at Manor House. I did not know much about London beyond my barracks in Woolwich, far away over the River Thames in the south of the capital. So when I got on a bus after exiting the Piccadilly Line station I had to ask the conductor, 'Can you put me off at the Tottenham Hotspur ground, please?' And, thankfully he did.

It was twilight as I stood on the pavement by the bus stop on Tottenham High Road opposite White Hart Lane, but as I looked across the road I could make out the huge, now replaced, West Stand with the legend 'Tottenham Hotspur Football Club' emblazoned in white letters right along it.

The stand was like a big grey, shadowy battleship rising above a row of modest terraced buildings. My jaw dropped. I had never seen anything like it. Scarborough were to go on to win three FA Trophies and, in the late 1980s be promoted into the Football League under Neil Warnock, but I'd only known the far-from-grand stage of Midland League football with them.

Army football was also a modest arena in comparison. As were, of course, the friendly games I had played for Malton Grammar against local rivals in front of one man and his dog. It was absolutely light years from either kicking a ball about on the streets or slipping on to the big farmer's field back in Malton not that many years before. We might have pretended to be our footballing heroes of the time playing at one of the great stadiums. But it was all pie-in-the-sky kids' stuff.

Now it was happening. I walked down the lane between the White Hart pub on the left-hand corner and the Red House – which dated back to when the stadium was first built in the 19th century and which housed the club's administrative staff – on the right, to the black wrought-iron gates which stretched across the lane and acted as the main entrance to the stadium.

I said to the fellow on the gate, 'I'm playing in a trial.' He directed me to the dressing room. It had been a dry day and the temperature not too low for late in the year as evening descended while I took my steps towards an outer door at the back of the West Stand. I wasn't shaking as I opened it, but it was a big ordeal for me. I kept thinking, 'Blimey, I'm at Tottenham Hotspur.'

I moved down a corridor and found a second door which led into the dressing room. I opened it. All the other players were in there, milling around and chatting. They must have privately wondered, 'Who the hell is this?'

Jimmy Anderson, who had become temporary manager because Arthur Rowe was ill, grabbed me and introduced me to the players, like Alfie Stokes and Johnny Brooks. It was largely a reserve team. They were all friendly, welcoming and encouraging as I was shown where I needed to change.

Suddenly it was time to leave the room. There were some steps down and we shuffled along a corridor underneath the stand before taking more up and out on to the pitch in the corner at the far end. Gulp! This was it.

The trial match was to be played against Crystal Palace under the White Hart Lane lights. It was a mind-boggling as I stepped out to face them in front of quite a few thousand. Not only was I donning the famous Spurs white shirts and navy blue shorts for the first time, but I'd never played under lights.

We drew 1-1 with quite a good side. Players like Alfie and Johnny continued to be helpful and encouraging as I ran around trying to get my bearings and doing the best I could. I don't remember doing anything spectacular although I made our goal from a corner.

They must have been reasonably impressed because Jimmy Anderson offered me another invitation to play. He said, 'I want you to play in a friendly against Cambridge University next week.' It was one of the two annual fixtures Spurs played against the Oxbridge universities before they played each other in the Varsity match at Wembley. I immediately gushed, 'Yes, please.' I did and played quite well, scoring two against Cambridge and then one in the second of the fixtures against Oxford. I joked with myself thinking, 'I'm a bit of all right, me.' Nonetheless, I was happy with the way I'd played.

It was a positive beginning to something I had not even dreamed about a month or two beforehand. I had only known Spurs from when I listened to the football results on the radio as a youngster.

I quickly started to read up on their history. I discovered how they had always maintained a reputation for playing good, attacking, entertaining football from when the club was formed. And they had had a string of iconic figures playing for them.

Sandy Brown, who scored in the 1901 final, was one. He got loads of goals. There was the famous amateur Vivian Woodward, a bit of a Corinthian figure. I don't think there had been that many amateurs since the club went professional. George Robb was to be one I'd soon come across, a teacher who played on the left wing, mainly for home games (more later). There was Arthur Grimsdell, who captained the winning 1921 final, and George Hunt who took the goalscoring record in the 1930s which Bobby Smith would break in the Double-winning season.

There was also another winger called Fanny Walden who was supposed to be good. And Willie Hall. I remember Willie, who got the fastest ever hat-trick for England in four minutes and eventually had both legs amputated. He was ill in hospital after I'd joined Spurs and I was asked to go along with Eddie Baily, a member of the Push and Run side who was still playing at the club, to see him.

THE BRITISH Army had marched into my life when I was 18. I had been happy playing football for Scarborough.

But National Service – a government military service programme – was compulsory in those days so I bade farewell to Scarborough and had to give up my job in the Malton estate agent. I was disappointed at the time.

Life was okay back home but my country needed me to report to the Royal Artillery at Oswestry at the start of a two-year stint (they offered me three, an offer I swiftly declined). Six months of basic training – what a culture shock. And I don't mean getting used to the small Welsh town, one I'd never been to or knew much about. The culture shock – as you might have guessed – was the Army life! It was terrible. So regimented.

The sergeant major came into the barracks and bellowed 'get out of bed' at silly o'clock. We made our beds and then they would come in and tip them up so we had to make it again. Then there were your boots. You had to pile on the spit and polish until they were shining. Then the sergeant major would pick them up and throw them out the window. You would have to retrieve them from the dirt they had fallen in outside and start again.

That sort of thing didn't last long and it eased off, but it was long enough. Did I give them any lip? You must be joking. You just got on with it. But I HATED it. I thought, although I knew I didn't have a choice in the matter, 'I can't handle this for two years.'

You didn't know what day it was at first after being kitted out. We had to march down to the NAAFI to get something to eat and march back. There were marching drills with a pack on your back and more.

We had to get our hair styled into a crewcut. There was one guy from Liverpool who had long hair. Remember it was before the Beatles, also Scousers of course, and the Rolling Stones inspired a generation of youngsters to grow their hair. And the sergeant major did not seem impressed. He shouted, 'Look at that' as he pointed to the guy's lank locks, adding, 'Get THAT sorted out.' It was. By the Army. The Liverpudlian joined the rest of us in the cropped brigade.

I wasn't frightened of the Army life. It was just so completely different to what I was used to. I kept going back to that thought of not being able to deal with it for the next two years. I don't know how but I managed to survive it in the end.

They tried their best to get me to stay on beyond the three months I was due to spend in Oswestry. I'd gone to the gym and did acrobatics over boxes. They were impressed and thought it might be worth extending my stay in order to go on a course to become a PTI. I said 'no'. But I learned how to take apart, put back together and set up a 25lb gun – and fire it on the range. That was a good experience.

I think National Service was useful to a few kids. There were a few villains in Civvy Street. They couldn't mess about. If they did they'd be sent off to Colchester where the Army nick was (and where I would play

31

for the town team). There were a few characters who were good blokes. They weren't all villains.

I was offered a clerk's course job in Woolwich in south London. I could, of course, already type. I wasn't that good at the skill but I was considered a Class One typist. It didn't matter as there was little or no competition for the post. My fellow National Service colleagues were useless at typing. They couldn't do it at all.

I accepted the post and after six weeks on a course the Sergeant in Charge told everyone where they were going next. Everyone that is apart from me. The Army had stations in Korea, with a war there coming to an end, Egypt, where the Suez Crisis was brewing up, and Germany, where the Cold War was going on and squaddies tuned in to hear Jean Metcalfe broadcast on BBC and British Forces Broadcasting radio, 'The time in Britain is 12noon, in Germany it is one o'clock, but home and away it is time for *Two-Way Family Favourites*.'

My mates were sorted for postings abroad. I asked the sergeant, 'Where am I going?' He told me, 'You are staying here.' They put me in charge of all the documents under a civil servant. I had to type out the soldiers' names, numbers and other relevant details to take with them to these foreign lands. Strange to think, my abilities on a keyboard saved me putting my life at risk in service to Queen and country abroad.

The fact I played football too was probably another reason I didn't get to go and possibly get my head blown off. I turned out for the Royal Artillery who had a guy called Mick Grice in charge of the team. He played for West Ham United, a right-winger, like one of his successors at the Boleyn Ground, Harry Redknapp.

We had quite a good team. It included Phil Woosnam, Mick's team-mate at West Ham who went on to captain the Hammers and play internationally for Wales. He was a good inside-forward, bright and talented. Phil, of course, was also one of the pioneers who got football going in the United States of America. He was commissioner of the North American Soccer League from 1969–83, no less. Phil was also inducted into the US National Soccer Hall of Fame – proof there were trailblazers for the game over there before David Beckham.

Phil was an officer and I was only a bombardier. So I had to salute him whenever I saw him! But we were equals when we played together for the RA and the Army Amateur XI.

More significantly, Ron Henry was also a team-mate in the RA. He played outside-left to my inside-left then. I recommended Ron to Spurs. We were both set on the same path.

4

Am-Dram

MOST OF the players in Arthur Rowe's Push and Run team were still at White Hart Lane when I first arrived in December 1954 as an amateur on leave from my National Service stint with the British Army. I'd been aware of Tottenham Hotspur growing up but they were just like any team I had either read about in the newspaper or heard about over the radio. But when I turned up I soon got to know about what they stood for first hand, especially with the legacy laid down by Rowe's side just a few years earlier.

What a team! It was full of good players who played for each other while employing Rowe's philosophy of making it simple, making it a quick and fluid system in which players worked in triangles to retain possession and edge towards an opponent's goal. They'd 'push' to a marked colleague and 'run' for the one-touch return. The wingers, Sonny Walters and Les Medley, would drop deep and link up with their full-backs Alf Ramsey and either Arthur Willis or Charlie Withers, to bemuse opposing full-backs who were unsure about tracking them from their position, thus giving Spurs vital space and time to work in.

The fans loved the Rowe Way, with more than 50,000 regularly flocking to White Hart Lane to watch the Push and Run team achieve back-to-back title triumphs in 1950 and 1951.

The Rowe Way influenced Ferenc Puskas's Magical Magyars who stunned England at Wembley in 1953, Johan Cruyff and Holland's Total Football of the 1970s and Lionel Messi and Barcelona's tiki-taka of the modern day.

And of course, the fact Bill Nicholson and Alf Ramsey, who were still playing on my arrival, were members of the side and went on to show how informed they were by Rowe's ideas as managers; with Bill Nick producing our glory team and Alf, of course, the only England side to lift the World Cup.

Eddie Baily, one of the team's key players, used to tell me when he was Bill's assistant that although the side was always 'Arthur Rowe's Push and Run team', it had nothing to do with Arthur. It was the players. He told me, 'We did it. We showed how it should be played.'

But Rowe, who played for Spurs in the 1930s, had worked hard to fully form ideas he had thrashed around while on a coaching lecture tour of Hungary after being forced to retire prematurely through injury.

He managed to instil them in the team largely made up of players from graduates of Spurs' Northfleet nursery under Peter McWilliam – who managed the club to the 1921 FA Cup – like captain Ron Burgess, Les Bennett, Les Medley and Bill Nick himself, who were, fortunately for Rowe, adept at putting them into action.

But Les Medley retired at the end of the 1952/53 season and returned to Canada where he had been posted by the RAF and met a girl who became his bride. That must have been a big blow to the manager as Les was a prolific scorer for a winger. He top-scored with 18 as Spurs were promoted from the Second Division as champions in 1950 and bagged 11 as they lifted the top-flight crown the following season.

And inspirational left-half Burgess had returned to his native south Wales to play for Swansea in May 1954. I got to hear a lot about Ron from Bill Nicholson. Bill loved him. He thought Ron was as near perfect a footballer as you can get.

Ron has been described as a human dynamo, up and down. He never used to stop. Sadly, I heard he ended up penniless and his wife couldn't afford to bury him when he died. Terrible when you see what players today who couldn't even lace his boots are getting. Eddie Baily organised it so his family got some money (£5,000) from a fund set up to help the Push and Run team players who were struggling financially. The departure of those players left big holes in Rowe's team.

Although I didn't think of it at the time, Medley's departure left an opening that I might have been able to fill as Spurs saw me as a number 11 rather than a number 10 due to my pace. Arthur Willis joined Ron at Swansea while inside-right Les Bennett departed to West Ham in the month I arrived.

But the rest of the famous side were still at the club as players, namely goalkeeper Ted Ditchburn, right- and left-backs Alf Ramsey and Charlie Withers, right-half Bill Nick, centre-half Harry Clarke, right-winger Sonny Walters and centre-forward Len Duquemin, plus Eddie Baily at inside-left. They all treated me well.

Ted had a newsagents. He used to ruck with the customers if they were slow giving over their money. 'C'mon, c'mon', he used to say impatiently having got the right needle. Bit hot-headed was Ted. You could whack your opponents and get away with it back then. That happened with Ted. He used to come out and smack 'em! Brilliant! But a good goalkeeper, a fun lad and great company.

Alf might have finished up managing England to global glory, but back then we used to take the mickey out of him. He was out of Dagenham – where Jimmy Greaves and Terry Venables came from – which was a working-class area of London. People generally spoke with a Cockney-type accent. But Alf had had elocution lessons and spoke poshly. Eddie told him, 'You don't really speak like that, Alf, do you? Come on, Alf, you are talking to us now!' Sonny Walters did a lot of work for Alf when they played together, getting back to be available for a short pass from him.

Harry Clarke didn't miss many matches. He had so many stitched scars from heading the heavy ball with laces which often caused his wounds. He got his eyes cut as well as his head! Eddie Baily was irrepressible, a real character. They were all lovely fellows.

I was honoured to be at a club with such players. A club with such a highly-respected manager who had got the team that mirrored the Spurs tradition for producing teams that entertained while playing an attractive, short passing game. I was proud that I had been able to impress the people in it enough to become a part of it.

But not everything in the garden was rosy at White Hart Lane. The Push and Run team had got old together with some feeling Arthur had remained too loyal to the players due to what they had done for the club – and he was ill. Arthur was a lovely man who loved Tottenham but he took things personally and that, I believe, is what affected his health.

Other teams were reluctant to adopt the style. Maybe because it was a hard system to implement unless you had the right players. And opponents were working out ways of nullifying the tactics.

But the Push and Run team was without doubt the main inspiration for the Double side of which I became a part. That was because it provided the foundation stones for how Bill Nick got us to play. He had been a pivotal part of Rowe's team. He believed in the style played and he was determined to carry on from where Arthur had left off.

For me, as an amateur on leave from National Service in the British Army, just being thought worthy of consideration by a club which only three years earlier had been champions of England was enough.

I HAD enjoyed my trial against Crystal Palace and goals against the Oxbridge universities. But I was to experience something beyond my wildest dreams.

I had been with the club for six weeks and we were playing Luton Town in a reserve match. I had got quite confident with how to get to White Hart

Lane across London from Woolwich by then. I reported to the ground to join the team travelling up to Kenilworth Road to take on the Hatters on their own patch. When I arrived I met Jimmy Anderson.

He told me, 'You are not going to Luton today.' I asked him, 'Why is that?' He said, 'Well, you are playing here against Sheffield United for the first team.'

I'd experienced a bit of amateur dramatics at school playing Bottom the Weaver in Shakespeare's *A Midsummer Night's Dream*, but this am-dram was a whole other world away and I said, 'Whoa.' I was stunned.

Jimmy must have noticed my state of shock and explained, 'I didn't want to tell you yesterday because it would have given you too much time to think about it. You'd have got yourself into a nervous state and might not even have slept that well.' Fair enough. He had a point. I had only come out of my teenage years a few months earlier. And, of course, I was still an amateur with the club tight on expenses such as travelling to and from my barracks in Woolwich. But any monies meant nothing compared to the thought of playing for and being a part of the famous Spurs first team.

I went into the dressing room. Although most of the Push and Run team were still on the books, Arthur and Jimmy had decided to put in a few new players for the First Division fixture.

It was getting towards the end of a disappointing season with the club in the lower reaches of the First Division table but safe from relegation – and knocked out of the FA Cup by the team I used to watch as a lad, giant-killers York City of the Third Division North.

The management must have thought it a good time to try something fresh. Eddie Baily, Len Duquemin and Harry Clarke were the lone representatives of the old guard. Alf Ramsey was in the dressing room with us. He was out injured but kindly helped me get my socks sorted out. They were navy blue and white. The idea was to wear them showing mainly the navy blue with the white bit folded at the top. Hopefully they didn't look too bad after Alf's input!

I sat in the dressing room with my nerves jangling. I was quite quiet. It was a massive thing for me knowing I was lining up with three of the players in Spurs' greatest team up to that point. I was thinking, 'Wow, I'm playing with Tottenham legends here.' Going out in front of tens of thousands of people. Others were relaxing me by chatting in a friendly manner.

Then it was show time. Just a few months ago I was playing in front of one or two for the Royal Artillery in the Army. But there were 26,678 watching this one on a sunny Saturday afternoon as I ran out with the rest of the team.

I will never forget that day – 19 March 1955. Not that I will allow myself to as I've got a framed black and white action picture of me from it hanging on my wall at home. I am trying to head the ball while jumping with an opponent with a packed stand in the background.

I was put in – just as Mr Rolls predicted back at school – as a number 11 with my wing partner Johnny Gavin bagging an outstanding four goals that day. Johnny, though, was gone in the November as part of the £28,000 which brought Double-winning centre-half Maurice Norman from Norwich City.

Johnny Brooks, a talented inside-forward, got the other goal in a 5-0 win. And he too was involved in a swap deal which brought another member of the Double side to White Hart Lane, Les Allen, although that wouldn't be for another four years.

It was unbelievable for me as I took in the crowd but I soon got involved in the game. I put in a few good crosses and the supporters clapped them. Also I felt my being small also helped me gain their favour. The small bloke up against a load of big ones!

I thought I played well, got up and down the wing and Spurs scored from one of my corners. It was Johnny who got on the end of it. I was over the moon with that! It was helpful to have the experienced Harry Clarke and Len Duquemin lining up with me. And it was especially helpful to me that Eddie Baily was too.

Eddie had been playing inside-right for much of the season but was switched to inside-left – number 10 – for the game, which helped me out. Having someone like him just inside me was fantastic. He was a great passer. If I made a run he found me.

Significantly among other newcomers were Peter Baker, Danny Blanchflower and Tony Marchi, who would all become part of the squad throughout the Glory Years.

Peter was the first of the Double team to join the club. He came as a junior in 1949, turned pro three years later and had spent the time in between largely understudying Alf Ramsey at right-back. His full-back partner against the Blades was Mel Hopkins, with Harry at centre-half in front of goalkeeper Ron Reynolds.

Danny and Tony were the wing-halves. Tony became a reliable stand-in for the first team during the halcyon days of the early 1960s. But it was Danny who made the biggest first impression of the three on me.

I was one of the first of the Double-winning players to arrive, although it is a tight call for who was second to Peter Baker between myself, Ron and Danny, who Arthur Rowe signed for the club record fee for a wing-half of £30,000 from Aston Villa in the same month I arrived for that trial against Palace.

I remember sitting in the stand watching one of Danny's first games. He was brilliant. He had this long stride, was a good passer and always wanted the ball. Playing alongside him against Sheffield United it was clear straightaway my observations were right. He was a good player.

For the record, the Spurs line-up that day was: Reynolds, Baker, Hopkins, Blanchflower, Clarke, Marchi, Gavin, Brooks, Duquemin, Baily, Dyson.

It was the start of an incredible journey. And amateur dramatics would soon give way to professional glory.

5

Pro And Cons

I USED TO go over the road to the cafe opposite my barracks in Woolwich regularly for a cup of tea. On Thursday 31 March 1955 I had visited it for a reason beyond drinking a beverage – and reading the latest on the UK locomotive engineers and firemen strike and freak Arctic spring weather sweeping North America in my morning paper – to break up the routine of being a National Service soldier.

I was due to meet Jimmy Anderson. He was deputising for Arthur Rowe, the ailing Spurs manager.

The reason? Mr Anderson had a form he wanted me to sign as a result of Mr Rowe being sufficiently impressed with my efforts to offer me terms as a professional footballer. Bombardier Dyson 22867193, aged 20, was about to be demobbed and he was demob happy, let me tell you, due to the prospect of earning his living playing for a club with the stature of Tottenham Hotspur rather than any negative thoughts on Army life.

I'd dipped my toe in the Spurs world for a few months as an amateur. My trial in that reserve game against Crystal Palace kicked it off before displays against Oxford and Cambridge universities added to the experience. And it all led up to that winning debut for the first team in an actual Football League game against Sheffield United.

But sipping tea across the table from Mr Anderson I was about to enter the world of White Hart Lane for real. The form was a one-year contract worth £15 a week in the season and £12 in the close-season. It had a one-year option, which they would take up, although my weekly earnings were then reduced to £12 and £10. I quickly signed while the hot steam was rising from my cup. I was flattered Mr Rowe had considered me worthy.

There were plenty of things to adapt to in my new life as a professional footballer. I had to get to know the players, the management, the rest of the staff, the regime, the philosophies, the expectations inside and outside the club.

The training was the hardest thing I'd ever done. It was a world away from anything I'd ever experienced. Given a golden opportunity I was determined not to waste it. I gave it everything and hoped it would pay dividends by me one day reaching the first team and playing at the top level in England.

There was also the question of my life outside of the day job. I was a 20-year-old and had got used to being away from my parents, having had two years in the Army. But I still needed to adjust.

There were no barracks packed with fellow squaddies to share the realities of being cooped up at the behest of the government full-time. The shared banter, confidences and friendships. Or mum and dad to feed, clothe, protect, encourage and generally look after my best interests.

The married players were given club houses to rent for about £5 per week. They were also allowed to buy them, interest-free, out of their wages. That's what Cliff Jones and Dave Mackay did. I wasn't able to do that, though, being as I was single.

Us 'singletons' had to get used to living in 'digs' with a family trusted by the club to look after players.

Tottenham first put me in accommodation at Ponders End, a few miles from the ground. I was in there for the last few weeks of the 1954/55 season after leaving the Army and becoming a pro. It wasn't very good. I used to spend the evenings in darkness except for the light from the television, a new 'toy' in households. The family were saving money on electricity. What broke the camel's back and led to me leaving only a short time after I'd moved in was that they still wanted rent in the close-season. Even though they knew I would be back home in Yorkshire during that time. I thought that was a bit much.

Anyway, there was this chap called Alan Woods, a Tottenham player, in 'digs' down the road with this other lad. Spurs didn't sign this other guy on and Alan said, 'Why don't you come to my place?' So I did, moving into the family home of insurance worker Peter Adcock and his wife Wynn.

The weekly rent was £3 or £4, which included clothes washed and meals – usually meat and two veg – cooked by the landlady. Sometimes I ate out if I was socialising (never back late by the way, because I was dedicated to my new career and wanted to be mentally and physically fit).

I got on so well with the family that when they upped sticks for Hoddesdon in Hertfordshire, just north of London, I went with them. They couldn't get rid of me! I spent my whole ten years at Spurs living with them. And I became great friends with their two boys, Michael and Steven.

I wasn't able to drive so had to hop on the bus to White Hart Lane to either train there or pick up a lift from one of the lads when we went to the training ground at Cheshunt. I did that for a few years. A pal of mine up in

Malton taught me to drive in his car during one summer and I took my test near Tottenham. And I passed first time. The guy who tested me, Dave, was a Spurs fan and I got him a couple of tickets for a match we played against Birmingham. I gave them to him AFTER the test, by the way!

It meant I could come off the buses and I bought myself a brand-new Ford outright off this pal of a pal and got a bit of a deal. At least, I thought I'd got one because I didn't have a clue whether I had. It was a few hundred quid. I heard Ron Henry was only able to put a down payment on his first car with the bonus we got from winning the Double. But I was able to pay for mine outright through savings.

JUST BECAUSE I had signed this bit of paper called a contract, it did not mean I would be figuring in any more 5-0 wins for the first team – like I had done against Sheffield United – in the near future. Or any first-team games, for that matter.

I had an inkling of what lay ahead. A week after the elation I felt following my first-team debut – in which I'd laid on that goal and seemed a hit with the crowd – I found myself dropped for the next match. And George Robb, another amateur, took my place – and scored in a 2-1 win over Cardiff City at Ninian Park. George, a schoolteacher, was a strong player. He used to bomb down the wing. Didn't pass it much from what I recall but a lovely fellow, like all of the players.

I had to get used to life as a reserve player. I accepted I had to pay my dues – but it was to go on a bit. About FIVE years. Those days the first team had a 12th man, with no substitutes during a game. So if you weren't in the 12 you got matchplay in the 'stiffs'.

Jack Coxford, a trainer who worked under first-team trainer Cecil Poynton, was in charge of the team (occasionally with Johnny Wallis, who ran the A team and juniors). Jack had come to Spurs after serving as a player-coach at Northfleet United, our nursery club which helped produce so many of Spurs' Push and Run team, including Bill Nick.

Ron Burgess wrote in his autobiography *Football My Life*, 'We were a young side at Northfleet, for the average age of the lads, with the exception of our skipper and centre-half, Jack Coxford, could not have been more than 19 years. Jack was the 'old head' amongst that bunch of sprightly youths, and what he didn't know about the game wasn't worth knowing! He did his best to impart some of his knowledge and experience to us by his grand example and influence.'

Coxford had to pick the players the manager, either Arthur Rowe or his deputy Jimmy Anderson, wanted for each reserve game. I liked Jack. He was all right. I got to know him quite well before he was eventually replaced as reserve manager by Harry Evans after Bill Nicholson became manager and made Harry (who was also to become the father-in-law to my future team-mate John White who married his daughter Sandra) his assistant. I remember going to Jack's funeral a few years later.

We weren't coached, but the players around from Arthur Rowe's great side naturally knew how to play. It was a wonderful experience for me playing with the players who had really helped put Spurs on the football map a couple of years beforehand – like Ted Ditchburn, Alf Ramsey and Bill Nicholson himself.

I remember one Combination match with Bill, who played left-back to my left-wing, against Arsenal. He was pleased I had scored given the Gunners were our north London rivals. It had been in front of about 10,000 – we always got big crowds for our reserve games – at White Hart Lane. Afterwards, I said to Bill, 'That was my first competitive goal for Spurs.' And he replied, 'Let's hope it is the first of many.'

With Ron Henry and Peter Baker, I helped the reserves secure ten victories in a row in the Combination. Perhaps you could say it was a dry run for my experiences in helping the first team to a record-clinching sequence en route to the Double (much more later). Alan Woods, my 'digs' mate, also played. I scored as we won 3-0 in Cardiff.

I managed a hat-trick as I helped the reserves batter Bexleyheath and Welling in the London Challenge Cup, a midweek competition which we won a few times. A precursor to the scoring success I had in knockout competitions for the first team down the road! I also helped Eddie Baily to complete a trio in a 5-0 Combination win over Coventry.

I was striving to make the grade and lucky to be learning the game with so many of the Push and Run team players involved. I would push the ball to a colleague and run and the ball was back there at my feet and got my crosses in. And the experienced players were quick to say 'well done' at every opportunity. The standard was so high that you couldn't help but develop. The influences certainly rubbed off on me and would stand me in good stead when I stepped up to the first team. I had put my own stamp on things too with the effort and enthusiasm.

Jimmy Anderson took over full-time for the 1955/56 season after Arthur finally retired following more illness. My debut against Sheffield United in the March had turned out to be my only appearance in 1954/55. But this following season I got three. I had to wait until the 12th league game to get my first chance of the campaign. And when it came things did not go so well. It was against Chelsea at Stamford Bridge in front of 48,195 on 15 October 1955 and we lost 2-0.

I did not get another look in until the following February. It was against Newcastle United at St James' Park. George Robb played but Anderson switched him to outside-right, allowing me to put on the number 11 shirt.

George and Len Duquemin got the goals which gave us a 2-1 win in front of close to 30,000 football-mad Geordies. I must have done all right because the manager retained me – and kept George at number 7 – for the next game, a home fixture against Birmingham City.

But my first appearance for the first team at White Hart Lane since figuring in the 5-0 demolition of Sheffield United 11 months earlier was not a happy one. The visitors stole the two points with the only goal of the game.

And it marked a return to reserve football for the rest of the season for me as Spurs made the FA Cup semi-final and finished fifth from bottom, two spots lower than the previous term.

The limitations for any first team appearances in 1955/56 were largely caused with George pretty much a fixture at number 11, and the number 7 shirt being shared between Micky Dulin, Dave Dunmore, Sid McClellan and, in a deep-lying role, Tommy Harmer.

I managed a whole eight league appearances in the 1956/57 season – and even an FA Cup debut for the club. The first four were all consecutive with me wearing the number 7 shirt and George back on the left.

The first was on Boxing Day and we drew 1-1 with Everton thanks to a George Robb goal at Goodison Park, after Spurs had walloped them 6-0 at home on Christmas Day. I remember going up on the train to Liverpool after the first game and having Christmas dinner on the train with the Everton lads. I don't think you would see that today!

The second provided a milestone moment for me – my first goal for the first team. It was in front of 42,000 at White Hart Lane. It was the first of four as we overcame Bolton Wanderers 4-0, with Tommy converting a penalty while Bobby Smith and George completed the scoreline.

We also kept a clean sheet beating Aston Villa 3-0 at home after losing by the same score against the strong Wolverhampton Wanderers side at Molineux.

My second and final clutch of four-in-a-rows saw me return to outside-left in place of George with Terry Medwin, the Welsh international, on the right.

It was quite daunting to play in front of 60,000 at Old Trafford in the first of the successive quartet. Spurs were looking more like their old selves, championship contenders rather than potential relegation survival fodder trying to hang on to the coat-tails of a United team en route to the title.

The hosts' line-up was made up mostly of Busby Babes, including Tommy Taylor, Liam Whelan, Eddie Colman and Geoff Bent, who were to tragically die in the Munich air disaster the following February. Also, Jackie Blanchflower played for the Reds opposite his brother Danny.

We had a decent side out ourselves that day with four members of the team that would win the Double four years down the line, including myself,

Peter Baker, Maurice Norman and, of course, Danny. We did well, coming away with a goalless draw. Perhaps the absence of the mighty Duncan Edwards – another to perish as a result of the crash – in the home line-up might have helped us.

A week later I managed my second first-team league goal in a 5-1 home win over Birmingham City with Terry Medwin proving Spurs had two wingers capable of finding the net.

I helped the team draw at Charlton before bagging my third goal in a 3-0 victory against Cardiff City at Ninian Park.

But helping Spurs go on an unbeaten run of four games and scoring twice was not enough for me to keep my place. George came back in for a couple and Bert Wilkie was preferred to me in the final fixture – one of only two appearances he made – as we finished runner-up and eight points down on United.

I managed my FA Cup debut that season. It was in the third round against Leicester City at White Hart Lane – and again I was on the right and George the left. We won 2-0. That must have been an omen as we beat the same opposition by the same score when completing the Double.

THERE WAS also an Anglo-Scottish floodlit tournament competition in 1956/57. We played teams like Heart of Midlothian, Hibernian and Partick Thistle. I got to play in the games we played in Scotland. George Robb was unavailable for them due to his commitments as a teacher in the London area. One match against Hearts at Tynecastle stands out particularly because Dave Mackay was in the opposition's line-up. Dave, of course, was to become such a crucial part of our Double side.

I scored in that one. And I was also on target against Hibernian at Easter Road. I really enjoyed those matches. They provided brilliant experience for me. But I still had plenty to do in order to consider myself a regular in the first team.

THERE WERE also the club tours at the ends of those early seasons for me to try and impress. I went on one to Austria, Hungary and France a few months after I had signed pro. It was the 1955 close-season. I didn't get a game with Sonny Walters, Johnny Gavin and George Robb sharing wing duties in the five games.

We went to North America in the summer of 1957 at the end of a decent season for the first team who Bill Nick had coached to runners-up. The club were thorough in preparation for the trip. Every little last detail was thought about to help the players in an itinerary booklet. We were informed that a ten-hour laundry service would be provided at our hotel, 'So that it will not be necessary to carry excessive underwear.'

We were also told, 'A light overcoat or raincoat may come in handy. Club Blazers, Flannels are appropriate dress at any time. Baggage: labels supplied should be used so that baggage can be easily and quickly identified. A number of spare labels should be carried to replace worn labels, or for attachment to any new luggage required.'

The booklet revealed we could only take a maximum of a tenner in notes and two quid in silver out of the country. It said the exchange rate was $2.80 to £1 sterling. We were also told to behave ourselves and attend official functions.

It stated, 'All players are reminded that the Club's prestige is just as much at stake on Tour as in League games, and they will be subject to the requirements of this Itinerary. It is considered an obligation for all members of the party to attend official functions.'

We travelled by ocean liner to New York. We had about a week on it and suffered terrible weather conditions for three days. The Atlantic cut up rough and we were going up and down. Some of the lads were sick, like Tommy Harmer, who had become a good pal. Fortunately for me I was okay. The first match was against Glasgow Celtic, who had also been invited over. I was on the left wing but Bobby Smith was the star of the show, getting a hat-trick, and we won 4-3. We took in the sights in the Big Apple and walked down Broadway, famous for the big theatre shows it puts on. I'm a big fan of American entertainment and it was everything I imagined it to be. It was a shame I was unable to catch one of the shows running at the time. We even strolled by Jack Dempsey's Restaurant, owned and run by the great American world heavyweight boxing champion.

For the next leg we crossed the border into Canada. I missed an 8-1 win over Essex County All Stars in the Canadian equivalent of Windsor, but figured in an 7-0 victory against Ontario All Stars. Bobby was on fire with his goals. He bagged four against Essex and went one better against Ontario to make it 12 goals in three games. That was some going, even if these were just friendlies.

We flew to Calgary for a 6-1 win over Alberta All Stars. It was just a week before the town's famous Stampede. We'd have loved to have seen that. I missed the next couple of games. Bobby bagged another couple as we made Celtic suffer again, this time in Vancouver.

Then the lads took on the British Columbia All Stars in the same stadium where the British marathon runner Jim Peters repeatedly collapsed at the end of the 1954 Commonwealth Games while leading and failed to finish. I saw a plaque inscribed in remembrance of what is one of the most famous of athletics stories. We lost that one 2-0.

Recalled, I helped us take on Manitoba All Stars in Winnipeg. And it proved a big game for me. I netted a hat-trick, although Alfie

Stokes managed two more in a 12-0 win. We overcame Celtic yet again, this time 3-1 in Toronto. Guess who got all of our goals? Yes, Bobby. He bagged 18 in eight games on that tour. He didn't mess about, did Bobby. He obviously loved North America. Celtic were choked, although the Scottish giants managed a 2-0 win over us in Montreal – a game I wasn't involved in – in our final clash before we travelled back.

This time the Atlantic was like a mill pond. I remember there was some good entertainment on board. It was a fantastic trip and Canada, in particular, was such a beautiful country.

SPURS HAD been the first team in close to 20 years to bag 100 goals in a league season in 1956/57, so there seemed little need to change much about the attack.

And Jimmy Anderson maintained the momentum – eventually – the following season by finishing third, beating Matt Busby's Manchester United, who had Duncan Edwards in their side this time, at Old Trafford, along the way; a match which marked the last appearance of Danny's brother Jackie for the old Red Devils.

But I was able to increase my number of appearances in that campaign. I got my first opportunity on 14 September 1957 against Tom Finney's Preston North End at Deepdale after George and then Micky Dulin had been given three games each at the start.

What a player Tom Finney was. He could play on both wings and through the middle. An amazing performer – and a loyal one as The Preston Plumber stayed at North End for his entire career. What a nice man too and I was sad to hear of his passing in 2014.

Unfortunately we lost 3-1 – with Tom showing an ability to drag the ball past his full-back – and it left us with just one win in the opening seven fixtures. But our fortunes changed the following week against Birmingham City. Alfie Stokes equalled a Football League record for goals scored in one game by netting five. More significantly, from my point of view, I got on the scoresheet in a 7-1 win. I made it two in two in the next game in a 4-3 win against Sheffield Wednesday.

It seemed the team had rediscovered its mojo. And perhaps maybe, just maybe, I might have taken vital steps to finally breaking through into the first team on a regular basis. Sadly, the very next game proved both hopes were illusory. We got walloped 5-1 by Manchester City at Maine Road and my bad ball led to their fifth. I was history – as was goalkeeper Ron Reynolds with Ted Ditchburn recalled – for the time being and Spurs completed a run of three losses in a row.

But I was able to force my way back in 11 days before Christmas. It was against Stanley Matthews's Blackpool. I lined up with Danny Blanchflower,

Maurice Norman and Bobby Smith while Ditchburn, en route to a league club appearance record of 418, remained in goal. We managed to leave Bloomfield Road with a 2-0 win thanks to Bobby banging in a couple in typical style.

Like Tom, Stan was one of the true greats. I played against him two or three times. He was tall for a winger with long legs. You didn't look at his feet as you were distracted by how far he would lean right over. In the blink of an eye, he'd gone the other way and was past you while you remained stock still. He could put 10,000 on the gate. It was why he got paid for turning out in charity games. I remember seeing him at Beverley Races. He had been given a horse and it was running this day. It didn't do very well. The horse wasn't very good.

Stan and Tom were two of the best players in Football League history. Money couldn't buy them today. They'd be great in any era.

The Blackpool match sparked my longest run of consecutive appearances in a first team Lilywhite shirt to that point. I helped us complete a hat-trick of victories with a 4-2 win at Chelsea and 1-0 home success over Wolverhampton Wanderers, who ended up as champions.

Three-all home draws against Newcastle United and Preston – with Finney playing centre-forward – mixed with away defeats against Burnley and Sheffield Wednesday completed my not so magnificent run of seven league games on the spin.

In between I'd also played in Spurs' two FA Cup games, helping them lash Leicester City – again – 4-0 and crash out 3-0 at home to Sheffield United.

In the February, George Robb came back in for a couple and then Cliff Jones was bought from Swansea by Jimmy Anderson for a record £35,000.

It meant myself and George had to play second fiddle to the Wales winger for the rest of the season with Terry Medwin largely on the right. George and I managed one more appearance each – mine coming in a win over Leeds immediately after Cliff had debuted in a 4-4 draw at Arsenal.

Again, there was another obstacle in my way. I had worked for years to get in the first team as a new one was being built out of the ashes of the great Push and Run side – and I'd this rival from the Land of the Red Dragon.

It was a shattering blow to my ambitions. I thought, 'Blimey, what do I have to do now?'

6
Breakthrough

I DIDN'T BEGRUDGE Cliff coming in as a rival for a spot on the wing at Tottenham. He was an established international player.

It was said he was unable to put in consistently high performances in the nine remaining games of the 1957/58 season, but Spurs were playing well and, besides which, the club had spent a lot of money on him.

It was how it was. Unfortunately for Cliffy, he fractured his shin in a training ground practice match collision with Peter Baker before the start of the next campaign.

It would not have been the way I would have chosen to secure a spot, but it led to Jimmy Anderson putting me in at the start of the term. As my luck would have it, it was not an ideal beginning. A better word would be disastrous. I figured in the opening three fixtures – and we lost all three!

We were beaten at home by a decent Blackpool side in front of over 57,000 at White Hart Lane. Five of the Double team were included; my old Army pal Ron Henry at left-back, with Maurice, Danny, Bobby and myself. But the Seasiders had us all at sea as they pipped us 3-2.

It got worse against Chelsea at Stamford Bridge, we went down 4-2 and the legendary Ted Ditchburn suffered a broken finger on what proved to be his final appearance of a fantastic career for Spurs. And nearly 36,000 Geordies had fun at our expense when we lost 3-1 against Newcastle up at St James' Park. It seemed I was becoming a 'bad luck mascot'. George Robb took my place in the next game – the return fixture against Chelsea. It proved quite a day for the Spurs wingers, George scoring and Terry Medwin hitting a hat-trick in a 4-0 win.

But I took over from George as Newcastle came south and beat us 3-1. That was me done as far as the first team was concerned until late October with George wearing the number 11 shirt.

That defeat by the Magpies proved to be my last appearance under Jimmy Anderson. Overall, he did not impress me as a manager. He might have signed me, but, as I've said, that was on Arthur Rowe's say so and I believe he found management difficult.

Jimmy had been at the club for years, coming up from the boot room. It worked at Liverpool in the 1970s with Bob Paisley and Joe Fagan emerging from the Anfield equivalent after Bill Shankly. But I don't believe it worked with Jimmy at Spurs.

He had a few run-ins with Danny Blanchflower. The manager made Danny captain but got upset when his new skipper changed the pre-arranged tactics chasing the game in the 1956 FA Cup semi-final against Manchester City and in a relegation encounter against Huddersfield Town. He was so upset he stripped Danny of the captaincy.

Jimmy didn't have a clue on certain things. I remember when we were trying to get the hang of a throw-in routine and Jimmy just came across and stopped it. He was a nice fellow, but management was a whole different ball game.

That said, he made some crucial signings. In his first full season in charge, 1955/56, he brought in Maurice Norman from Norwich City and Bobby Smith from Chelsea while allowing Alf Ramsey and Eddie Baily to go to Ipswich Town and Port Vale respectively. And, of course, Cliff, in February 1958, another member of what became the Double side.

But he also made some poor signings, like Jim Iley from Sheffield United. Jim was a nice lad but he used to hit a lot of long balls. He wasn't a player in the Tottenham tradition of playing a good, quick passing game.

And the team finished in second and third after struggling to stay up in his first season before a return to the wrong end of the table at the start of 1958/59.

Jimmy Anderson, though, like Arthur Rowe, suffered bad health. Having the pressure of expectation as a Tottenham manager could not have helped his well-being. After all he was in his 60s when he took over the reins. And he resigned in October 1958 after joining the ground staff a half-century earlier. His replacement was Bill Nicholson.

Bill had taken his first steps to the role in the Second World War. He had spent most of it as an instructor in infantry training and at the Army Physical Training Corps at the end of the conflict when he was sent by the British Army to teach sports, especially football, to coaches in the Central Mediterranean Forces in Italy. It was a great grounding for management, getting him used to handling people. It also got him thinking about coaching routines he could employ if the situation arose. And it encouraged him to qualify as a coach.

He got his FA badge swiftly and coached the Cambridge University team during his downtime from playing and training with the Spurs first team. And a few months before I turned up he had persuaded Arthur Rowe that he was unable to maintain the physical fitness required to play league football and was taken on to the coaching staff.

I played with Bill when he felt his body could still cope with reserve football, but it was clear in his coaching sessions that here was someone who was full of ideas. Exactly what the club needed.

Tottenham were in transition from Push and Run and it was hoped Bill could be part of the link to better times. It was natural many of his thoughts were based on the way Arthur Rowe got the team to play, although he had plenty of his own.

He obviously made a good impression because he had been appointed first-team coach when Jimmy Anderson finally took full charge. Bill was popular with us players. His sessions were always interesting and effective.

It was ironic that another of my reserve team-mates, Alf Ramsey, had ambitions to coach with Spurs. Nicholson's progress obviously blocked that path, although Alf didn't do too badly in the end, did he? He managed Ipswich Town to the Football League title in 1962, denying us a second successive Double, as well as England to the World Cup four years later.

Bill was promoted to assistant manager to Jimmy Anderson in 1957 and the greatest era in the club's history began a year later. He took over the hotseat when the board made their decision to appoint him in succession to Jimmy a few hours before Spurs kicked off against Everton at White Hart Lane on Saturday 11 October 1958.

It has gone down as one of the most extraordinary games in the club's history. Spurs won 10-4 with Bobby rattling in four and wingers Terry Medwin and George Robb were also on target. But it was completed without me. My name had not been on the team list put up by the new manager in the dressing room.

I had played with Bill and trained under him as my first-team coach and assistant manager. But even though I'd been born just a handful of miles away from his place of birth, it made no difference. I might just as well have been the other side of the planet when it came to Bill deciding whether to include me in his opening line-up.

None of it cut any ice with an individual who had loved the club and its supporters from the day he first took the train down from Yorkshire to London and on to White Hart Lane before the Second World War. They came before any considerations to players. That's how it should be, I know. But I so desperately wanted to establish myself.

I also found myself out when Bill named his second team for a 4-3 victory at Leicester. Jeff Ireland, who had debuted in the game before Bill took over (a 1-1 draw at Portsmouth), got the nod on the right in place of Terry Medwin while George was at outside-left.

But it proved third time lucky – at least in respect of my name appearing on the team sheet. Bill Nick decided I was up to the task for the visit of Leeds United.

I believe my inclusion again was aided by more misfortune to another player. George Robb had suffered an injury in a five-a-side training session, a problem which eventually forced him to retire prematurely as a footballer, although he had carried on a teaching career even after turning pro following years of maintaining his amateur status.

Unfortunately, my Jonah tag returned to haunt me. Bobby Smith and Jim Iley managed to score for us but Leeds scored a 3-2 victory to inflict on Bill his first defeat as Tottenham manager. The manager, though, kept faith in me as we took on Manchester City at Maine Road. We got our backsides slapped that day! City went nap and thumped us 5-1. So, if you are counting, that makes it six appearances by me in this season and six defeats.

I was out. Again. Bill switched Terry Medwin to the left and even tried Johnny Brooks, an inside-forward, in the position before Cliffy recovered and ended the number 11 debate through to the end of the campaign.

I managed to pull the shirt on once more – with Jonesy absent – in a draw against Aston Villa at Villa Park in what turned out to be a miserable season for us. Even Danny Blanchflower went off the boil. He had been brilliant the previous season, so good that he had been named the Football Writers' Player of the Year. And that summer he helped Northern Ireland to a shock run to the quarter-finals at the World Cup finals in Sweden, as did Cliff with Wales. But, as he himself admitted, his efforts for his country had taken their toll on him and Bill dropped him.

Fifth from bottom after two more than solid seasons under Jimmy Anderson was not the start Bill Nicholson would have wanted in his first season as a manager. But there was some good news with Bill going on a secret trip to Hearts to sign Dave Mackay in March 1959 when most mistakenly thought his main interest at the time lay in the capture of Mel Charles, brother of legend John, whose preference turned out to be Arsenal, whom he joined in the same month. How lucky was that for us given what Dave did for Spurs.

Getting Davy on board was crucial. Cliffy has said his signing turned a good team into a great one. And Bill himself said it was his greatest signing. I wouldn't argue with either of them. What a presence he would prove to be.

I was still doing okay in the reserves, which gave me confidence. It helped me feel more settled. The fact I was also friendly with a few of the lads away from the club added to that feeling. Also I felt I was quite popular with the supporters because they could see I was giving EVERYTHING every game. And I was scoring a goal or two.

But the changes in coaching and management did not seem to heighten my prospects of playing regularly for the club's main side.

Nor did the maximum weekly wage of £20. The club could afford to have a lot of players vying for a spot and there was no need for those players to move on in search of more money. Besides, they knew it was a good club and a potentially successful one.

It was disappointing to largely be still out with the club trying to build a new side to follow Arthur Rowe's super team. What added to the negatives was around this time I might have lost the chance to be part of what proved to be such a pivotal period in the club's history.

There was talk of Bill wanting to sign a promising teenage striker. His name? Denis Law, who was to find fame with Manchester United and Scotland. He was at Huddersfield Town at the time. The word was that Bill was willing to swap myself and Dave Dunmore for him, but Terriers manager Bill Shankly, who eventually earned legendary status bossing Liverpool, put a block on it. Yet I wouldn't have agreed to it if I had known at the time.

WE WERE delighted to learn that we would be going abroad for a tour after the 1958/59 season finished. I know Cliff was pleased when he heard. Cliffy thought he might be packing his sun cream for warmer climes. But instead he needed warm clothing. We were off to Russia. Remember the Cold War was going on, building from the end of the Second World War between the Soviet Union and Britain, the United States and France. And it was not the most attractive of propositions to venture behind the Iron Curtain.

It was a very different world to what we were used to in England, but the hotels were all right and we were treated with respect.

And there was plenty to do. We went to the circus when they were allowed to use animals – which is not the case these days anywhere as far as I know. It was superb. Brilliant.

There was also an optional visit to see the Bolshoi Ballet on the itinerary. Some went – I chose not to – and Bill Nicholson said he was impressed with the level of fitness of the dancers, and their techniques. These dancers had been working since they were young to achieve the high standard they had reached. Rudolph Nureyev was among them. Bill said he could use bits of what he picked up to use with us in training. A few of the lads also saw Lenin and Stalin lying in state in the mausoleum in Red Square. And visited the Kremlin.

But I didn't enjoy the tour as much as other ones I'd either been on or would be going on. Russia wasn't the greatest country to be in. It was dull, drab and grey, along with being a bit of a police state. I felt for the people who lived there, even though they must have been used to the conditions there. It would be a similar atmosphere when we went to Poland – also behind the Iron Curtain – to play Gornik in the European Cup in 1962.

I did not get to play and we had three games with mixed results; Cliff playing in all the matches at outside-left, and, on the opposite wing, Terry Medwin performed in the first two matches and Tommy Harmer in the third.

Terry Medwin scored as we beat Torpedo Moscow 1-0 in front of 50,000. Then we travelled to Kiev and won 2-1 in front of another big crowd, 60,000. And there were a staggering 100,000 watching the team as it was beaten 3-1 against a CCCP Selects in Leningrad.

Bill was over the moon at how things went for the club. The thing that most pleased him was how the trip gave the players a big opportunity to bond away from most distractions. It was largely training, playing, sleeping and spending the rest of the time in each other's company.

Eight members of the Double side were on it with Bill Brown, John White and Les Allen yet to be signed and Bill Nick told Phil Soar in *And The Spurs Go Marching On*, 'I cannot overstate the value of that trip in terms of getting things together.'

THREE MORE pieces to the jigsaw towards completing the Double team were put in place in the 1959/60 campaign. Bill Brown joined us from Dundee for £16,500 – a massive fee for a goalkeeper at the time – as we returned from the USSR. Ron Reynolds had done okay in place of Ted Ditchburn, but Bill Nick thought the position needed strengthening.

And John White, who had become known as a talented midfielder, was signed from Falkirk for £20,000 in October 1959 after Bill had consulted the player's Scotland international team-mates Dave Mackay and Bill Brown, as well as Danny Blanchflower, who had played a Home international against John.

Two months later striker Les Allen arrived in that swap deal with Johnny Brooks joining Chelsea. There was just ONE more piece left to be thumbed into place to complete the puzzle, but I would have to wait to become it.

It was clear Tottenham were going places with a brilliant start to 1959/60, going unbeaten in the first 12 matches, although ironically it ended when John White made a scoring debut in a 3-1 defeat at Sheffield Wednesday.

I managed to play a bit part in the unbeaten run by standing in for Cliffy in a 2-1 win over West Ham United at the Boleyn Ground, although it clearly did not go as well when I took over from him again in that Hillsborough reverse.

I had to wait until the following March to make my third appearance of the season, again deputising for Cliff and again helping the side to victory, this time 3-1 over Nottingham Forest at the City Ground. I hadn't done too badly in my cameo appearances for a side being tipped for the title.

I was determined to make the most of any opportunities by working hard in the reserves. I knew putting in the effort in second string games could provide a firm launching pad.

Second strings these days tend to not be so strong because they are often made up of youngsters being tried out and players coming back from injury. But we had largely regular line-ups which included many experienced players.

The reserve team was a good one playing at a high standard. The Football Combination we played in was a good league. So was our cup competition, the London Challenge Cup, which attracted good crowds under lights in midweek. It contrasted to the lesser competitions of today.

But when my opportunity came to perform in the Football league side through either injury or whatever I had to take it with both hands. You HAD to play well because of the competition for places. Ideally, you had to help the team win. If not you could be back in the reserves. It was tough.

Well, even though I had done all right – and helped the first team to a couple of victories – it clearly wasn't enough to keep me in. Not enough to stop me bouncing back to the second string.

It became so frustrating I felt forced to ask for a move. I did not want to go. To quit such a great club, a club that had given me a chance – out of the blue – when I was not enjoying National Service and had not even considered a career in professional football was a realistic proposition.

I spoke to a *Daily Express* reporter, Desmond Hackett, telling him, 'This is no good to me. I'm sick of it here. I might as well ask for a move.' The next thing an article appeared in the *Express* with the headline 'Dyson might seek move'.

Bill pulled me about it, saying 'You've been speaking to Desmond Hackett, then?' I said to him that I had told Desmond I'd reached a point where I was so frustrated with not being in the first team that, although I didn't want to go, I might have to in order to get first-team football.

It was left at that with Bill. He didn't inform other clubs. Would there have been a long queue to sign me? I don't know. Bill never said any more about it. I decided to stay and fight for my first-team place.

Eventually, at long last, my big breakthrough came – right at the end of the 1959/60 season. I've read Bill had decided Terry Medwin had not been playing up to form – something I don't remember, believing it was just a lucky break – and put me in at outside-left, with Cliff switching to the right in Terry's place for the final two games of the season.

Cliffy was predominantly right-footed so it suited him. Danny told him, 'You can do just as well on the right. In fact, you might do even better for yourself. When on the left you cut in and sometimes run straight into players.' He was clever, Danny. He knew the game and how it should be played.

Bill had been looking for a solution to his 'out-of-sorts strike force', or so it was suggested. Whatever the reason it was a move for which I would be forever grateful. It sent my career into orbit. The timing couldn't have been better as it turned out.

I was ecstatic to be that last piece of the puzzle in forming the Double team. But in the meantime I knew, of course, in order to be viewed that way I had to impress – big time. If I could be part of a winning team it would be a major boost to my prospects of establishing myself with managers reluctant to change that sort of side.

SPURS HAD led the way in the First Division from December – when Les Allen scored twice in a 4-2 win at Leeds – to March before the wheels came off their title bid with two shock 1-0 home reverses against lowly opposition over Easter.

The first was against Manchester City, in which Tommy Harmer played his last game for Spurs before he went to Watford. Cliff scored a goal that was disallowed with the referee blowing for half-time in between him putting in a rebound and his penalty being half-saved by Bert Trautmann.

And I was involved in the second two days later versus Chelsea. The result against Ted Drake's Blues could have scuppered everything for me. Fortunately, Bill kept faith in my talents for the next fixture against Wolverhampton Wanderers with Terry Medwin out.

Wolves were rated odds-on to not only complete a hat-trick of successive championship triumphs but the Double too. A win for Stan Cullis's men could have sealed the first half of an historic achievement with Blackburn Rovers awaiting them in the FA Cup Final.

The pressure was off Spurs, who had slipped three points behind their Molineux hosts to put themselves virtually out of the frame. And we beat them 3-1. Danny gave us our team talk out on the pitch rather than inside the changing rooms and within two minutes he made a goal for Bobby Smith. Dave Mackay headed us back in front after Peter Broadbent put Wolves level.

I thought I was playing well and proved it by laying on the third goal for Cliff with a cross he headed in at full stretch. And all in front of more than 56,000 spectators.

It was a much-vaunted win. Some said they could 'sense history turning'. Out with the old, in with the new. The long ball replaced by the quick-passing game reliant more on ball skill and flexibility. Deputies for departed heroes falling short of the mark against the new kids on the block.

It was a changing of the guard which would be confirmed by an even more emphatic scoreline in Old Gold country the following season, which was to become Spurs' most momentous one.

All I knew was that I was beginning to feel part of something special instead of viewing it from afar. And helping Spurs say au revoir to our supporters – close to 50,000 of them – for another campaign with a 4-1 victory over Blackpool underlined the emotion.

It was reported that my form had reached 'astonishing heights'. Whoever wrote that knew what they were talking about!

There had been talk that the side in that campaign might be good enough to complete the Double, especially after crushing Crewe Alexandra 13-2 in a fourth-round FA Cup replay. Les scored five, Bobby four and Cliffy three, with my mate Tommy getting the other one. It was and remains (as the deadline for this publication passed) a record score for Spurs in professional competition. It was a hell of a performance which provoked the legend of how the Railwaymen of Crewe arrived in London by train on to Platform 2 and left from Platform 13.

But the pundits were soon silenced when Blackburn Rovers visited White Hart Lane in the next round and returned to Lancashire with a 3-1 win.

Yet the chattering classes would again have cause to speculate in a positive manner soon. Very soon. And yours truly would be right in the thick of it, lapping up every second.

7
Cheshunt

TOTTENHAM MOVED into their latest training ground on Hotspur Way, Enfield, in 2012. It seems £30m has bought the club a fantastic state-of-the-art facility that is one of the best in Europe. Its 77 acres has 'a covered artificial pitch, world-class player preparation areas, pool and hydrotherapy complex, altitude room, large-scale gymnasium and specialist sports rehabilitation suites'.

This is according to the brochure, or rather the club's website, which adds, 'There are 15 grass pitches across the site including four dedicated solely for First Team Training and one and a half artificial outdoor pitches with floodlighting. The First Team Match pitch is built to exactly the same specification as the pitch at White Hart Lane. The new Training Centre has been designed with environmental protection and sustainability in mind.'

It talks about 'restoring historic hedgerows and field boundaries as well as significant additional planting, an organic kitchen garden and orchard… enhance the ecological habitat'. There's even an installed pond to 'establish a wetland'. Right on for the players, coaches, auxillary staff and right on for the environment.

It has had a little embarrassing publicity with some 61-year-old IT chap accused of trying to have sex with a sheep in a field nearby. But overall the only red faces as the team prepared for the start of the 2014/15 season were those of the players putting in the sweat and toil under Mauricio Pochettino, a modern-day successor to Bill Nick.

It is like the club have returned home as far as their training base is concerned after one or two moves in recent years.

The complex is just three miles north on the A10 of the training ground Spurs used while I was there during the Glory Glory Years at Brookfield Lane, Cheshunt.

That facility did not, of course, compare with the one the club possesses now and which they sold to developers who built the Brookfield Farm shopping centre in its place in the 1980s. M&S before Push and Run; Tesco before tiki-taka.

For a start, the site only stretched to 11 acres and had just three pitches which the groundsman looked after well. We benefited from his expertise when we had our practice games there. One of the pitches had a stand alongside it. He provided such a good surface for us.

I remember the fans used to watch us training through a wire fence, the sort of thing which I can't see happening today at the big clubs.

I still have a lot of affection for the place as do those who followed us in my day. One supporter, who called himself 'Spurs reveller', posted on the internet, 'I lived a little north of the old training ground alongside the A10. Used to make it a day out during school hols and cycle with puncture outfit at the ready as a boy along the A10 and watched a few training sessions through the fencing with a couple of mates, one who had trials for Spurs as a 13yr old schoolboy. And I got autographs of a few as they drove out of the gates into Brookfield Lane. These days at many clubs, got more chance winning a biggy on the lottery than gaining access to watch a training session. Well it does seem like that now. For youngsters in such areas a real shame.'

Most significantly, Cheshunt will go down in Spurs history for being where their most famous season was plotted.

Bill Nicholson was delighted the side which I'd hopefully broken into on a regular basis had improved from 18th to third and tightened up sufficiently to have conceded 45 less goals in the league than the previous campaign, his first in charge.

When we had defeated Blackpool on 30 April 1960, ten of the side which would win the Double were playing with Tony Marchi, our former captain and ever-dependable wing-half, stepping in for Les Allen.

That campaign was, of course, to prove merely a dress rehearsal for the biggest of blockbuster seasons. And there were new lines to learn to ensure it was, at the very least, a better one than the last as we set the stage for it at Brookfield Lane.

We reported back in mid-July for the 1960/61 season. It was a Thursday. Bill picked that day so there were a couple of comfortable days to shake out a little rust and allow the weekend to remove any stiffness in the muscles before the pre-season training began in earnest on the Monday. We trained pretty well in that pre-season but it was hard.

On the first morning we got together and sat on the grass chatting about what we'd been up to in the summer and reflecting on how we'd got so close to winning the title, just two points off champions Burnley.

I read later that Bill had said in *And The Spurs Go Marching On*, 'It felt in 1960 I had a side well prepared to do something. You cannot put into words; it's a feeling you get. And I had a strong feeling around that time.' And Danny famously told the chairman Fred Bearman when he visited the training ground later on that pre-season, 'We'll win the Double for you this year – the league and cup.'

I think he had seen how close Wolves had come to achieving it the previous season and Manchester United in 1957. We've heard what happened to Stan Cullis's troops, but United's attempt had got them within touching distance of being the first team in the 20th century to lift the Double.

The Busby Babes suffered an ailment which had been so often associated with the FA Cup Final: injury. Their goalkeeper Ray Wood was crocked in a collision with Peter McParland – a tough competitor – early on against Aston Villa.

Two lots of nearly men in three years. It made Danny think what had always been thought of as impossible was, indeed, possible.

Danny said in his autobiography, 'I felt that it [the Double] couldn't be done with a weak heart and that the team which might do it would have to really believe it could do it. "We can win the double," I said to one or two of the players. "Yes" they said as if they did not disbelieve it. I mentioned it to Bill Nicholson. He looked at me cautiously, he might have been thinking the same. "I think it can be done too," he said.'

But there was NO talk about doing the Double – from either Danny, Bill or anyone else there – on day one of four weeks of pre-season prior to the 1960/61 campaign.

Bill spoke to us collectively about how well we had played the previous season. But he felt we could do a lot better and could win the title. He felt the club had waited long enough since last lifting it with the Push and Run side he played for, and we should experience competing in the European Cup.

He said he had been happy the defence had proved itself a lot tighter and that he hoped the forwards would be able to score more goals. Bill emphasised that it was up to all of us to ensure that happened. We also had a general discussion about how the championship could be brought back to White Hart Lane after a ten-year wait.

He also underlined his opinion that work brings success and that we were going to put plenty of it in to make sure we were successful.

Bill warned us that no one was guaranteed a place in the first team and said that everyone had to earn the shirt.

As for the FA Cup, well winning that as well would be in the lap of the gods.

Training during the season usually finished just after 1pm but in pre-season we spent a full working day at Cheshunt. We set up camp.

It was the period a lot of clubs used to focus largely on getting the players fit. We would do a run out into the country over the roads and hills. Danny Blanchflower and John White were superb at it. Bill led us. He was as fast as anyone and faster than a few.

Bill described it more as a fast walk. He thought it got our muscles going without straining them. Towards the end he would signal for us to run, and Danny and John used to gallop away. We had some good athletes but Danny and John were exceptional.

John was a superb cross-country runner. That ability was one of the reasons Bill signed him. Funnily enough, he had been concerned about John's stamina because he was, like Tommy Harmer, slight. But he was reassured after phoning up John's Army barracks where he had been on National Service. The chap told him he wasn't able to play football that weekend because he was competing for his regiment in a cross-country event.

Another running exercise involved us going around a big circle. We moved in intervals of ten yards. We walked one, jogged one and sprinted one, then two, then three, increasing the number by one each time we went round. It was tough but useful. Bill thought it replicated what we would do in a game. Bill was good at thinking things out like that.

Yes, we worked on getting in condition for the upcoming season. We would be as fit as any of our rivals. But we also spent a lot of time on improving our abilities with competitive training, practising ball skills, working on tactics, developing passing movements and talking about which roles each of us would be undertaking in the coming season.

Bill exposed weaknesses and organised how they could be covered. It was all for the sake of the team as a whole. It was long, thorough and tough – and it went on that way solidly for all of the four weeks.

I had played with Bill, along with Peter Baker, Ron Henry, Tony Marchi and Danny, and our manager mingled in naturally with the players as we worked with the ball. The drills involved heading, passing and shooting, which we all enjoyed. You'd get the ball under control, pass and move quickly. We worked on Bill's take on the Push and Run.

He used his phrases to get over his point like, 'When not in possession get in position.' All it meant was that if you didn't have the ball you get in a position to get it – not rocket science. Bill wanted us to mix the short passing game his Push and Run team used with a long passing style.

We went over tactics and strategies like ensuring players in possession were supported with the help of a sectioned practice pitch. We spent a lot of time on all this in pre-season in contrast to what we did during the campaign.

Bill was keen on his stats. He had figures which revealed a third to a half the goals scored came from set pieces. I think we were the first to put a player in front of an opponent taking a throw-in. Conversely, a Dave

Mackay throw-in was a weapon which Bill wanted us to exploit. We'd practise Bobby Smith flicking the ball on to either me, Les, John or Cliff in the middle.

We also worked on Maurice Norman coming up from centre-half for corners. I think we were among the first to do that too. Bill was also keen on devising free kick routines. He had loads. There was one he was particularly fond of where the dead ball would be chipped up for a team-mate to turn and shoot.

We played 'ghost' football. It was Bill's first team against the second team of his assistant Harry Evans. But each side just let the other have the ball so they could work on patterns of play without pressure.

Bill was big on space. He had related sayings on the subject like, 'The man without the ball makes the play' and, 'Time equals space.'

There was one exercise he drilled into us about how to create and use gaps. When one of our team-mates had the ball as many of us forwards as possible would run in different directions to give him options of where to pass the ball.

The more options the more bemusing it was to opponents trying to guess where the ball was going. It was hard work because we were always on the move but it was to prove effective.

On the Saturday morning we reported to White Hart Lane and went on runs around the streets and through the park nearby before returning for soap massages given to us by either Cecil Poynton, Jack Coxford or Johnny Wallis.

It was intensive stuff but once the season had kicked off, Bill eased up on us. He knew a competitive game was a whole other thing to training drills. He had drummed into us the basics and then trusted us to apply them and improvise as the occasion demanded.

During the season, we only spent Tuesday each week at Cheshunt and the rest of it at White Hart Lane where we developed our style with ball work each day through five-a-side sessions in the court at White Hart Lane under the old West Stand.

It was a far cry from the experience Danny had at Aston Villa. He used to say one big reason for leaving them to join Spurs was because the players were deprived of the ball in training, and were told it would make them hungrier for it on matchday.

We had a final practice match before the league programme began in front of spectators at White Hart Lane. It was an annual thing: the Probable First Team v Probable Reserves. The Firsts usually won, but not this year. We in the Firsts led 4-1 and drew 4-4. Bill was not impressed. He wasn't satisfied very often as it happens, although he had cause to be none too pleased about us giving away a three-goal lead.

I had only just nosed my way back into the first team at the end of the previous season. I had tried to make the most of it, largely in Terry Medwin's place. There had been no animosity with Terry. He was a good lad and we were all pals together. Whoever was in was in. That was that. And, as I've mentioned, I played well enough the final three games of 1959/60.

But Bill's comments about selection being made on merit alone was a reminder I could take nothing for granted. We were back to a level playing field. I had to prove myself all over against during pre-season to make sure I was still wearing the shirt when it came to the season kicking off.

I trained as hard as anyone and, I believe, did well in practice matches. I had been known for the hard work I always put in for all 90 minutes of every game. I was about 100 per cent industry. But I also felt Bill was looking for a bit more than that. I did not know his thinking but thought if I could improve my overall game in the lead up to the big kick-off it might give me the edge.

I think I did and that's why Bill took a chance and kept me at number 11 with Cliff again donning the number 7 shirt, leaving Terry Medwin having to sit it out as we started the campaign against Everton at White Hart Lane on Saturday 20 August 1960.

8
A Flyer

I WOKE UP on a dry, fine morning on Saturday 20 August 1960 feeling good. It was to be a momentous day, the start of something great. I had a breakfast of egg on toast with the Adcock family at my digs in Colmore Road in Ponders End, north London, before hopping on the bus for the three-mile trip to White Hart Lane.

Bill Nicholson had pinned the team sheet for our opening game of the 1960/61 season up in the changing room at White Hart Lane at the end of our training session the day before.

My name was on it along with the other ten names who have gone down in legend: Bill Brown, Peter Baker, Ron Henry, Danny Blanchflower, Maurice Norman, Dave Mackay, Cliff Jones, John White, Bobby Smith and Les Allen.

It is remarkable to think this was the first time this 11 had played together in a competitive game, considering what they went on to achieve a few months later.

Les Allen had been the last of the team to have arrived at Spurs, shortly before the previous Christmas, but yours truly had spent most of the 1959/60 season as a reserve. I'd got the 'Bill wants to see you' message from trainer Cecil Poynton which meant I was to be told the axe from the first team had fallen.

Yes, I had got in the first team with Les once before when we played together in that victory against Nottingham Forest in March. But Cliff Jones was missing from what would become the famous team that day, with John White playing wide on the right and Tommy Harmer occupying the number 8 shirt John was to make so famous.

I might have made my impression in the three games which wound up a decent campaign that April. And put in everything I had on the training field since we had reported back. But until Bill had stuck up his list it all meant nothing.

Now it meant something, everything. It seemed appropriate that Everton provided the opposition, given that the Toffees were the visitors when Bill made his debut as Spurs manager. His counterpart John Carey had himself only been in his job for ten days before the Lilywhites inflicted that record 10-4 drubbing. It was a far cry from the days when Johnny captained Matt Busby's Manchester United to the FA Cup in 1948 and the league in 1952. And the former Republic of Ireland defender must have had revenge on his mind.

Carey had rung the changes since that loss in October 1958 and only goalkeeper Albert Dunlop, centre-half Tommy Jones, forward Jimmy Harris and captain and midfielder Bobby Collins remained in the line-up to make up for what I'm sure was one of Everton's most embarrassing scorelines.

There was a big crowd – more than 50,000. It was an unbelievable atmosphere. Everton were a good side and Bobby Collins was a terrific schemer for them. And their new-look forward line had cost £100,000 to put together, including Roy Vernon who went on to be a prolific goalscorer for them with 101 goals in 176 games. He even captained them to the league title a couple of years later.

Some said we weren't at our best, that the side were running in like a brand new car. But we must have played well. Danny Blanchflower and Dave Mackay were superb at half-back, Danny going forward while Dave helped in attack and defence. Maurice Norman was totally dominant at centre-half whenever Everton counter-attacked. There was talk that Maurice showed the sort of form which could get him a call-up when Walter Winterbottom picked his next England team.

Bobby Smith had a go and even Danny and Maurice had chances, but we just could not find the net for most of the match. Albert played well for them and made a hell of a lot of saves.

We got better as the game went on and went in front five minutes from time. There was an unsuccessful penalty appeal for a foul on Bobby but Les smashed the ball in.

Shortly afterwards Bobby headed in a cross from John White and we completed a 2-0 win. It was well deserved and people were already saying we would be champions. Some were even encouraging punters to put their money on us. After one game! Slightly premature perhaps. We had a private belief it could be our year to emulate the 1951 side but no one among our group was getting carried away.

TWO DAYS later it was a Bank Holiday Monday and we went to Blackpool, not as tourists to enjoy either the beach, the donkey rides or the tower, but as professional footballers to secure a second victory against a side which included a 45-year-old Stanley Matthews, the legendary Wizard of the Wing.

Under the Bloomfield Road floodlights, I got two goals. The first belied my small stature and proved I was capable of heading goals, as I had been encouraged by Bill to practise my heading. It was all about timing. I used to time a run to get to the ball first and employ the decent natural spring I had which had also helped me with my gymnastics in the Army and at school. Often the ball used to sail over my head.

This night by the seaside I kept my eye on a cross from John White, who had collected a short corner from Les, before beating their giant goalkeeper Tony Waiters to the ball and head it home. I've got a picture of that goal and Tony had no chance! It was the cue for my goal celebration which has been called War Dance, both arms aloft, jumping up and down. I just loved to score.

We escaped when Peter Baker fouled Ray Charnley and Arthur Kaye missed the spot-kick. Terry Medwin had got back in the team – with Cliffy being clattered by his old Army pal Alex Parker in our opening game and suffering ankle ligament damage after fearing he might have had another broken leg – and put us two up, again with John the architect.

Then I got another with my head. Peter had come up from right-back to get a cross in from the right, which Bobby allowed to come through for me to score. The War Dance got another outing.

Blackpool had a good line-up, besides Matthews, who Ron Henry kept quiet. There was England international Jimmy Armfield, who was my marker, at right-back, and Jackie Mudie, the Scotland international striker who went on to manage Port Vale with Matthews. And Mudie got a goal back but we played some super stuff that day. In fact, the *Daily Mirror* used the same adjective in its match report, written by Frank McGhee. I'm told it was the first time we had been described as Super Spurs!

Often the star names in our team would get the headlines, but this time it was me getting them with one, in the *News Chronicle*, declaring, 'Two-goal Dyson streaks in for slick Spurs.' And, I must admit, I rather enjoyed it. All those years spent striving to make the main side seemed worthwhile.

A HAT-TRICK of wins was completed at Ewood Park five days later. Our hosts Blackburn Rovers had won their opening two fixtures. They had also knocked us out of the FA Cup the previous season, you may recall, although we had not wasted time getting our revenge in the league a week later.

And, with me now in the side, we repeated the 4-1 scoreline to make it three out of three. I scored our fourth after Les had got one and Bobby had bagged a couple. Three goals in two games – now that's what I call a goalscoring winger.

No, seriously, I remember my goal clearly. I was up against Mike England. Mike went on to become a centre-half and moved to Spurs a year after I left to win the FA Cup, two League Cups and a UEFA Cup, while serving his native Wales despite his surname! But he was at right-back this Saturday afternoon.

So with me at number 11, Mike was my marker and quite young – 18 – and inexperienced. I managed to take advantage of all that by reacting quicker to a ball and beating him to it before hitting a right-foot shot into the net. And it was only just after half-time.

Rovers had been in form but we were really into our stride. What people spoke about afterwards was not so much the goals but the way we won. John Oakley of the *London Evening News* reckoned it was 'a dazzling display which would have overpowered any team in the country'.

And Tom Finney agreed. Tom was writing for the *News of the World* and thought we were 'breath-taking' and our performance was, 'English soccer at its most superb…which would have sent even the fabulous Real Madrid home rubbing their eyes.' He even picked me out for individual praise, saying 'how well wee Terry Dyson played'.

Coming from someone of Tom's stature in the game that's the highest of compliments. I had a reputation for effort, fighting spirit and not allowing an opponent to settle on the ball. Now, through comments such as Tom's, I believe my all-round abilities were starting to be recognised.

The league table was compiled for the first time that season – and we were top of the pile, one point clear of Sheffield Wednesday and Wolverhampton Wanderers.

I HELPED Bobby extend a Spurs record he had created earlier in the game when we defeated Blackpool 3-1 in the return fixture under the White Hart Lane floodlights the following Wednesday in front of nearly 46,000. Bobby needed just one goal to beat the Spurs goalscoring record set by George Hunt at 138 in the 1930s. Bobby already had a history of threatening the club's records, having equalled Ted Harper's league-goals-in-a-season mark by netting 36 in 1957/58.

It took him just four minutes to go beyond Hunt's milestone that night before I assisted his second around 15 minutes from the end. I linked up with Danny to put Bobby in. It put us back in the lead with Leslie Lea having equalised. It was reported our front line struggled to get into gear, but that we had a quality which champions need – fight. Well, we put in plenty of sweat, none more so than Bobby and he deserved to complete his hat-trick, a chance laid on for him by Terry Medwin. Cliff was still out due to that X-rated Parker challenge.

A FLYER

BOBBY CLEARLY had his shooting boots on at the start of this campaign. And he bagged a couple more in the next game on 3 September – our fifth of the season and, yes, it was another win. This time it was against one of the biggest names in football, Manchester United, managed by Matt Busby, their most successful boss before Sir Alex Ferguson came along and set standards unlikely to be emulated. More than 55,000 at White Hart Lane saw us put in a display that earned us rave reviews.

We were superb that day. It felt brilliant to be part of such a side at the peak of their powers. Les got a couple and Danny Blanchflower and Dave Mackay drove us forward all the time and John White had a fantastic game.

It was no mean feat. United had not got off to the best of starts that season but still had plenty of top performers including the likes of Bobby Charlton, Dennis Viollet, Maurice Setters, Johnny Giles and Harry Gregg.

Danny, Dave and John dominated at a pace and style to suit themselves and their passing was slide rule for myself, Terry Medwin, Bobby and Les.

John floated over the ground and popped up in positions which left the opposition wondering how he had got there. He showed his tremendous command of the ball as well as awareness of those around him.

John was capable of scoring goals too – although he proved a maker rather than taker against Matt Busby's team. What more do you want from a midfielder?

Bobby Smith was scoring goals for fun in the opening games. His brace against United meant he had already netted eight goals in just five matches.

Les had only got two from the first two, but he doubled his season's tally against Busby's side rebuilt from the Munich air disaster two years before.

Mr Allen was proving himself a good player and a regular goalscorer for Spurs since being plucked out of Chelsea reserves for Johnny Brooks, a skilled player who I felt was a bit of a bottler.

Bobby Charlton tried his best for United that day as we turned it on. He was two-footed, had a hell of a shot, could make the ball swerve and, clearly, was always capable of scoring goals. I know Bobby used to put in a lot of practice trying to make sure his shots were on target, although a couple of long-rangers in this game came to nothing.

United's best player on the day was Harry Gregg in goal. He was out of this world. I lost count of the saves he made. It would be getting on towards a cricket score but for him.

Cliffy was still out and watched from the stands and was quoted saying that he thought it was 'an outstanding performance'.

And author Julian Holland said in his book *Spurs – The Double*, 'It was a pyrotechnic display that made the watchers' blood race in the heat and their hair stand on end in excitement. If it was not clear what heavy revolutionary and inspiring new ideas were being expressed at White Hart

Lane in those early matches, there was no doubt after the 4-1 defeat of Manchester United.'

Still there was no Double talk among the players and, indeed, the rest of the camp, about us winning the title despite all the outside expectation. It might sound clichéd, modest and unlikely, even boring, but we just played each game as it came along.

There wasn't really a sense of anything building. I don't think players do sense that kind of thing. Their job is to play and try to win. It's what we did. Train, play, train again, play again.

We had no thoughts about trying to beat the record winning start to a First Division season of six games held by Preston North End since 1888/89, when the club's Invincibles became the first Football League champions and first to achieve the Double when also securing the FA Cup.

Yes, we had been confident of winning each game. And we had won one, then two, then three, then four, then five. Our thought was, 'Blimey, I'm looking forward to the next game, going back to even Stevens, 0-0 and starting again to try and win again.'

We were playing well. We didn't realise how well ourselves apart from Danny because he was so far ahead of all of us players in his thoughts. We just prepared for the next game and played it, and we knew that if we prepared well and played well we would win. We never thought we would lose. And we were particularly confident when Dave Mackay was in the side. That was our mindset.

People outside saw more in it than we did. We were totally relaxed about it all. There was no tension. And part of that was because we didn't fully appreciate what was happening beyond playing and winning games. We all worked hard and were pleased for one another, and were just having a good time.

9

Eleventh Heaven

W E MADE it six of the best at Burnden Park against Bolton Wanderers in front of nearly 42,000. We knew we had to show our steel as well as skill. They were a kicking side and gave us plenty of stick. Boy, were they hard. Just looking at their line-up on paper brings it all back: Roy Hartle, John Higgins and Tommy Banks were hard-as-nails defenders; notorious. Cliff was still injured and I'm sure wouldn't have fancied coming up against them. I'll tease him about it when I next see him!

Tommy Banks was at left-back and known for kicking you like mad. Peter Brabrook, who played for Chelsea and West Ham as a winger, told me a story of when he was with the Hammers and had to take on Banks. The full-back, said Peter, told him, 'Don't even flipping try to come near me. Don't even try to flipping get past me, otherwise I'll kick you in the flipping stand.' So Peter says he never went near him, adding that West Ham used to get beat 4-0 and 5-0 up there because his side were frightened to death of Bolton's tough tactics even though they murdered the Trotters at the Boleyn.

Tommy did have his redeeming features. The younger brother of fellow defender Ralph, who was in the Trotters side beaten by Blackpool in the Matthews Final in 1953, was to help end the maximum wage in 1961 and get us professional footballers better pay and conditions. But on 7 September 1960 he did not appear to have any as he set about his work.

Yet Tommy didn't try it on with me as I was on the other side of the field. Fortunately we were too good for them even though Tommy himself had to go off with a torn right thigh muscle after they took the lead. We turned on the form which had earned us so many plaudits, pleasing on the eye and ruthless in its efficiency. We might have been in the backyard of a team with a hard image but we adopted the same approach home or away. This was no different.

It only took us five minutes to equalise after Tommy went off. John floated over a cross which their goalkeeper Eddie Hopkinson was unable to get to and reliable Les was on the spot to nod home. John made it 2-1 to seal the points and equal Preston's record when he took a cross from Danny on the turn and hooked it in.

Frank Saul did well on his debut in place of Bobby who had an injury. Frank had only celebrated his 17th birthday a couple of weeks before but Bill thought a lot of him and viewed him as a successor to the likes of Bobby.

He did not do so badly and always got goals. Remember, he went on to score in the 1967 FA Cup Final – the Cockney Final – win against Chelsea. He was a fast mover, was Frank. His ginger hair was often a blur to the naked eye!

WE JUST needed another victory to crack that Invincibles' record. And that had to be obtained against our local rivals Arsenal.

And, as it happened, a triumph would equal our own best winning start, which came in 1919 after politicking from Gunners chairman Henry Norris got Spurs relegated and his club promoted for the first competitive season after the First World War.

The fact the Gunners had only been voted up after finishing just sixth in the Second Division when hostilities brought the Football League to a halt stuck in our throats.

Norris's only argument was that Arsenal had been a league member longer than Spurs but he sweet-talked the body around with the assistance of president John McKenna, of Liverpool, who happened to be a pal.

It is no surprise, then, there remains a rivalry between the fans of the clubs, particularly when you also think Gunners also upset Spurs by moving north from Woolwich, my old Army stomping ground, south of the River Thames, to become unwanted neighbours just before the Great War.

So our visit to Highbury on Saturday 10 September 1960 in search of a seventh straight win caught the imagination.

There was a crowd of nearly 60,000 packing out the Gunners' old stadium that Saturday afternoon. And what they saw was us putting on the style which seemed to be attracting big crowds wherever we went, especially in the first half. It was exhilarating just to be a part of it. But to score as well put the icing on my cake.

Frank made the most of another chance to deputise for Bobby. He hit a cracker to give us an early lead and put in such a good performance you forgot he was only an inexperienced homegrown teenager in a side being lavished with plaudits. I, of course, could be considered 'homegrown', although it was via Yorkshire and the British Army. And I was delighted to fly the flag for the few members of the team who had not cost a fee.

Again I put my heading ability to good use to put us 2-0 up and a photographer caught the moment, as the framed snap on my wall confirms. I had an excuse for what was becoming my trademark celebration. I was having the time of my life in a side that deserved the adjective 'super' in spades.

We should have been about six up by the time we went in for our half-time cuppa, but Arsenal's Wales international goalkeeper Jack Kelsey was in brilliant form. It was shades of the experience Harry Gregg had endured against us just a week or two earlier.

Arsenal drew level with goals from David Herd and Gerry Ward in only four mad second-half minutes.

But we had built up such a wealth of confidence that we came forward and Les hit the winner. Lovely.

I WAS the centre of a moment of controversy which, to all intents and purposes, secured our eighth triumph. You did not have to wait for the second half of the season to complete home and away fixtures then like you do generally now, so we welcomed Bolton Wanderers just seven days after we had left Burnden Park with both points a month after finishing our league meetings with Blackpool in the space of nine days.

The Trotters went home the same way as the Seasiders – pointless. And I enjoyed my central role on a wet night as the rain poured down on the 43,500 fans at White Hart Lane.

Bobby was back in the number 9 shirt in place of Frank and Cliff returned as the soon-to-be fabled 11 played together in competition for the first time since the opening day. Terry Medwin had stood in really well for Cliffy and Jonesy's return could well have seen me lose my place. Bill might well have decided to put Cliffy back to number 11 and retain Terry on the right. But, thankfully for me, he decided with continuing the experiment of playing Cliff at number 7. I liked to think my form and goals played a part in that decision.

It did not take Bobby long to find the net. He cancelled out an early lead given to the visitors by Billy McAdams, the striker brought in to somehow try and replace the legendary Nat Lofthouse, the Lion of Vienna who was a one-club man associated with Bolton like Tom Finney with Preston North End.

We had a few chances but their goalkeeper Eddie Hopkinson kept denying us with a string of saves.

Then we got a break which decided the game. It was midway through the second half and Bobby had drifted out to the left and I moved into the middle, into the penalty area, as he crossed. I went for the ball. A challenge came in and I lost my footing and fell into the mud. The ball ran loose and

Les got a shot away which went wide. But then the referee pointed to the spot. He had awarded it for the challenge on me, deeming it a push.

There was contact and I'd slipped, but did not appeal. No one did. I admit there was a certain bemusement among us for a decision reckoned to be suspect as well as late. What a good ref! Danny ignored all the fuss and was as cool as a cucumber as he beat Hopkinson from the spot.

It sparked off a lively ten minutes with Bolton clearly left seething at what they perceived as the injustice of the penalty award.

Their right-winger Brian Birch seemed particularly hot under the collar. He fouled Dave and was booked. And not long after that he took down Cliff. It was a bookable offence and when the ref took his name the winger should have got his marching orders. But the official just booked him again, allowing him to play on.

Hopkinson also had a wobbly. He waved his fists at us and then refused to take a goal kick with the fans relentlessly booing him, with those behind his goal throwing paper at him. He was a good goalkeeper, Eddie, at a time England produced lots of them, including Ron Springett at Sheffield Wednesday and Alan Hodgkinson at Sheffield United.

We just kept going and Bobby hit the third a few minutes from the end to give us a 3-1 win.

THE PRESS reports were full of how we could equal the Football League record of winning starts set by Hull City if we sealed two points in our next game against Leicester City in the days Gary Lineker's hometown team played at Filbert Street rather than the King Power Stadium.

It was a reunion for me with Colin Appleton from when we both played for Scarborough. We had gone our separate ways when I left Yorkshire to do my National Service and I had not seen him since.

Fortunately for us, and unfortunately for Colin, he had a big part to play in us extending our winning start to nine.

Leicester weren't a bad team. Bobby had put us ahead but the Foxes came back at us. Their crowd was going crazy as they thought their favourites were going to end our winning run and topple the glamour boys from the capital. Ken Leek missed a couple of opportunities for them before their right-winger Howard Riley made it 1-1.

But we were playing well and Les thought he had scored before Colin's fellow defender Tony Knapp cleared off the line.

In the end, we netted our winning goal when Cliffy caught Colin in possession not far from his own goal and gave the ball to Bobby to score his 12th goal in just seven appearances.

Danny, Dave and John maintained a high standard of class to keep us in control and gave the media another reason to eulogise over us. Even the away fans showed their appreciation of the performance even though we were beating their team, something we had noticed at other grounds.

WE WERE in new territory when we took on Aston Villa at White Hart Lane seven days later. Another victory and we would be the sole holders of the Football League record for winning starts.

And I was more than pleased to do my bit in a 6-2 success by making goals for John White and Dave Mackay and scoring one for myself.

I remember my goal vividly. Les got to the byline and pulled it back and I lashed it in from four or five yards. I am able to recall a lot of my goals. I don't go round thinking about them but if someone mentions it, it will trigger the memory.

Spurs always seemed to beat Villa around that time. John had put us in front after Danny and Cliff set him up. And I helped him make it 2-0, although Bobby assisted by unsighting their goalkeeper by running across his line of vision as John shot.

Bobby grabbed a third and I got the fourth. Villa kept going but Les made it five without reply. They got a couple of goals back but Dave managed to complete the scoring when I lobbed the ball to him after he had called for it.

The press lapped it up. 'From goalkeeper to outside-left, every man was playing with a wealth of confidence. There just isn't the semblance of a weak link anywhere,' said reporter Harry Ditton who added that we were 'immaculate and irresistible' and that 'in their present mood there is not a team in the country that can live with the Spurs'. He knew what he was talking about, did Harry.

Joking aside, we murdered Villa that day in front of 61,000. We found plenty of space with our versatile passing game. All that hard work at Cheshunt before a competitive ball had been kicked in anger that season was continuing to pay off in our magical start.

Was it our best performance of the season? Well we got the most goals in one game in it but I wouldn't say it was our best win. I still didn't think, 'Ooh, we're going to win the league.' We liked being top. And there was quite a bit of celebrating in the dressing room afterwards. Bill even had the chairman's hat on as we posed for pictures with the champagne flowing to signify the achievement of passing Hull's record. Yet there was still a long way to go.

Bill would not let us think the job was done. We just got on with our games. As for the Double, well we were going to have to wait until the New Year before we even started considering the FA Cup.

We read the reports. They were brilliant. It was nice to get positive mentions, but it really didn't turn our heads.

Were our opponents frightened of us? Did they go out with the attitude 'we'll show you lot'? I didn't know what they were thinking. We were probably better than all of them as a team and played some good football. As I have said, we entertained the crowd. The away supporters at White Hart Lane enjoyed watching us. There was no booing or catcalling against us, just applause.

That's certainly how it was against Villa. They were a good team who put up a good performance. Gerry Hitchens, their centre-forward who went to Italy, did well against Maurice Norman in the first half and his side did create chances. One hit the bar and they scored a couple of goals. But with Danny and Dave controlling the midfield, we were just too good for them.

WE EXTENDED the run to 11 when we tore apart Wolves at Molineux. The corresponding fixture the season before – which had been such a breakthrough match for me – had hinted there was a changing of the guard in English football taking place. This performance was deemed confirmation of the power changing hands and I was personally delighted because it was further proof I had been accepted as a regular in a 'super' side.

The first thing I recall from that day was Eddie Clamp – who also played for Arsenal – getting me with a terrible foul. He was a tough, uncompromising defender and caught me right across the shins. Luckily I had seen him coming and tried to jump out of his way. But his challenge was high enough to whack me. And, boy, did it hurt. The dirty so-and-so. He would have been shown a straight red these days but on that afternoon Eddie escaped.

I also managed to make the crucial second goal, have three efforts which went close and net yet another for myself. Jonesy put us ahead from a ball by Les but then I supplied the ball for Danny to hit a second from long range before half-time. Les got the third and my one completed the scoreline. My goal was a bit of a pot-shot which hit a defender but they all count.

There were some superb individual performances with Danny and Dave dominant as usual and Wolves found it hard to contain John. He seemed to be involved in every passing move. Wolves struggled to cope overall and it was only their England left-half Ron Flowers who seemed to put up any resistance.

When we had to defend, Maurice Norman was outstanding in central defence. 'Monty' had to play his early days at Spurs playing right-back because the then manager Jimmy Anderson had bought John Ryden to replace Harry Clarke at centre-half. But Maurice kept at it and when Ryden was sold he came into the middle.

Wolves manager Stan Cullis conceded we were 'the greatest team I've seen'. Cullis was the perfect person from whom to seek an evaluation. He had established Wolves as the best team in the land with two successive title triumphs. He also had first-hand experience of the Magical Magyars, with many of the great Hungarian team which humiliated England in 1953 playing for Honved under floodlights in pioneering friendlies Wolves staged against top continental teams. Such games and Cullis's strong emphasis on fitness showed he was a bit of a progressive thinker. And he could speak three languages. Yet his football philosophy was largely about employing the long-ball game.

We provided a contrasting style with our version of Push and Run, which included more pizzazz and variety.

Against Wolves, although wearing the number 11 shirt, I swapped places with Cliff. Peter Baker, our right-back, even got himself in the opposing area. We were constantly on the move looking for space and supporting our team-mates, all the while tip-tapping quick passes around.

Cullis was like a lot of our opponents in being unafraid of praising us. There were 53,000 there and it seemed all of them cheered us to the echo. We enjoyed that.

The press thought us 'magical' and suggested a meeting with European giants Real Madrid, who had recently won another European Cup with legends like Alfredo Di Stefano and Ferenc Puskas. The thinking was that as no one in Britain could match us, perhaps continental giants might.

The club gave each of the players an engraved silver oval tray to commemorate our record. It states, 'Presented to T Dyson to commemorate the outstanding achievement in creating a new Football League record by winning the opening eleven First Division fixtures of the 1960-61 season.'

I was one of 14 players to receive the tray, with Bill Brown, Peter Baker, Ron Henry, Danny Blanchflower, Maurice Norman, Dave Mackay, Cliff Jones, John White, Bobby Smith, Les Allen, Terry Medwin, Tony Marchi and Frank Saul. We were all mentioned with chairman Fred Bearman, directors F. Wale, S. Wale, John Bearman, D. Deacock and R. Jarvis, plus Bill Nicholson.

They listed the opponents beaten and the results under the heading 'The Record'. It is one of my proudest possessions.

10
Bonding

THE CAMARADERIE among the players was developing at a tremendous rate. It was brilliant in the dressing room. We used to sit in the bath together after the match, which is something you can no longer do with all the health and safety regulations in place. But we enjoyed doing it, chatting about the game and having a laugh. There was no 'us and them' in the squad. The so-called big stars like Dave Mackay, Danny Blanchflower and John White mixed in. We were one unit.

We were a nice group but not so nice that we wouldn't have a go at each other if something was wrong. With Dave about we were never likely to be too nice. He wanted to be a winner and made sure we did as much as we could to make sure we were. And winning certainly helped bring us even closer together.

We looked after ourselves but also enjoyed each other's company socially. After a home game we would go to the Bell and Hare pub close to the ground and have a couple of halves of lager. No more! Dave and I and others used to park around the back and go into the bar meeting people who had just watched us play, discussing the game or whatever topic of conversation cropped up.

It has been suggested we had our own section but we weren't elitist like that. We used to mix with the supporters. Looking back I guess that is why they felt so close to us. They felt a part of what we were doing. We didn't think that at the time. We just saw having a chat over a drink in the pub with the fans as something perfectly natural for us.

Some others used the nearby Corner Pin pub where Push and Run players like Len Duquemin and Les Bennett used to have a snifter and a natter with followers.

There's still something like that going on in non-league, but as for the top clubs, it has all gone. The players have lost that closeness these days. Supporters don't even see the players after a game. The conversation would be difficult anyway I guess because so many players playing in the Premier League now are from abroad and thus do not have English as their native tongue.

I spoke to one press man who said, 'We never see the players. They get in their 4x4 or whatever and – boom – are gone. So we have to make up the stories.'

I was single and used to enjoy nights out at the dogs. I'd meet up with Dave and Bobby for the greyhounds at Haringey, Walthamstow or, as I did on one occasion, Clapton. Bobby only lived in Palmers Green and Dave was in Southgate. With me it wasn't far to travel to these venues for any of us. We either met there or I'd pick Dave up in my car and meet Bob there.

I used to go out to the dogs a couple of times a week. Greyhound racing was very popular then, although all those stadiums have now closed down as times have changed. The fact that the Hackney Wick track was replaced by the hockey arena for the 2012 London Olympics is another reflection of that. I used to love the dogs, going out in the fresh air and having a little punt.

After training I'd often join Dave, Bobby, Bill Brown and Maurice for lunch, to have a round of golf or have a bet on the horses, not surprising as I'm from a racing family.

The lifestyle of the day meant there were quite a few smokers in the team, including myself, although I've long since given up.

It was more the thing to smoke back then. The health warnings you see today weren't around. The ban on indoor smoking in enclosed public and work places had not reduced those who smoked to grubby outdoor spots at either their pub, restaurant or office.

We're much more health conscious these days, as is shown in modern-day football dressing rooms with their energy bars and protein shakes. In my day I don't remember anything bar the half-time tea.

A few of us smoked after games but Tommy Harmer, when he was with us, smoked a lot before because he got very nervous. But he had to do it out of the dressing room. We had two toilets attached. Tommy was always in one of them puffing away. Maurice Norman used to joke that the only way to get him out of the cubicle was to shove a piece of paper under the door saying it was time to go and play a football match. I think goalkeeper Bill Brown also used to light up on his way to the ground. He used to say it was to ease the butterflies in his stomach.

Ron Henry smoked after the game and even got into our communal bath with a fag on. It was with Bill Nick's blessing. He used to allow a post-match cigarette or two.

I ended up in court because of my then smoking habit. I got some cigarettes on the cheap. It came about when I bumped into a pal of mine, Jimmy Burton, as I was leaving my digs in Ponders End and he said, 'I've got loads of cigarettes. Do you want some? Take 200.' So I did. I was just being nice and doing Jimmy a favour by taking the cigarettes off his hands.

I didn't really want them and gave them to Peter Adcock back at my digs. He didn't smoke them but gave them to a pal who ran a tobacconists shop. The friend put them out the back. A customer came in and asked for this particular brand of cigarettes. An assistant who was serving went out the back and found the ones I had given to my landlord and sold a packet to her.

That night on *Police Five* – the television programme fronted by Shaw Taylor in the 1960s which tried to help the police solve crimes – I heard about this £20,000 robbery involving 2,000 cigarettes. They showed that on the bottom of each packet it said 'packed for the United Nations'. The customer must have seen it and gone to the police as her packet had the UN note on it. I wish she hadn't!

The next thing was the police came around and asked me questions. I didn't want to drop Jimmy in it and just said I had got the cigarettes for my landlord, hoping it would stop at me. I was advised to get myself a good lawyer!

I said, 'Oh, all right.' So I saw one and was told I had to elect to go for trial as I had a better chance of getting off with a jury. The papers were full of it with headlines like 'Spurs star sent for trial'. It was unbelievable as it was something I'd chosen to do.

So the day arrived and off we went to court. In we went. I looked behind me as I stood in the dock and saw the steps which led down to the cells. I thought, 'Bloody hell, I don't want to end up walking down there!' That was a sobering experience.

The judge involved had asked to preside because he was a Tottenham fan. My barrister said I had been given the cigarettes by a fan as a thank you for my performances. The judge joked, 'He wouldn't have got any this week.' And he was right because we had just played terribly.

Then this policeman handed me an autograph book and said to me, 'Just before they throw this out, can you sign this, please?' The next minute the judge said he wouldn't proceed further with the case. I was told that receiving stolen goods was very difficult to prove if the recipient didn't know at the time. Earlier a policeman backed me up with his evidence, saying I'd been unaware that the cigarettes were stolen.

After it was dismissed I saw the prosecution and defence barristers walk out together having a good old chin-wag and thought, 'What a game this is.'

Like with a lot of these kind of things, the fans on the terraces give you a bit of stick. David Beckham got lots of it after being sent off against Argentina for England in the 1998 World Cup as we went out. Likewise Luis Suarez in more recent years when with Liverpool, first over the 'racist comments' controversy he got involved in with Manchester United's Patrice Evra and then the biting incident with Chelsea's Branislav Ivanovic.

All that was serious and nasty. There was a lot of hostility for both Beckham and Suarez and it would not have been easy for them to take. Becks came through it all to become the international icon he is now, although the jury is still out on Suarez at the time of writing after another biting incident playing for Uruguay in the 2014 World Cup finals in Brazil.

The banter against me was light-hearted in comparison. I remember going up to Anfield just after the case to play Liverpool and copped plenty from the Kop. They were chanting, 'Ee-aye-addio, Dyson nicked the ciggies.' And it wasn't just on the Kop, it went all around the ground. If I had reacted negatively it would have aggravated the situation. I did not want to dig myself into a big hole. I'd have struggled to get out of that.

After all they were only taking the rise out of me during the pre-match warm-up. I just laughed it off. I joked with team-mate Jimmy Greaves about it, saying, 'Listen to that lot!' Jimmy had a good sense of humour and quipped that the chanting might be justified as I had nicked the cigarettes! I pointed out that wasn't the case, that I had only received them.

I know Jimmy has told quite a few funny stories from his playing days relating to players having scrapes with the law in a column for *The People*. He learned about how my old Spurs club-mate, the late Alfie Stokes, was up before the beak in the late 1950s for fare dodging on the buses. Bill Nick, apparently, had told Alfie to try and keep the club out of the headlines but, quite innocently I'm sure, he turned up in court wearing a Spurs blazer.

Jimmy related another one when we were together at Tottenham. There were certain supporters who hung around the players. They were genuine fans but known to be involved in petty pilfering. Jimmy told the paper, 'We had a band of followers at Tottenham and we all knew a lot of them were villains and petty criminals. They'd always be saying, "I've got a few washing machines, do you want one?" You'd ask what sort and they'd say, "Well, what sort do you want? I'll get you one."' We didn't get any free washing machines, though. We had to pay.

OUR RECORD run of 11 consecutive victories at the beginning of the 1960/61 season remains, as we publish, a top flight best all these years later. That, of course, gives the achievement perspective.

Just think of some of the quality of teams which have followed our one in English football. There have been the great Liverpool sides of the 1970s and 1980s under Bill Shankly, Bob Paisley and Joe Fagan, the Arsenal team managed by Arsene Wenger and dubbed the Invincibles for going through a whole season unbeaten, Chelsea under Jose Mourinho, the ridiculously successful Manchester United sides under Sir Alex Ferguson and the modern-day Manchester City team which Manuel Pellegrini led to the Premier League title in 2013/14.

They have all achieved great things. But our record-winning streak has been beyond all of them.

All good things come to an end, we are always reminded, though. But the way our run finished still irritates me to this day. We ended up drawing 1-1 with Manchester City, but God know how because we absolutely murdered them. We had the side that every Spurs fanatic knows by heart firing the bullets almost non-stop.

It was a Monday night fixture under the White Hart Lane floodlights and our level of form had not dropped off one iota. We were still hot. We had prepared as normal and believed as much as ever in how Bill wanted us to play.

There were nearly 60,000 roaring us on. What an atmosphere those lights created. We swarmed forward and littered their goal with shots. A report had it that we had fired in 25 to City's five by half-time. But we had just one goal to show for it with Bobby banging one in.

Even so the fans were delighted with what they had seen. They gave us a fantastic ovation as we disappeared into the tunnel for a ten-minute breather at half-time. There was a buzz. The mood gave no hint about any other outcome than a 12th victory on the bounce for us. Bobby and John had a couple of chances at the start of the second half.

They had a decent side. Their goalkeeper was the famous German stopper Bert Trautmann, the former Nazi soldier who had come back from breaking his neck in the FA Cup Final. Ken Barnes, the father of City legend Peter, was at wing-half. Denis Law wore the visitors' sky blue shirt prior to his going off to Torino in Italy the following year and then carving out a brilliant career at City's red neighbours at Old Trafford, although he was quiet that evening.

Suddenly City were level from an unlikely source, a winger called Clive Colbridge. And his goal was controversial to say the least. We thought he handled the ball before blasting home. But the referee Gilbert Pullin was having none of our moans and groans.

We picked up from where we'd left off before this bolt from the blue and all told had 39 attempts on goal against City's nine. We were so unlucky. We were good at a lot of things that season and one of them was the ability to take our chances but we just could not do that against City apart, of course, from Bobby's effort.

THE RESULT was a blip as in our next game five days later we took our opportunities. Our performance level yet again was high. Each display maintained our momentum. We looked forward to the trip to the City Ground to take on Nottingham Forest. We played well in front of Forest's biggest crowd of the season. Danny, Dave and John were at the core of our success, while the rest of us weren't too bad either.

I helped John put us ahead, Dave got one and Cliffy a couple, one being a header as I recall. It was another good day and a 4-0 win. One reporter from *The People*, Ralph Finn, who wrote several books about Spurs, gave each of us ten out of ten for our individual performances. Another writer suggested there needed to be a Super League so 'giants' like us could get the competition we deserved rather than having to be part of 'cruel, painful spectacles' against 'minnows'. That would be selling Forest short. It was just we were in the purplest of purple patches

Danny reckoned we were lucky to win game number 14 against Newcastle United at St James' Park. Well, Cliff scored a controversial goal to put us 3-2 up after Maurice and John had got our openers. Newcastle were not happy. They thought Cliffy was offside. Referees, like all of us, make mistakes, although this one, F.V. Stringer, told the media he was right. But we still needed another goal – from Bobby – to win it after they made it 3-3. It was a hell of a game. There was a massive crowd – more than 50,000. I remember the stadium was open at one end with St James' only having stands on three sides. What an atmosphere it had.

Newcastle were up for it. Jimmy Scoular was in their side. He had captained them to the FA Cup five years before and, I've read, the late, great Duncan Edwards described him as the 'finest tackler of the ball I ever saw'. Well on this Saturday afternoon up on Tyneside I would describe him as a dirty so-and-so.

They had some decent players, like Bob Stokoe, who later managed Sunderland to the 1973 FA Cup by stunning Don Revie's Leeds United, and Len Allchurch, a winger who was brother to Ivor, a Welsh legend and an old Swansea team-mate of Cliff's. There was also Bobby Mitchell on the left wing and Len White who managed to get a couple of goals against us.

We were lucky to get away with both points the following Wednesday. Cardiff City were in the lower half of the table when they arrived at White Hart Lane for the evening match.

There were close to 48,000 there, most expecting us to roll over our visitors. The temperatures were dropping and the club had invested in plastic covers to protect the pitch, which had been showing signs of wear and tear.

Reports had it that Danny and Dave were taking unnecessary risks when they helped the defence. Generally it was viewed that our performance had dipped in comparison to previous games. Not surprising, given how consistently good our displays had been.

Cardiff put us under a lot of pressure and forced us to come from behind. I managed to get back on the scoring trail to make it 1-1 with another header. I had drifted from outside-left into an inside-right position and got to a cross from Dave. I was described as 'little Terry Dyson' by one newspaper. It was not an uncommon description, emphasising, I suppose, how surprising it was that a small chap like me could get so many goals with his head against all these big defenders.

Terry Medwin, who had come in for injured Cliff, scored the second from a ball by Les as we got our noses in front before half-time. We had good fortune when we got a penalty as their number 4 Steve Gammon handled my cross – with the visitors claiming it was accidental – and our number 4, Danny, calmly converted it before Cardiff pulled one back late on in our 3-2 win.

I made a couple of goals as we showed more of what we can really do – particularly late on – when Fulham came to White Hart Lane one Saturday afternoon.

I thought I put on quite a good show but Walter Winterbottom, the England manager who was in the stands, did not pick me for his next squad as a result. I wondered, 'What more are you looking for from me, Walter? I should have been first on the team sheet!'

Cliff came back in – despite some doubts about whether he was over a knee problem – and, although I don't want to swell his ego, he did well and got two, the two I made! He was brave for the first. Fulham full-back Jim Langley, who was to become a team-mate of mine at Craven Cottage, swung his boot to clear my cross as Cliffy dived in with his head. We had missed him.

Johnny Haynes was in the Fulham team. He was such a good player, Johnny, a good passer. He was another I would get to know as a team-mate at the Cottage and in non-league.

But we showed, particularly with three goals in the last 15 minutes, that we remained in good shape. The headlines described us as 'slick' and we ran out winning 5-1. Again, we pulled an impressively-sized crowd and those wearing lilywhite rosettes and rattling navy blue and white rattles left the ground smiling as the media typed their complimentary write-ups.

But I did not agree with every word reported by the scribes, like the suggestions there was a bit of needle and tension between the teams. That's rubbish. Hogwash. One thing we never were was tense and I don't remember any particular hostility between us and Fulham. Maybe, because it was 5 November, on-the-field fireworks were assumed to have been let off because we had won so many games pressure must have been getting to us? It was all in the imagination of whoever was writing all that rubbish.

That win, though, meant we had totted up an incredible 31 points out of 32, while scoring 53 goals and conceding just 18. You'd think it couldn't happen. But it did. It was like a Roy of the Rovers story.

I read a quote from Bill, viewing our achievement with hindsight years later in the book *The Double*, saying to its author Ken Ferris, 'Looking back it was almost won after those first 11 matches. You draw the 12th and then win the next four and you are in with a great chance. At the time there was such a great feeling among the players. They did their work, got stuck in and enjoyed it. It was hard work but they were keen and conscientious.'

Bill did not make those feelings known at the time. We as players were still not thinking about the league. It was just the next game, despite what we had already done that campaign. But a record start like that must have knocked plenty of the stuffing out of our rivals. And it had given us an incredible amount of confidence while building the greatest of spirits among the players.

11
We've Got A Chance

THE START to the 1960/61 season had been fantastic for everyone. As far as I was concerned it could not have gone better. It was an absolute dream. No, beyond a dream. I had played in all of Spurs' 16 games from the first minute on day one against Everton to our nap hand against Fulham – and we had dropped just a single point.

I'd spent half a decade trying to prove myself good enough to play in the first team. There was a time, which I have mentioned, where I had been on the verge of wanting a change of scenery in order to establish myself as a regular performer in the Football League.

Yes, we were a team together when we won and sometimes lost, but I believe there were a few reasons why Bill had finally decided he wanted to make me a part of his team. I scored goals for a start. And I worked hard, made goals with crosses and passes, supported team-mates and tackled as aggressively as I could in a fair manner.

It was a roaming role. I'd give Ron Henry, my Army colleague at left-back, a hand defending. Or I would swap wings with Cliff, be Dave Mackay's wingman in his left-half role, or pop up in the middle alongside Bobby. I never waited on the left touchline like I often see wide players do today.

I often turn to my wife Kay when we watch either *Match of the Day* or a game on Sky Sports and say, 'Why is he out there? Get involved. Get in the box.' I'm sure they think if they do one good thing they've earned a little break. That wasn't for me.

Also, I put my heart and soul into it. Bill said I refused to be bullied – and he was right. I was so determined. I wanted to try and to make it impossible for Bill to leave me out.

I was flattered when he said of me, 'If I had to nominate a player who had the attitude I wanted it was Terry Dyson. He needed no motivation.' He was right, I didn't need any. I don't know why any player would not give it his all if he is playing to 60,000 people. But I think the main reason I'd remained a fixture in the side was because we had been winning.

WINTER WAS drawing in as we got deeper into November 1960. The pitches had lost a lot of grass and there appeared to be more brown than green on the surfaces. But it did not seem to make any difference whether we were playing on the pristine surfaces of late summer or a cloying mudheap. We just kept playing super football in front of full houses and had got full points bar one game. Yet even while we were romping along at the top, there was one team trying to hang on to our coat-tails. Sheffield Wednesday had made an impressive start to the season. They had one which would have been considered a flyer in most campaigns; going unbeaten in 12, although they had drawn three before their 13th proved unlucky with a 4-1 loss at Wolverhampton Wanderers.

Even though Spurs had opened up a seven-point gap with the victory over Fulham while Wednesday could only manage a 0-0 draw against Manchester United, we knew we faced a stiff test against the Owls at their place on 12 November.

It was a classic in as much as Wednesday were known for their mean defence – conceding just seven before their visit to Molineux – while our image was one of attack with our 53 goals against 18 impressive evidence.

Finding a way past uncompromising defenders such as Peter Swan and Tony Kay, soon to be caught up in a betting scandal but giving 100 per cent against us, along with rock-solid full-back Don Megson, would not be for the squeamish, although with players like Dave Mackay and Bobby Smith in our side we were hardly a bunch of wallflowers.

Hillsborough was packed to the gills. Nearly 54,000 squeezed in and it was thought if anyone could stop us it would be Harry Catterick's team. They were not only big and strong, but could play a bit and had the sign over us in their own backyard. Spurs had only won once in the league there – and that had been as far back as 1937.

More relevant was the fact they had ended Spurs' run of 12 unbeaten games – while I was largely still in the reserves and fighting for a first-team place – the previous season. On top of that, the Owls had given a bloody nose to all of the eight previous opponents who had left pointless after visiting Hillsborough since the start of the campaign.

With an even better unbeaten streak to protect and a dismal away record against them – plus Wednesday having turned their ground into a fortress that term – an argument could certainly have been put that we might just taste that first reverse.

People spoke about how defeat might act as a release valve for the pressure building up because of our unbeaten run, and would benefit our side's championship bid as a result. Well for a start, contrary to what some might think, we were still not feeling the tension even though recent performances had not been so consistently good as our opening games. We were still going game to game and enjoying our football. And we were confident of victory and did what we always did: try to play like we did at home. That was to go for the jugular.

Wednesday's defence lived up to its reputation with Swan and Kay helping to ensure the hosts were the most physical team we had faced all season. They stonewalled us in the first half. And they managed to hit the front after catching us on the break. Les had a shot saved by their reserve goalkeeper Roy McLaren. Roy cleared wide to Nobby Craig who crossed for Billy Griffin to beat Bill Brown.

We got level a couple of minutes later through Maurice with the help of a bit of good fortune. Les went down the left and the ball went out of play as the linesman flagged for a goal-kick. But the ref had already awarded us a free kick. Dave found Maurice's head and it was game on.

We clicked into gear. In fact we murdered them in the second half. Unfortunately, out of the blue, Megson, father of future Wednesday boss Gary, pushed the Owls forward and crossed. Maurice tried to cover it but Keith Ellis headed the ball over him and this was where Wednesday got lucky. Ellis hit the ball against one of our defenders and it rebounded to John Fantham who fired it past Bill. We gave it a go – and it got a bit fiery – but we just could not get that equaliser. We had won ten away games on the trot but not this one. We were forced to reflect on defeat for the first time that season.

I've read that we weren't upset as we got the coach to Sheffield Midland station for the return train trip to London, that we sang and cheered. Ron Henry has been quoted as saying that we were relieved to be beaten, that it was a load off our back. That's not how I remember the mood being. It was terrible.

We were not in a very good humour as we had our post-match meal on the train back. Us players were a bit down. We were disappointed with how we had played. We had had our chances and couldn't get the equaliser but the manner of the performance was a bit of a let-down for us. We'd had a sobering experience.

We were sombre. The mood reflected how much it meant. We were absolutely gutted, ALL of us. We weren't invincible. Who is? But we weren't used to getting beat.

We got our revenge later in the season but the Owls had proved that afternoon they were the one team in the league who could stop us. They proved a good team. But, at the risk of repeating myself yet again, there was no thought about the league being won or lost, just the feeling of looking forward to the next game. We learned our lessons from the defeat and soon got back on track.

In fact, it took just two days. A friendly against the Russian Cup winners Dinamo Tbilisi was just what we needed. We beat them 5-2 at White Hart Lane – and I got a couple. There were 46,000 there – and that was just for a friendly – and they saw us more like our old selves in terms of a result as well as performance.

FIVE DAYS later we underlined we had not suffered any hangover from the loss at Hillsborough in a match that mattered – our 18th league game of the season.

And I enjoyed myself with another two goals in a 6-0 win over Birmingham City at White Hart Lane. We were three up in a quarter of an hour and I managed to lash home the second high into the net – from a delivery by Les after Dave had picked up the ball – either side of goals by John and Cliff. We played some great stuff.

One report said, 'This is Spurs at their irresistible best…no defence can live with them when they are in this mood.' We had another burst of goals near the end which I started with my second before Bobby and Cliffy completed the scoring. And we could have got a few more but for their keeper. He made some great saves from Bobby and Cliff.

The performance reflected how we could play in the present and not think about what had gone before, like, of course, that defeat against our biggest rivals.

We maintained our form up at The Hawthorns as we overcame West Bromwich Albion 3-1 with Bobby scoring twice and Les once. They reckoned Bobby was offside for the opening goal, but we played smoothly enough to deserve another win.

The high standards we were setting were obvious in the first half in a classic home game against reigning champions Burnley on 3 December, a wet Saturday in front of nearly 59,000 creating an amazing atmosphere. We got chances and took them. We got three in as many minutes and were 4-0 up in 40 minutes. Bill, who did not take things for granted, thought it would be enough to secure both points. We were playing so well. But Burnley came back at us.

Ron had a hard time against their winger John Connelly, who pulled one back before half-time and then hit a late equaliser after we had made a couple of defensive errors to gift Burnley two further goals. I also remember their captain Jimmy McIlroy being dangerous with free kicks just outside our box.

The best game we took part in all season? Some described it as the 'match of the century'. Superstar journalist Ian Wooldridge colourfully wrote that it was 'the most thrilling match I've seen since Stanley Matthews turned a Cup final into a one-man mutiny against fate'. Others praised all 22 players for proving glory was more important than money with the row over the maximum wage between our players' union and the Football League raging. It was a brilliant match for the neutral on a muddy, sticky pitch. Burnley were a good side but it was galling to be 4-0 up and only draw. Bill was far from happy we let it slip.

We completed half our league fixtures for the season by showing how well we could defend with a 1-0 win against Preston North End at Deepdale. On paper, they looked a team we should beat as they had been struggling. But games aren't played on paper. We were a good side but even so we could not expect to win every match by a landslide. That's where the likes of our full-backs Peter Baker and Ron Henry came in, along with centre-half Maurice Norman.They did not bomb forward. They just defended. And when Preston managed to get through Bill Brown was in good form with some great saves.

We were running away with the league but refused to loosen our grip. Preston was the first of five straight victories which rounded off the year in a hectic December in which we crammed six games. It was a period we underlined how poor pitches and adverse weather conditions were not about to stop us playing the brand of football everyone in the country seemed to be enjoying.

WE BEGAN our second half of an unforgettable season on Saturday 17 December by coming out of our dressing rooms at Goodison Park greeted by fog coming in off the River Mersey. It was a stark contrast to our opening-day win at White Hart Lane in rather brighter conditions back in the August.

With the floodlights on, it looked like a yellow smog. It was wintry and miserable. Our hosts Everton had become our closest rivals, having moved into second, and there were 61,000 who braved the conditions for what was being revved up to be some contest.

Everton were a good side. Jimmy Gabriel and Brian Labone were top defenders. Billy Bingham was an international winger who went on to manage Northern Ireland. There was left-winger Derek Temple who made his name by scoring as the Toffees came back from 2-0 down against Wednesday to lift the 1966 FA Cup at Wembley shortly before England won their only World Cup there. There was also Alex Young, the Golden Vision, up front.

But it was their Scotland international midfielder Bobby Collins who was running the show that day. Dave Mackay swapped over from the left to contain him, and it worked. Danny was superb that day too. Dave deserved to get the goal of the game – he belted it in from 35 yards as we came away 3-1 to the good.

It was quite a full-on time because after we returned to London from Liverpool the club held its Christmas party. That's where the 14 of us got presented with those silver trays to commemorate our record start of 11 wins on the bounce.

It was a fun night and I also got presented with a copy of the book *Little Women*, a famous Victorian classic by Louisa M. Alcott. The joke was, of course, that I was only 5ft 4in, single and on the lookout for a little lady! My big pal Bobby Smith was presented with a model of a petrol station. He had this reputation for borrowing our cars and not replacing the petrol he'd used!

Our chairman Fred Bearman, aged 88, was given a copy of the racy and infamous D.H. Lawrence novel *Lady Chatterley's Lover*. The book had become a best-seller after an Old Bailey jury had the previous month overturned a verdict 30 years earlier that it was obscene. Dear old Fred had told the gathering, 'After I've read it I'll tell all you boys about it.'

IT WAS traditional to play derby double-headers at Christmas and this year it was against West Ham United. The first was on Christmas Eve and the second on Boxing Day. Two games – big ones at that – in three days, but we were up for both.

The Hammers had some more than useful players. John Bond and future manager John Lyall were their full-backs, with Ken Brown at centre-half. Phil Woosnam, whom I had played alongside in the Army, was in their line-up at inside-forward.

He was wearing a crew-cut hair-style, maybe left over from his days in khaki! We remembered each other, of course, but it was not an occasion on which to have a catch-up chat. The Hammers also had my old Spurs team-mate Dave Dunmore in their line-up. Dave left us for the Boleyn Ground the previous year. He was unlucky at our place as he was big and dangerous but he had had Bobby Smith in front of him.

They all played in both games – as did another, a blond lad called Bobby Moore. England's future World Cup-winning captain was only 19 at the time. He was a good player and a quiet, nice lad. A good passer of the ball, he never gave it away and tackled well. Not brilliant in the air or quick, but his positional play was superb. He could read the game so well. He certainly showed his potential against us over our holiday matches with the Hammers.

I always thought Mr Moore was shunted to the sidelines by the FA and by English football despite his leading our country to the biggest sporting achievement in our history. Like everyone, I was upset when he passed on so young. He was only 51 when he died of bowel cancer in 1993. They have put up a statue of him at the new Wembley – better late than never to get recognition. That statue should have been commissioned in 1966!

We overcame Bobby and Co 2-0 at White Hart Lane on Christmas Eve. And nearly 55,000 saw me head the second after John had nodded the first. It meant I had cracked double figures in the goalscoring department for the season. It also meant all five of Spurs' forwards had completed the achievement. It was also John's tenth, with Cliff already having reached that number. Les was on 12 and Bobby 18. It meant we had scored 73 goals in just 23 league games, 78 in all if you include our dynamic friendly defeat of Dinamo.

Bill Nick had to change the side for the return fixture in the East End with Cliffy damaging his knee in the first game while Bill Brown was suffering an ankle problem, so Terry Medwin and Johnny Hollowbread stepped in.

Johnny was another unlucky player. I'd played with him for the reserves a lot. Bill Brown had secured the number 1 jersey and Johnny had had Ted Ditchburn and Ron Reynolds as rivals before that which largely limited his chances of obtaining a first-team spot. But Johnny, who has sadly passed on, was a good keeper, a decent shot-stopper and athletic.

The reverse fixture with West Ham proved a memorable Boxing Day. I would come to know from personal experience that Bill Nick was not prone to overpraising performances, but he insisted our first-half display was the greatest he had seen from a Spurs side. If you also take into account that he was a member of the side which had been rated the best in the club's history until our lot got going, it was some statement.

He had a point. We played our familiar style of perpetual motion at a pace to suit ourselves, quick passing and cool finishing, with Danny outstanding. We got a couple of goals to show for it in the opening 45 minutes, with Les hitting the first off Ken Brown and the second directly into the net before John added the third. West Ham did have one great effort from Bobby Moore, but Johnny was up to the task and saved brilliantly.

We had one game left to finish off the year – and it was on New Year's Eve. I prided myself on my crossing and managed to play a part in three of the goals which helped beat Blackburn Rovers 5-2 to send most of the near-50,000 spectators at White Hart Lane off to celebrate the dawning of 1961 in good spirits.

Bryan Douglas put the visitors ahead in the unseasonal sunshine with one report stating we 'looked merely members of the human race'. But I was able to make the equaliser. I got fouled out on the left but still managed to retain possession. The referee waved play on and, as the Blackburn defence hesitated expecting to hear the man in black's whistle, I crossed for Bobby to smash in the equaliser. I slung over another cross, this from the right, and Les volleyed it in.

My third cross was backheeled by Bobby for Danny to make it 3-1. Les and Bobby wrapped it up with their second goals. We had had to battle for it, though, with Blackburn seeing plenty of the ball. Terry Medwin had come in with Cliffy injured.

Tony Marchi deputised for Dave Mackay and had to play most of it in pain after an early knock. Bill Nick must have been mindful of us having been knocked out of the FA Cup on our own patch the season before by Blackburn. And Tony, more defensive than Dave, helped out Maurice in the middle of our rearguard.

I'm sure Maurice was grateful – even with Tony not fully fit – because he was up against Derek Dougan, a Northern Ireland international striker, who was a real handful. A bit of a character was Derek, God rest his soul. He had plenty of chat, was dangerous and brave. Maurice did quite well against him and his aggressive style.

Tony usually filled in at left-half for Dave, while John Smith, another reliable stand-in, often deputised for Danny when our captain was unavailable at number 4. But Tony was definitely our first reserve.

Bill had bought back Tony from Italy the previous year. Tony was at the club in the days of Spurs' Push and Run team and became captain when Arthur Rowe tried to rebuild the side. But the club got a big offer from Juventus in Italy for him – £42,000 – in 1957 and took it. It was good business by Bill when Tony returned because he paid a fee which was less than half of that figure. Tony was classy, dependable and a lovely bloke. He'd have probably walked into most other teams.

We were ten points clear of Wolves and had only dropped four points in 25 league games, winning 22, drawing two and losing just that one against Wednesday who had now slipped to fourth, 13 points behind us. In total we had smashed in 81 goals, an average of 3.2 per game.

And it wasn't a case of leaving ourselves exposed at the other end because we only conceded 28. Arsenal, in their most frugal '1-0 to the Arsenal' phase under George Graham in the 1980s and 1990s, would have been pleased with that effort.

The bookies had stopped taking bets on us winning the league, yet it was only at this stage we started to think we had a chance of the title. We still did not think about the Double. It was just the league.

The analysts had it that Danny and John's partnership was the team's axis with John providing a 'broader sweep' than Tommy Harmer that helped vary our pace and power more efficiently.

Phil Soar wrote in *And The Spurs Go Marching On*, 'It was a one-horse race. The point and poise of the side was the Blanchflower–White axis, the wry, pale Scot having taken over Harmer's role to add a more urgent, broader sweep to a side now better able to vary pace and power.

'Mackay, who seemed to play with a skirl of bagpipes in his game, was the ideal blend of flinty, foraging pirateer opposite his skipper, and the so brave Jones with his jet speed was a scimitar aimed at the heart of any defence. And now Smith and Allen were proving Nicholson's point, that with all the style in the world it was still goals which won matches in the end.

'Little Dyson, small enough to be the son of his father, a leading northern jockey, had wrested the other wing place from Terry Medwin with a bit more dash and orthodoxy, while the defence had now bedded solidly down from keeper Brown and outwards to Baker and Henry, with Norman commanding in the air if occasionally reluctant to tackle on the ground.' Phil wrote that the defence, 'unlike the middle and front lines', was 'built on extremely conventional principles'.

12

Happy Cup Trails

THE POP charts were packed with song titles which some might have applied to Spurs on the day we begun our FA Cup campaign in the 1960/61 season.

The American performer Johnny Tillotson sung 'Poetry In Motion'. He was warbling about the girl of his dreams rather than describing our style of play, although any English friend might have made a transatlantic call to tip him off that the lyrics might have had a second meaning as far as English football was concerned!

There was the comedy record 'Goodness Gracious Me' by the British actor and *Goon Show* star Peter Sellers and Italian actress Sophia Loren, perhaps rather tenuously, reflecting the shock waves we had sent through it.

The legendary Elvis Presley was in the top ten having parked his interpretation of rock 'n' roll in a layby to move forward with the ballad 'It's Now Or Never'.

And anyone believing the Double could be ours might have been whistling that tune on either his or her way to White Hart Lane on the afternoon of Saturday 7 January 1961.

The crowd was gathering for our opening tie, a third-round meeting with Charlton Athletic. More travelled from our opponents' south London home than usually attended matches at The Valley. Among them was a pal of mine. When the FA had made the draw in their council chamber at Lancaster Gate in west London, he got straight on to tell me how excited he was that Charlton would provide our first opposition in the cup. He was a big fan of our opponents, although I'd had no idea. And his side gave us a run for our money.

We were overwhelming favourites given that Charlton were mid-table in the second tier of the Football League while we had totted up 46 out of 50 points at the top level.

It was even pointed out by those looking for an omen that it was our year to lift the cup because we had done so when the year ended in one in 1901 and 1921. The Second World War made sure it couldn't be done in 1941, but now, here in 1961 the 20-year cycle had come around once more.

We read and heard people talk about how victory was a foregone conclusion for 'super Spurs'. Us players chose to ignore the hype. We did not take anything for granted, not that Bill Nick would have allowed us to.

It was a little like our attitude in the league. It is a cliché, but we continued to take each game as it came without getting carried away. Of course, we had been doing so well in the league it was unsurprising our confidence was sky high.

But we had not kicked a ball in anger in the cup. We considered talk of a Double somewhat premature, particularly bearing in mind what had happened the previous season when there was a similar suggestion as Spurs went into the cup three points clear at the top and were dumped out by Blackburn Rovers in the fifth round.

And we expected Charlton to give us a difficult game despite the gap between us. We might have banged in more than 80 goals that season but the Valiants were hardly goal-shy. They had fired 57 and caught the eye with some entertaining football that season.

The weather was dull but 55,000 filled the stands and terraces. The old West Stand, which had three levels, with seats costing ten bob (50 pence in today's money) was packed. And everyone looked out on to a pitch which was a terrible mud heap.

The cup, without question, was the greatest domestic knockout competition in the world. Third round day was one of the biggest, if not these biggest, aside from the final, in the English football calendar. There was no thought of debating whether it had lost its allure, often a debate today with more competitions and distractions diluting its status. It was special.

Danny played brilliantly and laid on two goals for Les as we got a decent start. But Charlton were certainly not overawed and played some good football and reduced the arrears when Stuart Leary, a decent striker who had come over from South Africa, scored.

Then came a moment I will never forget. I managed to score my first FA Cup goal. I have Danny to thank for supplying the ball which gave me the opportunity to beat Willie Duff in the Charlton goal.

I tried to spin away to do my War Dance celebration, one that had stood me in good stead in the Football League and, lest you forget, the Football Combination. I was so pleased. As I've said, a goal is what you strive to get most as a player. And one I felt was justified, especially when you consider these days players go mad even if they just get a tap in. On this occasion, however, it did not quite go to plan. I lost my footing as I slipped on the muddy surface and got covered with even more mud.

But I was not bothered. I had made a vital contribution, scoring a big goal in what turned out to be the biggest of seasons. And it proved crucial because Charlton came back at us, made it 3-2 through Lawrie and gave us a lot of edgy moments as they forced us to hang on.

We weren't at our fluent best, but showed we possessed the vital ingredients of resilience and luck. If the Double was to be achieved, we would need those qualities along with our talent.

Our number in the bag for the fourth round draw was 17. When it was drawn out we knew it would be in front of our own fans again. There had been a pause as we crowded around a portable radio in our dressing room at White Hart Lane and listened intently. 'Number 32, Crewe Alexandra,' said the announcer after pulling out a numbered ball. Who would have believed it? The team Spurs had crushed 13-2 in the previous season's competition.

It seemed an even better draw than the one which pitted us against Charlton. Crewe seemed happy with it. Their manager Jimmy McGuigan told the papers, 'The cheers of the lads when the draw came through was instinctive. But all of us realise that this dream match could again turn out to be a nightmare.

'I would rate Spurs among the top three clubs in Europe. We cannot hope to beat them. But this time there will be no humiliation. No jeers that we heard last time from the Londoners.' Jimmy was the trainer the year before and admitted then to the media, 'I wanted the ground to open up and swallow me.'

The difference for me, of course, was I had not had any involvement in that club record scoreline. Now I was a first-team regular. I had not missed a game for the side in a season of all seasons. But any thoughts of the tie were put away to the back of our minds. Back to the forefront came our league campaign.

IN THE meantime, the players' union, the Professional Footballers' Association, led by chairman Jimmy Hill, was fighting to get the maximum wage lifted. A players' strike, backed by the likes of Brian Clough and Bobby Robson, was threatened.

Two days after we had beaten Charlton, the Football League made a rejected proposal to satisfy the players and avert the strike set for 21 January.

The story dominated the press and I know Dave Mackay was far from happy with the focus on such matters. He felt people were 'sick and tired' of hearing about the issue.

Jimmy Hill came round to try and get 100 per cent membership among all the players and I felt it was a good cause. Some clubs were earning fortunes, while their players weren't.

A TRIP to Manchester often entailed a visit to the dogs at Salford. Bill did not mind as long as we did not do anything to affect our fitness. I went with Bobby and Dave after checking into the Queen's Hotel on the night before we were due to face Manchester United for our first league game of the New Year. Unfortunately when I peered out of my hotel room bedroom the following day the view was obscured by fog and our match postponed until the Monday evening.

We had a few injury problems. Peter Baker pulled a muscle in training on Sunday and Ken Barton, a defensive-minded full-back and a nice lad, who sadly died when he was only 44 in 1982, was also ruled out.

John Smith, who had come from West Ham in the swap for Dave Dunmore, took over from Terry Medwin who himself had been standing in for the injured Cliffy against West Ham, Blackburn and Charlton.

The physical ailments didn't help on the night in front of a 66,000 crowd at Old Trafford. They made us struggle to find our natural rhythm. United's fans were incredible and as they cheered on good side with Albert Quixall, Maurice Setters, Bill Foulkes and Bobby Charlton.

But what stuck in my craw about that match was the way they treated Danny. I suspected Matt Busby of being a bit of a so-and-so with his tactics in this match. Danny believed they 'had' him up there. They had a couple of players who could put it about and Danny was whacked and it put him out of effective action. He stayed out there to make up the numbers with no substitutes allowed. And United were able to score a goal in each half through Nobby Stiles, who was to be in the England team which lifted the World Cup five years later, and Mark Pearson for a 2-0 win.

ON 18 January, two days after our loss to United, two days before John F. Kennedy became President of the United States and three before players were due to down tools, the maximum wage was abolished and the strike called off.

I believe one major reason the ceiling was finally lifted came about when all the Wolves team threatened to pull out of a prestigious televised friendly against foreign opposition.

The FA, though, refused to give up on the retain-and-transfer system. That meant players were still not allowed to move clubs at the end of their contract if their employers offered them 'reasonable' terms acceptable to the FA, even if they happened to be not as good as their previous ones. Jimmy Hill called it a 'slave contract'.

Two years later the High Court ruled it an 'unjustifiable restraint of trade' following the landmark case brought by Arsenal's George Eastham. George took former club Newcastle, with whom he had been in dispute, to court, with the encouragement of the PFA, to prove the system unlawful. The Bosman case in recent times gave players even more freedom with the doors Eastham had broken down.

But for now the focus was more on the lifting of the maximum wage. The players were more in the money. Hill's Fulham chairman Tommy Trinder went out and paid his club's star player Johnny Haynes, the England captain, £100 a week. And this has led, in the modern day, to some players earning £200,000 a week – a far cry from how much I personally benefited financially from the game. You'd have to multiply my earnings by 5,000 to reach that six-figure sum, although I'd doubled my weekly money to £40 as a result of the cap being removed! It was the most I EVER earned as a Spurs player, although our key performers Danny, Dave and John were on £60.

Spurs hung on to half my improved wages and gave me the other half in two lump sums at Christmas and at the end of the season. I found it a good system, one which remained in place for two or three years. It enabled me to pay for that car outright.

I had not been earning that much above the national wage, anyway, but even then I had enough to live on as I didn't lead an extravagant lifestyle, one I believe is a world away from the one led by the modern-day footballer.

The rent at my 'digs' was, you may recall, only £3 to £4 a week when these days the average prices in Ponders End are now around 100 times that amount. And I had to fork out a little extra to pay for restaurant meals when I went to the dogs with Dave and Bobby.

In the afternoons there were my betting shop visits with Bobby when I just risked small amounts compared to Bob, who was always a bigger gambler than me.

Another night I used to go to the cinema. I enjoyed that, especially the westerns like *The Magnificent Seven* with Yul Brynner and the other six and *The Alamo* with John Wayne. I even saw action films such as *Spartacus* with Kirk Douglas and Laurence Olivier.

Or else I would just stay in with the Adcock family and watch the telly and spend nowt. I enjoyed a quiz called *Take Your Pick* hosted by Michael Miles with its Yes-No Interlude and the Clint Eastwood western *Rawhide*.

I did spend a bit of money on suits. I used to know a tailor up in the East End of London who made them up for me. A sharp Italian style – I didn't mess about!

I was to wear them on our parades when showing off our trophies. But I don't think my sense of style in what I wore helped me when I was trying to woo Kay. She just remembers me in Marks and Spencer's suits off the peg. I only had a couple of those tailor-made combos!

I was into music and used to buy singles. You know what I mean. The vinyl discs which spun round your record deck at 45 revolutions per minute. You could hold about six above the deck of your Dansette before they dropped down individually on to it with the arm of the needle automatically moving on to the first groove.

One of my particular favourites was Louis Prima. He was a great singer and a trumpeter – and also acted in a few films. He was the King of Swing in the 1930s after having a New Orleans jazz group. Louis also had a big band and was a lounge act in Las Vegas. He became known for singing 'The King of the Swingers' in the cartoon version of *The Jungle Book* but when I was buying his music he was producing pop-rock music. I spent quite a time listening to his records in my bedroom at Ponders End.

There was also the Royal in Tottenham High Road. That used to stage dances with a live band that played rock 'n' roll and the twist, a dance craze inspired by Chubby Checker's big hit of the same name in 1960. It was a case of dance the night away. In the Double season there were only a couple of us single lads in the team, but the married ones used to join in the fun – without their wives.

It was all quite innocent. They were fun nights. Yes, I used to meet girls there, but there was never anything serious going on. No one special. I never messed about. There was no potential for kiss and tell exposés by WAGs in the newspapers as far as I was concerned.

A lot of girls seem to latch themselves on to footballers at social get-togethers these days. There was none of that stuff. We weren't even considered that famous by the clientele there. It was a different outlook back then. We used to go to a couple of clubs with 'bouncers' on the door in the East End. It was the time of the Kray brothers, who dominated the criminal world in that area.

The siblings had a feared reputation. The Krays were big boxing fans in the East End. A few of us players used to go to the occasional show in the area, Bethnal Green, or wherever, although we never met the brothers.

There was one show I went to with Dave Mackay when we had a little trouble – before we got there. I'd just got my new Ford car and drove round to Dave's place in Southgate to pick him up. As I waited for Dave to get ready, I heard a shout from upstairs from Dave.

One of his boys had got into my car and Dave had noticed from his window that the car was rolling back. His kid had taken the handbrake off and my car rolled into the parked car of one of Dave's neighbours. Fortunately there wasn't much damage done and Dave's wife Isobel diplomatically smoothed things over with the folk next door.

We did attract a few dodgy characters around the East End and north London. They used to like their football, like Johnny 'The Stick' Goldstein and One-Armed Lou, quite a nickname but also quite a literal one. The Stick was a ticket spiv who was mad on Spurs but absolutely hated Arsenal with a passion. We got to hear that he'd sold tickets to Arsenal fans for a cup final at Wembley one time and we questioned him on that. And he told us, 'You ought to see where those seats were – obscured views behind pillars.' But we didn't really socialise with them and they never caused us any harm.

We couldn't afford to go 'up west' much to the clubs there, especially when we were only on the maximum wage. These days you read about players going to these flash clubs as celebrities alongside film, pop and soap stars, spending thousand and thousands on one night out, not being content with one bottle of champagne when they can have TWO or more, or even having their own 'celebrities section' inside the club of choice. As I've suggested, we certainly weren't viewed as public figures comparable to those in the movie and music worlds.

But whatever we did it was never excessive. Yes, I used to go out for a few drinks with Dave and some of the other lads after a game, but we always looked after ourselves so we were 100 per cent able to perform at our peak for Spurs. I was so dedicated I sometimes used to come into the ground on a Sunday and do a bit of training. I kept myself fit, and looked after myself mentally and physically. My life revolved around the football so I could give of my best on a matchday. I owed that to everyone at the club, the supporters and myself.

OUR REVERSE against United was only our second defeat in 26 league games in 1960/61, but we soon got back on track with a result that the supporters especially enjoyed. We completed the double over Arsenal with a 4-2 win.

The animosity between clubs was pretty much down to the fans, which I've mentioned. Tottenham supporters absolutely loved it when we pulled off such results against the 'old enemy' while the players from both sides got on with each other. It was a tough old encounter with another mega gate. More than 65,000 saw a battle at White Hart Lane. We had Cliffy back but he took an early battering, when Billy McCullough brought him down in full flight. But Cliff just bounced back up and had a great game.

Tommy Docherty, Dave's Scotland team-mate, was also getting stuck in to us, largely hard but fair, although he eventually got himself a booking, an offence which was bigger news in those days when referees were less inclined to take names.

I got caught myself. It was by a young Arsenal defender, Terry Neill, who went on to manage Spurs and Arsenal. Terry's challenge on me was in the penalty area. Danny converted the spot-kick to give us a 2-1 lead. And the contest was killed off by a strike from Bobby and a second for Les after he had cancelled out a 1-0 lead for the visitors.

I don't think it was any coincidence we had rediscovered our form with all our main men back, Peter Baker returning to restore the Famous XI.

As Julian Holland put it in his book *Spurs – The Double*, 'On top Spurs played like peacocks, showing every rainbow feather, aloofly preening themselves before their adoring fans (many of whom had paid an illicit fiver to see the game). It was as though, after Monday's shaking at Old Trafford, they had determined to refresh themselves, to run over their scales, to go through their practice pieces, to rehearse their exercises. Restore to concert pitch.'

John Arlott wrote in *The Observer*, 'Wearing the air of conscious superiority which is now their accustomed strip, Tottenham brushed aside some strenuous tackling to beat Arsenal with time and breath to spare.'

Colourful writing, for sure. But it seemed we kept prodding writers to produce their best prose.

We had netted 48 points from a maximum 54 in 27 league games. The wagon was still rolling towards emulating Arthur Rowe's Push and Run team's title triumph.

THE FOCUS returned to the FA Cup and the second successive visit of Crewe in the competition on 28 January 1961.

Although there had been that freak 13-2 result in our favour 11 months before, we adopted a sensible 'confident but not overconfident' approach. We thought we would beat them because we were a good team. That we would try and play well and if we did we had a good chance. Bill, as I have probably said already, would NEVER let us get carried away. And if we did he would bring us back to earth quickly. We murdered them. It was comfortable.

The cup seemed to be becoming a lucky one for me personally. I managed to score for the second tie in a row. It was another header. I celebrated with Dave, who was all smiles. Dave managed one with his head as well and I made one for Cliff, while Bobby and Les also scored in a 5-1 win.

We were given an away draw in the fifth round to either Peterborough United or Aston Villa, who had drawn 1-1 before two goals by Peter McParland in the replay ensured we would be travelling to England's second city, Birmingham, to Villa Park to bid for a quarter-final spot.

THE CHAMPIONSHIP race was back in our heads for the following Saturday with Leicester City visiting White Hart Lane. We were 12 points clear at the top of the table and had scored NINE times in our previous two home league games.

The press also pointed out how success on the field was bringing a cash windfall off it. The *Daily Mail* reckoned we were 'within sight of the greatest money prize any British side has ever played for'.

And more and more were tipping us for the Double. But we were unable to prevent our second defeat in our three league games of 1961. The 3-2 reverse against Leicester City was our first at home, and our opponents were quoted predicting we weren't going to lift league and cup.

We would turn that around on the biggest English football stage of all at Wembley a few months down the line, but for now it was a small prick in our title-chasing bubble. It wasn't good.

Les and Danny twice put us back level but Leicester captain Jimmy Walsh scored their winner, his second, with Ken Leek also scoring for them. They weren't a bad side.

DANNY HAD continued to be a massive influence as a player, captain and on-field manager and did not deserve to be on the losing side.

His larger-than-life personality had also made him a household name in Britain. We saw him on the TV advertising a cereal, saying 'hullo there', an expression which became a national catchphrase.

It was no surprise *This Is Your Life* wanted to feature him. The famous television programme caught famous folk unawares by arranging a meeting under false pretences. Then they would tell their subject they were featuring their story live on air with the help of a 'big red book' after secretly bringing together relatives, friends and colleagues.

On the night of the Leicester defeat, we were all gathered in a London studio as the presenter Eamonn Andrews went out to trap his prey. The plan for myself and the other players was to come out from the back as a collective after all the other guests had appeared.

Eamonn told his producer, 'We've got him' as he walked towards Danny, saying to him, 'Hello Danny. See that light?' Danny said 'yes' and then Eamonn said to him, 'Well tonight Danny Blanchflower...' He was going to finish off by saying 'this is your life', but before he did Danny turned and ran out of the studio area. They tried to get him back in but he wouldn't return.

It was the first time it had happened to the show, which was a popular one. This geezer came out – it was Angus Mackay, producer of BBC radio's *Sports Report* – in an ordinary suit and told us and the audience who didn't know who the subject would be, 'I normally come out in a dress suit at this time but as you can see I'm not as, ladies and gentlemen, there will be no show tonight.'

I didn't know what had happened at this stage. When I did I thought, 'Flip me, I can't believe this.' Danny's brother Jackie, a Munich air disaster survivor, had come down along with so many of our captain's family and Danny wouldn't be seeing any of them.

Publicly, he said, 'I did it for personal reasons. If I told you what they were they wouldn't be personal anymore, would they?'

I saw him the next day at training and gave him some stick – a few of the lads did – and asked him why he had done it. He told me, 'I don't believe in the programme. They only say good things about you, but we've all done bad things. I couldn't agree to do it.' His actions impressed a few commentators. Ralph Finn said in his book *Spurs Supreme*, 'His refusal to put himself in the limelight of *This Is Your Life*, his masterly display of argumentative erudition at a *Face To Face* encounter [a television programme he did afterwards], his occasional radio and TV sallies have endeared him to a large audience and, in the process, have succeeded in doing more for the good name of soccer and its players than any man, club, league or organisation has managed to do since football began.'

Julian Holland in *Spurs – The Double* wrote, 'In walking out of *This Is Your Life* he was making another gesture – and one of the most effective he has ever made – in bringing dignity to professional footballers…that a celebrity, even if he is only a professional footballer, has a right to say no to the public when it wants him to do something he does not like.'

IT WAS important we got immediately back on track after the disappointment against Leicester.

We had the chance to do that against Aston Villa at Villa Park the following Saturday. We hoped to complete the double over them – at least – after that six-goal win over them earlier in the season.

It was billed as a rehearsal for our fifth-round FA Cup tie against them at the same venue the following week. Bill warned us not to view it like that as it was something completely separate and tactics would be different.

It was reported the players' minds were on the cup game and that we were sizing each other up for it. Observers thought it a tense affair, which meant we weren't as calm and self-confident as usual, and that our rhythm lacked its smoothness. I remember certainly that Villa manager Joe Mercer gave us a tactical scare early on by putting a player on Danny full-time. Danny took his marker – Bobby Thomson – on a walkabout into the Spurs defence but said afterwards he was frustrated the space created wasn't exploited enough in a goalless first half.

Danny told us at the interval to give him the ball even though he was marked and play Push and Run. That the quick passing and movement would undo Villa. And he was right.

He and Dave were magnificent as we won 2-1 to reach the 50-point mark quicker than any other team in the history of the First Division. Bobby headed us in front and I doubled our lead. I remember it clearly. I'd got in there, just outside the six-yard box and just caught the ball on the volley and it flashed in.

We were used to doing well in the league at Villa and delighted this game proved no different. They were certainly two welcome points after one or two erratic results.

THE LEAGUE victory clearly whetted the appetite for the cup game against Villa on their home turf. It attracted the second biggest crowd to watch us in a season of big crowds watching us: 65,474, just 61 fewer than witnessed our Old Trafford reverse.

It seemed everyone wanted to be there to bear witness, like when Matthews played in his winning cup final eight years before, or they would when Cassius Clay beat Sonny Liston to become world heavyweight boxing champion and launch of the legend of The Greatest three years later. Or even when champion jockey Tony McCoy more modestly rode his 4,000th winner over jumps at Towcester in modern times.

We might have done well against Villa themselves in the league, but Villa Park was a bogey ground for us in the cup. Spurs had lost three semi-finals to last-minute goals since the Second World War at that venue.

But we won it comfortably and played well, with Dave again magnificent. Reporter Ian Wooldridge, another to tout us as nailed-on Double winners, wrote that Dave 'performed miracles of delicate ball control, tackled like a battering ram'. His partnership with Danny was hailed as the 'greatest partnership in modern soccer'.

We took the lead with a five-player move which ended with Cliffy having a shot deflected past his own goalkeeper by John Neal, who became Chelsea manager down the road.

I started a move which gave us our second goal by feeding John before the ball went from Bobby to Les to Cliff and the back of Villa goalkeeper Geoff Sidebottom's net.

Joe Mercer was complimentary about us. That's how opposing managers continued to view us instead of the bitching that goes on between them these days. We continued to enjoy these accolades and even Bill admitted we had a chance of the Double.

One negative was when Villa's Peter McParland caught Dave. We crowded around Peter because we thought he had 'done' him. It was a terrible tackle. Even Maurice, who was generally even tempered, got hold of Peter as a result. Peter got spoken to by the ref – and he was spoken to by us, I can tell you that. He was a dirty so-and-so that day!

13
Balancing Act

THERE WAS no way, I guess, we could have kept up the league form we had shown up until the turn of the year. There was bound to be a splutter. Our defeats against Manchester United and Leicester City had shown that, although we had managed to bounce back straightaway with wins.

There were thousands locked out as Wolverhampton Wanderers called on 748 Tottenham High Road on Wednesday 22 February 1961. Over 62,000 were wedged into our home as we were still a big draw, the target to be shot at. Every opponent remained desperate to beat us and Wolves were no exception. We had put on a performance at their place earlier in the season which was considered symbolic of a new wave replacing the old with Wolves manager Stan Cullis insisting we were the best team he had seen, although before this one he hinted we might be cracking. We had also beaten them six times in a row at home.

Under the White Hart Lane floodlights I was thrilled to play a part in the build-up for Bobby to put us in front. But Wolves put in a lot of blood, sweat and tears to stifle us and they had solid internationals like Ron Flowers, Bill Slater and Eddie Clamp. Even when they lost their captain Slater after our goal they still managed to secure a 1-1 draw.

Julian Holland was of the opinion in his book *Spurs – The Double* that myself and Cliffy 'ran into trouble, and the hard thighs of Wolverhampton's defenders, as though drawn by magnets'. Thanks for that, Julian.

We managed to get back on the winning trail straightaway after a blip for the third match in a row. Manchester is known for its rain. And when we took on City – with Denis Law – at Maine Road in front of yet another full house the wet stuff was torrential. And it left the pitch swamped in water as we all squelched around as if running around in a glue pot.

The state of the pitch was terrible. It was not the only one we had played on that season of course, but somehow, typically, we were still able to play our football. Even though the ball was a lead weight in contrast to the flyaway balls of today and our boots heavier than the lighter-than-light versions worn now.

I don't know exactly how we managed to do it. It was just how we were taught by Bill and we just did. I suppose the style was natural to us. Terry Medwin was in again for Cliff – with the versatile Tony taking over from Maurice – and we were grateful to him for popping up with the only goal of the game. Terry always did well when he came in, a quick winger with an eye for goal.

BACK TO the FA Cup. You only had to look at the amount of people who watched our two games against Sunderland in the sixth round to appreciate just how important this competition was to English communities. There was a combined total of 126,000 squeezing the Victorian structures of Roker Park and White Hart Lane in the space of four days! That, though, wasn't the whole story.

It was the reaction of the people present and, indeed, those left outside, some with a ticket I'm told, that filled out the tale which does full justice to the magic of the cup. People talk about the magic of it these days, but there's a slight air of self-delusion in comparison. As I have already said, the FA Cup just doesn't mean what it did in March 1961.

We travelled up to Wearside on the fourth day of the month for the first game at Roker – Sunderland's ground before the modern-day move to the Stadium of Light – expecting a tough encounter. The hosts had lost their place in the top flight after 70 years not long before but had been storming along that season, having only lost one in 20 over the previous five months. They were a young side with some good players like their captain Stan Anderson and centre-half Hurley, who was a bit of a legend up there.

What we weren't prepared for was the reaction of their supporters. I would not experience anything like it in all my time in football. The Roker Roar among more than 61,000 inside their stadium was absolutely deafening and the excitement among their followers was incredible.

Even when Cliffy gave us the lead it failed to burst the fans' bubble. And their team were definitely buoyed by that support. The pressure was intense with the noise of the crowd, so loud we literally could not hear each other. It was backs to the wall.

We held out for as long as we could but they eventually got their equaliser through Willie McPheat. Pandemonium! Their fans surged on to the pitch, throwing their bobble hats in the air. It was just pure exuberance. Largely good-natured.

They were so happy they wanted to hug their heroes and offer personal congratulations, although I did hear of one story of a fan who went a bit too far. This particularly supporter, I'm told, came over to Bill Brown as he was getting the ball out of the net to ask him for his autograph! Cheeky so-and-so! We were forced to hang on – and were lucky to do so. Cup fever was raging for the replay at our place under our lights the following Wednesday. There were 64,797 crammed into White Hart Lane that night.

Thousands were locked outside no doubt trying to convince those on the turnstiles they either had a ticket or deserved entry. I read reports a few surged and pushed police back with a few helmets going flying! As the game kicked off many, I'm told, hung around and reacted to the sounds they heard from inside the stadium. The fans had gathered since mid-afternoon, even as early as when the schoolchildren left for home, with the education authorities deciding that in future the pupils would have a half-day off when we had a big midweek game in the evening.

Bobby only got into the dressing room about 25 minutes before kick-off. He'd had to abandon his car and got a lift through the crowds on the back of a policeman's bike while his wife had to walk to the ground. We had shown resilience at Roker, but mostly it had been about survival.

It was a completely different story this night with so much of the crowd with us. The atmosphere was brilliant under the lights and I thought to myself, 'I'll have some of that, let's go.'

Expectations were high along with the feeling in some quarters that Sunderland had had their chance and we were going to make sure that was the case. And we lived up to the opinions to slaughter them.

It went well for me personally with two goals as we won 5-0. Cliff made my first and our third just before half-time after Les and Bobby had scored. Les did brilliantly for my second which made it four. Dave got the other goal.

Julian Holland described it well in his book *Spurs – The Double*, giving Les deserved credit. He wrote, 'Almost unnoticed there suddenly danced into the Sunderland penalty area a white-clad figure, the ball immediately at his toe. Delicately he picked his way past not one or two of the red-and-white striped defenders, but four before he slipped the ball inside for Dyson to hammer home the fourth goal.

'For once the heavy, frowning uncertainty left Les Allen's face. His grin, as his colleagues mobbed him with their salty-lipped congratulations, seemed to reflect perhaps that he was worthy after all to rank as an equal in this team of stars.'

Our 'stars' also came to the party that night. John, Danny and Dave were magnificent. Dave proved he really was the heart of the club.

THE FURTHER we got in the cup the more hectic the schedule became as we tried to balance it with our league commitments. As we'd needed a replay to get beyond the Mackems, we returned to the league for our third match in a week.

On paper it was winnable, even though we were playing Cardiff City at their old home, Ninian Park. We had not lost to the Bluebirds for years. I remember it was on a Saturday night under lights because Wales were involved in a rugby international in our hosts' capital in the afternoon.

I gave us the lead. In fact, we were twice in front when Les also scored, but Cardiff came back both times to equalise. And Derek Tapscott, who I knew from when he played for Arsenal, hit their winner. The Gunners had signed him from his hometown club Barry, the setting of that great modern television comedy *Gavin and Stacey* (which features the actor Mathew Horne, a Spurs fan). Derek was a good striker. I can still picture the moment. He was right down the far end from me. It made most of the 46,000 crowd happy. It was reckoned to be the biggest shock of the season.

It was a choker, not only because it was a terrible result for us but because we had played so well in the first half that we should have had a comfortable lead. We had averaged one point per league game since the dawn of the New Year. It was the first of two successive defeats – the second came 11 days later.

FOR THE time being we had to put our cup heads back on to face the reigning league champions Burnley in the semi-finals on Saturday 18 March, 1961.

It was at the ground where we had lost last-four showdowns in 1948, 1953 and 1956. Blackpool did for us on the first two occasions, the second time leading to that most famous cup story when Stanley Matthews went on to pick up his first winners' medal. And Manchester City completed our unwanted hat-trick. The press made a lot of our Villa Park hoodoo.

We knew it would be hard as soon as we heard we'd been drawn against Burnley on the dressing room radio at the Lane. The memory of how they had come back from 4-0 down to snatch a point at our home at the start of December was still fresh in our minds.

Bill Nicholson booked a hotel for us in the lead-up to the semi so we could train and relax away from it all. The Caswell was in Mumbles on the south Wales coast. It was a lovely spot, not far from Swansea where Cliff and Terry Medwin were born.

Up to this point, as I've said, there had been no official talk of us winning the Double. But in the sun lounge of the Caswell there was.

Despite our wobble in the league, we allowed ourselves to feel confident enough to think that we would win the title. But the FA Cup on top? That was something neither myself nor any of the other lads had dared to bring up in conversation.

But Danny had an instinct for saying the right thing at the right time on and off the field. He displayed that instinct to us in that sun lounge. He told us there for the first time that he felt we had a good chance as we were only two games away from the cup and would only need to average just over a point from each of our final ten league games to emulate Spurs' title winners of 1951. We all agreed.

Danny's ability of saying the right thing was also evident in a chat he had with the opposing captain Jimmy McIlroy. Danny and Jimmy used to share a room when they were together on international duty with Northern Ireland, with McIlroy smiling as he told how his team-mate kept him up all night talking football!

And Danny spoke to him before the semi, believing their conversation gave us a little psychological edge. He told the tale in his autobiography *The Double and Before*. Danny wrote, 'We had the home dressing room and I kidded Jimmy McIlroy about it before the semi-final game. "We've got the lucky dressing room," I said, "and you never win at Villa Park – Burnley never do well there."

'"We've not been beaten here in our own jerseys yet," Mac jibed. "Burnley always have to change there as their shirts are the same as Villa's."

'"We've never lost against those jerseys here," I quipped back. We had not lost a league match at Villa Park since the war.

'"Where did you stay last night?" I asked Jimmy.

'"Droitwich," he said.

'"Poor sods," I smirked, "we stayed there before our 1956 semi-final here and lost."

'Jimmy smiled at my insinuations but I hoped they were making him feel uncomfortable.'

We kept our fingers crossed that the fact Burnley had lost 4-1 to Hamburg in the European Cup a few days before our meeting would also put them off balance.

It was blustery and sunny and the pitch was quite hard, but we normally had decent games against Burnley. And this was no exception, although slightly below the normal level because of what was at stake.

I think it was a harder game than it would have been at Wembley where the open spaces of the national stadium would have suited our more expansive team game. Burnley and ourselves were well matched.

We all knew that winning the league was a sign of a consistently high level of performance. But with the cup you have to factor in something you don't really have control over – luck. It seemed as if we'd need it judging by a practice we had against our reserves at White Hart Lane after coming back from Mumbles. The first team, minus Danny, were beaten 4-1. I got our consolation goal after the 'stiffs' had gone 4-0 up.

We'd got some good fortune as Sunderland threw the kitchen sink at us in the first game of our sixth-round tie.

And we certainly got some more against Burnley. Whatever Danny said to McIlroy, it seems their skipper did not let it affect him adversely as he pulled the strings in our opponents' midfield.

But our defence stood firm. Bill Brown cut out any crosses, Peter and Ron were calm and Maurice kept a tight rein on their blond striker Ray Pointer, while Dave made it difficult for McIlroy.

The wheel of fortune first spun in our favour after about half an hour during probably our first proper attack. Burnley captain Jimmy Adamson, at centre-half, was about to intercept a ball from Les, but the wind caught it and blew it by him to Bobby who lashed it in. Their goalkeeper Adam Blacklaw had no chance. Goals had dried up for Bobby and I was especially pleased my dog track buddy had proved himself on one of the biggest of stages. It changed the game and we came forward. I had a header which beat Blacklaw and was handled on the line by their right-back John Angus. Unfortunately, the referee didn't see it and waved play on.

But we had two massive slices of luck. Ron handled in our area, but the referee ignored Burnley appeals. And then the man in black disallowed a headed equaliser from Jimmy Robson following a corner, adjudging he had climbed on Maurice's back to get to the ball. I believed it was a perfectly good goal from where I was upfield. I thought, 'That's a touch fortunate!'

Burnley were not best pleased, as you would expect, but kept going and we had to block several efforts.

From one we broke, got a free kick and Danny guided it into the area for Bobby to get our second. He worked so hard, that day, did Bob. Some were questioning whether England should pick him but I felt national manager Walter Winterbottom should have no doubts about including him given my pal's contribution.

I combined with John to help Jonesy make it 3-0. We all crowded around each other saying, 'We're going to Wembley.' We had more than 20,000 Spurs fans roaring us on and quite a few came on to the pitch, many chairing Bobby off. We had just beaten a team that were no mugs in front of 70,000 – the biggest crowd to have watched us all season. And what Danny had said about the Double being do-able made even more sense. We were on a high.

The train journey home was brilliant. We had a big compartment booked for the players and staff, and had a meal and a few drinks. The champagne was flowing and we chatted away excitedly. Marvellous times.

WE COMPLETED back-to back league losses against Newcastle United at White Hart Lane the following Wednesday night; a match switched from Saturday because of the semi-final. It was only our second loss at home that season.

Some pointed out how two defeats in a row – against Manchester City and Chelsea – had all but scuppered our title chances the previous season and questions were asked about whether lightning would strike twice.

The fact we could now forget about any cup ties interrupting our league programme at last seemed a good one. The final date had been booked for 6 May and we would soon find out that Leicester City would be our opponents, although it took them two replays to get beyond Sheffield United.

But it did not seem to give us an advantage when the Toon Army turned up in London N17. Lady Luck seemed to desert us. We should never have got beaten. We gave Newcastle an absolute tonking in the first half. It should have been a cricket score. I had a chance. We all had a chance. Danny even had a penalty but the ball just would not go in until Cliff and I helped Les put us ahead just before the interval.

Newcastle were struggling for points, en route to relegation. They had only collected 24 points from 66 available and were third off the bottom. And they certainly fought as well as riding their fortune.

Magpies goalkeeper Dave Hollins, the elder brother of John, who was to play for Chelsea, Arsenal, QPR and England, made some great saves. And their second-half goals, which got them the points, were pretty much from their only attacks.

We tried to retrieve a point in a frantic finish but it was clearly not our night. It was reckoned to be a shock just slightly below our reverse at Cardiff on the football media's Richter Scale. Julian Holland insisted there was a hint of desperation 'like the panic of a surfacing diver who is too long in breaking water'.

Laurie Pignon was more reassuring when he told readers of the *Daily Sketch*, 'Now wait for The Dirt-Diggers to start tossing mud at shining White Hart Lane. I can hear the double talk already: Spurs are over the top...the strain is too much for them...they're falling to pieces like grandma's patchwork quilt...what rubbish...this was one of those Floodlit Nightmares when the whole soccer world turned upside down and white was proved black a dozen times....Newcastle had taken a bigger hammering than a blacksmith's anvil in the first 45 minutes. It seemed pointless to come out for the second half. Spurs' half-backs and forwards were carving them up and eating them alive.'

The result meant our lead at the top had been pegged back to four points ahead of Sheffield Wednesday.

Our winless league run extended to three when we were held to a goalless draw by Fulham at Craven Cottage. The press were full of it. They thought we were wobbling in our title bid. Giving Bill Nick the benefit of their 'wisdom'. One reporter, Bob Pennington, said in his report, 'If Nicholson is to claim the Cup, let alone the double, he must use the whip. The slipping stars in his shoddy attack must be told "graft – or you won't play at Wembley".'

In our change strip of navy blue shirts with white edging and white shorts, we had our chances against our west London hosts and their goalkeeper Tony Macedo – a future team-mate – did well. Bill wasn't too pleased. He told the media, 'We used to enjoy our football because we worked hard at it. But we are not working now.'

It was not the best time to go off the boil but we still believed in ourselves.

14

We Are The Champions

FRONT-RUNNERS the whole season, our lead had been whittled down to three points following the point dropped at Fulham. Opportunities hadn't gone in and our rhythm missed a beat or two with just one point from the previous six available, but we refused to press the panic button. As always, we just looked forward to the next game.

Earlier in the season, during our 11-game winning run, commentators were falling over themselves trying to find words to praise us.

Alan Hoby told his *Sunday Express* readers, 'Nothing I can write can remotely convey the majesty, rich theatre and sheer entertainment of Spurs' enchanting brand of football.'

But, as we've discovered, a few of them had become less than positive. I guess it was best to take the advice Rudyard Kipling gave out in his famous poem *If*, 'If you can meet with triumph and disaster and treat those two impostors the same…You'll be a man, my son.'

The team spirit we had built up was as strong as ever. We were still dominating teams. The belief we would take the title also remained firm even though our lead had been cut from the ten-point advantage we held coming into the New Year.

And with that we entered another purple patch. It came after Bill Nicholson had got us together to say he was happy with the defence but not the attack.

He reminded us we had to start finishing better again and said that we had to work as hard as we had done in the first half of the season so as to give support to the player in possession. The more options we gave that player for a pass the better our system worked.

Yet the first half in our next league game, against Chelsea, was the same as the one against Newcastle. We hammered the opposition throughout it but, unlike against the Toon Army, we were unable to make a breakthrough in that opening 45 minutes.

Around 65,000 were attracted to White Hart Lane on what was Good Friday to take on the Blues from west London, who included ace goal scorer Jimmy Greaves, a player who would soon have a significant role to play in N17.

It was clear that despite our lack of good results of late we had lost none of our pulling power.

But the fact we had been unable to get on the scoresheet as we went in for our half-time cuppa in the dressing room meant we had gone 185 minutes without a league goal. That was hard to imagine when you consider how we had been scoring goals for fun in the first half of the campaign.

But Cliffy scored soon after the restart and we went to town. The floodgates opened. We went 4-0 up with Jonesy netting a second, Les grabbing one and young Frank Saul, in for Bobby, getting the other before the opposition consoled themselves with two late goals.

It was ironic Chelsea should be our opponents as they provided a major banana skin to our title hopes in the previous campaign in the same fixture.

But there was no stopping us this time, even though we were also without Dave. To be honest Tony Marchi played well in his place, achieving the remarkable feat of keeping Jimmy quiet.

Easter continued to provide a more hectic schedule than the modern day with three games in just four days.

We had to play bottom club Preston North End at our home ground just a day after beating Chelsea. Our loyal supporters dug into their pockets for what must have been an expensive holiday period for them and were rewarded as we won 5-0 with Cliff scoring a hat-trick, the first being our 100th goal of the season.

Ten of the side who had played Chelsea turned out. The one who was absent? Me. I'd picked up a little hamstring injury. It was the first match I had missed all season and I was gutted.

My problem was bad enough to keep me sidelined for the final Easter match against Chelsea at Stamford Bridge on Monday.

The 57,000 attendance meant around 170,000 spectators saw our three holiday games and they witnessed the Lilywhites win all of them.

Bobby and Dave came back in for Frank and Tony. Bobby put us in front and my replacement Terry Medwin got the equaliser after Chelsea had gone 2-1 in front through goals by Frank Blunstone and someone who seemed to score quite a lot against Spurs back then, Jimmy Greaves. But Danny beckoned Maurice upfield and our centre-half got the winner.

I was frustrated at not being a part of it and hoped I could get my place back in a side that had been winning without me.

It is strange how things work out. I had fought so many years to get into the first team and then just as I thought I was not only a regular but a member of a team heading towards the title and, hopefully, the Double, I picked up an injury that could have meant me missing the run-in.

Fortunately for me it wasn't serious and I got back in for the next game.

THE EASTER of 1961 was just about the busiest ever for Spurs players. Not only were there three matches to fit in but a wedding too. Maurice got married to Jacqui in Hertfordshire in between the Preston and second Chelsea games. It clearly gave Monty a boost judging by his winner!

IT WAS good to be back as we took on Birmingham City at St Andrew's on 8 April. Our line-up was the one associated with the season due to my return. Brum had a reasonable team. Jimmy Bloomfield hadn't long arrived in Birmingham from Arsenal. He was a player I remember from my Army days when I played against him and his team murdered mine. He was a very clever player, a good passer of the ball and a goalscorer, and he was on good form.

Terry Hennessey, who was to become a Wales international team-mate of Cliff's the following year, was a good defender, although he gifted a goal to Les. And they had a good winger, Mike Hellawell, who was also a first-class cricketer with Warwickshire.

We got a flyer and were three up in just over half an hour, with John White having a brilliant game, making a goal for Bobby and hitting the third. As if we didn't know already there were no easy games and they came back at us with a couple, but we secured the points.

AS WE made our way to the St Andrew's dressing rooms, we knew exactly what it would take to lift the title.

Four wins on the bounce had ensured that a win over Sheffield Wednesday in our 39th fixture of a momentous season was all that was required to ensure our 'super' side, Bill Nicholson's 'super' side, would repeat the achievement of Arthur Rowe's Push and Run adventurers a decade earlier.

It would certainly be appropriate as the Owls had sustained a bid to wrest the title from our grip throughout the campaign.

Wednesday had that mean machine of a defence which had only conceded an average of one goal every league game. They were on a 19-match unbeaten league run and had only lost three of 18 games on the road. And they had been the team to end our winning streak of 11 at the start of the campaign, of course.

We knew it would not be for any faint-hearted souls. That it was more than us putting on the style which had proved so popular with clubs and supporters around the country as well as all of us at White Hart Lane.

It was a night when we all had to stand up and be counted. Wednesday remained the uncompromising outfit we remembered when they became the first team to beat us. And there was a vital added ingredient for our visitors, who knew that a win was the only way they would keep their own hopes of a title success flickering.

But we were up for it. We were ready for the physical battle, the blood, sweat and tears needed to ensure the triumph. We knew it might not be pretty as a spectacle, but the right result would see us win the top-flight championship for just the second time since the formation of the club close to 80 years before.

The showdown was under the White Hart Lane floodlights on Monday 17 April 1961. There had been queues at the ground all day, everyone hoping to get the ticket which would get them inside the ground to witness a moment of history first hand.

Us players got there about two hours early – like most of us tried to do before the Sunderland tie – because we knew it would be heaving. I managed to have an afternoon nap, something I always did before a night game.

I mingled with our backroom staff and other arriving team-mates and their relatives in the car park before heading into the dressing room. All the players chatted to each other. Everyone was quite confident.

Bill Nick gave us his final words before taking a seat in the stands because of its clearer view of the action in comparison to his previous habitat on the touchline, passing on instructions to Cecil Poynton pitchside via the recently-installed telephone system.

Bill was, though, confident Danny would play the role of on-field manager as well as he had done through the season.

It was important that Bill did not have any ego problems with that situation. And he didn't. Bill's number-one priority remained what was best for the team. He knew what Danny was: a motivator, tactician and shrewd judge who would act on words spoken and his own thoughts. And he trusted him. Danny respected Bill. Ever since his manager told the board he would recommend they turned down a transfer request from Danny after Bill had dropped him soon after becoming boss.

As we ran on to the recorded strains of McNamara's Band blasting over the Tannoy, I sensed the electric atmosphere. There were 62,000 in there and all but a few down from my native county, Yorkshire, had come to witness a coronation. More so, I suspect, than seeing 'super' Spurs give a display to prove how super we were.

Wednesday were aggressive and there was little opportunity for us to present evidence of the free-flowing football which had characterised our game that season. The intensity of the visitors limited the creativity of Danny and John, while Dave was kept occupied marking their busy inside-right Bobby Craig. Cliff had a couple of runs.

But the Owls turned up the intensity. They had players like Peter Swan, their centre-half, who could put it about a bit. Fortunately, again, we had a few players capable of matching them physically like we had at Hillsborough. Bobby, Maurice and Dave were not shy of fighting fire with fire. Wednesday players might have thought that they were hard themselves but they weren't that hard in comparison. I could show my aggression too. Players were going in hard and there was a series of flare-ups.

It was a difficult match for the referee to control. Tommy Dawes, from Norwich, was nicknamed 'Smiler' but he had little to smile about as he tried to keep control. Officials those days might not have sent off that many, but Dawes had to get the book out a couple of times to take Dave's name and Wednesday's Peter Johnson. He gave Wednesday captain Tony Kay a lecture. Dawes was quoted afterwards as saying, 'I certainly knew I'd refereed a match.'

Then Wednesday took the lead from a free kick that should not have been given. Their striker John Fantham, who had got the winner to end our unbeaten run in the away fixture, hit the ground as Maurice came in to tackle him. Boos rang around the ground. The home fans were obviously convinced the referee had been hoodwinked and that John had dived. I remain convinced Monty appeared a couple of yards away from challenging John when he hit the deck. Was it a dive? Was it a slip? We'll give John, who sadly passed in June 2014, the benefit of the doubt this far down the road.

But one thing beyond doubt was that their full-back Don Megson eventually converted the set piece after his first effort had rebounded off the wall. And our hearts were in our mouths when Wednesday hit the post. Coming back from 2-0 would have been a tall order. Suddenly we were level and I was delighted to play my part in it.

I might only be 5ft 4in but as I explained before I'd developed an ability to win the ball in the air by timing my run to get into the thick of it. That's what I did as I saw Peter Baker pump up a ball from defence to get above Megson and nod the ball to Bobby.

My pal still had plenty to do with Swan right by him. This is where he proved he was not just a bulldozer of a centre-forward. He flicked the ball over Swan with his right foot, then got behind the defender to lash the ball into the net with his left. It was Bobby's 26th in the league and was he pleased! He danced around as we rushed to congratulate him.

A minute later Les put us ahead. Danny was standing over the ball waiting to take a free kick and he told Maurice to move into the penalty area. He found him and Monty headed into Les's path and Les volleyed it in for his 23rd in the league.

We had a few walking wounded in the dressing room. It had been a bruising 45 minutes. Cliff had to have two stitches in a knee and Dave was patched up after a couple of X-rated tackles on him. But they were both as brave as lions and we all went out there to finish the job.

Danny managed to slow the tempo to frustrate Wednesday but the challenges were just as intense. Bill had told Bobby to make a nuisance of himself and he whacked their goalkeeper Ron Springett, the England stopper, into the post and hurt his back. It was not malicious. Just a reminder that no Wednesday player could switch off even for a moment.

Bobby gave everything for the club. He put himself on the line – and proved it that night. Dave was a warrior. But even in the heat of battle had managed to retain a sense of humour. He made out as if he was going to blast the ball past Bill Brown at one point. Another moment, I've read, he had time to crack a joke to Ken Jones, Cliffy's cousin who was a reporter for the *Daily Mirror* and was sitting on the touchline as there was no room in the press box for him.

Ken said in *The Double*, 'The ball went out of play where I was sitting for a throw-in to Spurs. I put my foot on it as Mackay came across to take the throw. Just before he took the throw he said to me "you can have 6-1 Smithy won't get his head to this". It was amazing that in the midst of such an important game he would think of chatting to me on the touchline.'

It was, though, tense as the second half wore on. Clive Toye wrote in the *Daily Express*, '[It was] a heart-lifting, blood-pounding period of fear for Spurs' hysterical fans as Wednesday fought on and on in the shredded-nerve atmosphere built up by the baying-for-victory crowd.'

He wasn't far wrong but the crowd – and all of us in the Lilywhites corner – got what they wanted as Smiler blew the final whistle. There was an incredible roar that must have been heard for miles. We'd done it. I felt grateful to be a part of the special team doing something so special. I had given it everything as I always did. I played well and helped the team win. I was buzzing. The team went down the tunnel into the dressing room as the fans flooded on to the pitch and the champagne flowed. The chairman Fred Bearman came in to join us.

We heard the supporters chanting 'Danny, Danny' for our captain and we came back out and filed up into the directors' box as Danny said a few words to those either on the pitch or who had remained in the stands and on the terraces as we stood alongside him.

Bill Holden, the *Daily Mirror*'s chief football correspondent, said, 'As I write these words pandemonium reigns at White Hart Lane. The song is ringing in our ears "glory, glory – the Spurs go marching on".'

There was no Twitter, Facebook nor any kind of social media on which to spread the news globally in seconds. No internet or live television either. The news did not filter out until the late night news on radio and perhaps TV. And the first full reports were not read in newspapers until the following morning at breakfast.

We had scored 111 goals in 39 games and fielded the same side in 22. THE side. The 11 which beat Wednesday on a wet but unforgettable Monday.

BILL NICK immediately set a new league target with the title in the bag. He wanted us to go for the record number of points in winning the First Division crown. We needed three points from our remaining three matches to break Arsenal's all-time best total of 66.

Our first opportunity to gather them was five days after sealing the title. All of that Monday's heroes played bar Cliff, who could not overcome that knee injury which also put him out of a Wales international.

It wouldn't be easy: Burnley at Turf Moor. The new champions versus last year's champions. Our hosts had forced that 4-4 draw at our place after being 4-0 down and no doubt in the mood to gain revenge for our FA Cup semi-final win over them.

I helped us get a great start. After Peter Baker had scored his first and only goal of the season, I supplied a cross for Bobby to head us two in front. Danny was playing well but so was his Northern Ireland team-mate Jimmy McIlroy, the home skipper. And Danny's erstwhile pal ensured Burnley roared back to win 4-2, with Bill Brown limiting our opponents with some great saves.

Four days later we did get a couple more points on the board. Terry Medwin got the winner as we beat Nottingham Forest. It equalled Arsenal's tally from 30 years before.

And we hoped to go beyond it with West Bromwich Albion coming up at White Hart Lane on the final day of the season, Saturday 29 April 1961. There were 52,000 packed in on a sunny afternoon; many no doubt attracted by the fact the Football League president Joe Richards was handing over the glittering silver prize of the First Division championship trophy to Danny after the match. The Throstles – as they were commonly called those days rather than Baggies – beat us 2-1.

Bobby Robson, who was to become my manager at Fulham and go on to boss England, got their second goal after Derek Kevan had put the visitors ahead. I can still picture Bobby's shot deflecting off Dave and passing by Bill Brown even though it was all those years ago. Some images just stay with you even though you might wish they wouldn't! Our Bobby pulled one back and we really should have got a point. It would, of course, have been enough to go past the Gunners' mark. So we had to be content with sharing the record with Arsenal.

The West Brom defeat was blamed on the belief we had half an eye on the FA Cup Final on Wembley the following week, and that no one wanted to be injured and miss out. I don't buy any of that. We tried our hearts out to get at least a point. The result was just one of those things.

Bill said in his speech to the crowd how we had shown we weren't a wonder team on the day. As always he had wanted to delight the fans.

15
The Double

A LOT WENT on in the week building up to the FA Cup Final. We got measured up for suits and were presented with new Puma boots. We felt like Jack the lads!

The press wanted pictures of us. We had to pose on a ladder on the White Hart Lane pitch. All 11 of us stood on this blessed thing. I posed about halfway up, hanging on to the arm of Les Allen below me and Ron Henry above. A bit precarious. Fortunately nobody fell off it and hurt themselves! Can you imagine if that had happened? It would have been a bit like the story Ken Jones told when Danny wanted to get away from Eamonn Andrews a few months earlier. Ken said, 'When they said "this is your life" and Danny pulled away, Angus [Mackay, the producer of BBC radio's *Sports Report*] grabbed the sleeve of Danny's blazer as he tried to get away and Danny fell backwards down some stairs. You can imagine the trouble the BBC would have been in if Danny had been injured and couldn't play football for Tottenham.'

On the night before the final the club took us up to the West End to see the film *The Guns of Navarone*. Funnily enough I saw a re-run on television the other week and it brought back all the memories of our night out all those years ago. Of course, it also reacquainted me with the final words of the film.

It was a conversation between Gregory Peck's character Captain Keith Mallory and David Niven's Corporal Miller talking about an adventure they had come through successfully. Niven says, 'To tell you the truth, I didn't think we could do it.' Peck replies, 'To tell you the truth, neither did I.'

Just as well that didn't have a negative effect on us the following day after viewing it at the Odeon in Leicester Square all those years ago!

We stayed overnight at the Hendon Hall Hotel. I shared a room with Les and didn't sleep too badly that night. We had the treat breakfast – bacon, egg, tomatoes, toast and marmalade and coffee – in bed.

Then we went for a walk around the grounds before going back to the hotel. We hung about waiting for the coach – some of us watching the final build-up on the TV – to take us on the short journey around the North Circular to Wembley with a police motorbike escort.

In the meantime, Bobby, unknown to us, paid a couple of visits to his doctor in Palmers Green, a few miles down the North Circ. He had kept an injury secret – twisting his knee during the West Brom game – and left his room-mate Maurice asleep while he drove the 20 minutes to his doctor for an injection.

His physician had told him he would need a second one. Bobby wanted to make sure he was spotted at the hotel so no one would suspect anything, so he drove back to Hendon Hall and saw our trainer Cecil Poynton and told him he was going for a walk around the grounds. Instead he got back in his car and was Palmers Green-bound once more for the second injection before finally returning in time to clamber on the coach with the rest of us. What a way to spend the morning of a cup final – but he so desperately wanted to play and was such an important part of the team.

We all sat down to lunch. There was steak on offer but I settled for egg on toast.

We boarded the coach just before 1.45pm – including Bobby – for the short journey around the only ring road for north London before the M25. It was an amazing trip. The crowds along the way were incredible. Everyone was waving at us and we were waving back to them. That was a marvellous feeling. We were otherwise subdued among each other. The match was on my mind and I'm sure the same applied to the rest. There wasn't much banter flying around.

We arrived and eased into the tunnel inside Wembley Stadium by the dressing rooms. Our party all filed off and had a look at where we were changing. I remember there was a big bath, although, of course, those sort of communal facilities are a distant memory these days. They looked fantastic.

Each one of the players wanted to take in the early atmosphere and get a feel of the pitch so wandered up the tunnel on to it in our tailored suits.

We took balls on to the pitch to get an idea of the bounce and pace of the turf and strolled around. I wasn't looking around for anyone in particular, although I knew family, including my mum and dad and brother John, and friends were due. I just wanted to take in the experience as a whole. I turned to Bobby and said, 'We're here. Isn't it brilliant?'

I just thought of how many people would have swapped places with me at that moment. They would have loved to have walked out there to experience such an occasion. Bobby thought the same way while the Spurs supporters were cheering around us.

Leicester were soaking up the atmosphere as well. I spotted their defender Colin Appleton, the guy I had played alongside at Scarborough in the Midland League all those years before. I called over, 'Hi Col.' We had a friendly chat, talking about how it had been a long time since we had been at Scarborough together. We wished each other all the best.

After we went back into the dressing rooms to get changed, a guy in a white suit got on to a platform to conduct a band which provided the pre-match live entertainment.

Bobby wanted to hear their rendition of 'Abide with Me', the song which is still always played and sung before FA Cup finals in the modern day. And is always a moving communal experience with everyone joining in. Bob came back out of the dressing room on his own to listen to it.

Bill had given his team-talk the previous day, going through the Leicester players in detail. Now he went round all of us wishing us well and giving little reminders about who to mark closely and other tips. He used to natter on while we just thought about what we would be aiming to do rather than worrying about what the opposition might try. Then it was time to leave our inner sanctum. It hadn't seemed five minutes since we had arrived.

We walked out the dressing room and lined up alongside Leicester in the tunnel. I wasn't superstitious about what position I took up, although one or two others were. The nerves twitched.

From where I stood at the bottom of the tunnel, it was pretty dark. All I could see was a little bit of daylight between the roof of the tunnel and where the floor curved up towards the exit. Then Bill and Leicester manager Matt Gillies were given the signal to start walking towards it. The gap got wider and brighter as we neared the point where we would leave the tunnel and be seen by the 100,000 crowd.

The butterflies continued to race around my stomach, but it wasn't because it was THE cup final. They were the ones I experienced regularly in any game, whatever the importance. They came about by me hoping and praying I'd give a good account of myself and that we'd end up getting a good result.

When we walked on to the world-famous turf we were guided to a spot in front of the Royal Box in the stands for the pre-match introductions to the great and the good. Quite often it was the monarch who did the honours. That had been the case the previous time Spurs were in the final – in 1921 – with King George V present along with his son the Duke of York, who was to become George VI and father Queen Elizabeth II.

The Queen wasn't there to greet us, but there was a royal personage in the shape of the Duchess of Kent, the lady married on the day I was born.

The Duchess spoke to Danny at the presentation, saying, 'The other team have their names on their [track] suits.' And Danny smiled and joked, 'Yes, ma'am, but we know each other.' Then we peeled off to run towards one of the goals for our warm-up.

We were massive favourites, the biggest since Wolverhampton Wanderers in 1939 when they took on Portsmouth – and came unstuck with a 4-1 defeat! At least that fact gave us a reality check.

Matt Gillies sprung a surprise by revealing Leicester would not be playing Ken Leek, a centre-forward who had got a lot of their goals. In his place was a young Hugh McIlmoyle, more of a deep-lying striker. I know Maurice Norman was pleased Leek wasn't playing as he'd had some battles with him.

It was a grey day, with rain threatening, as the wind got up after a sunny morning. The surface was lush. It forced us to play a slower passing game than usual. Then it bucketed down, which we could have done without given our fluid style.

I managed to create an opening for John but he fired over from the very spot he'd predicted he'd score from the day before when we'd paid a flying visit to the stadium.

Leicester left-back Len Chalmers was injured after 19 minutes. Les Allen tackled him fairly and squarely but Len fell awkwardly and twisted his knee. Remember it was in the days before subs, so it was a case of the Wembley hoodoo striking for the EIGHTH time in ten years.

Poor Len limped on out of harm's way on the left wing and poor old Les took it to heart and played a more subdued role. Danny and Dave weren't as dominant as usual but our defence was superb. Peter Baker got knocked out stemming one attack while Ron Henry earned the man of the match accolade.

Cliffy had a goal disallowed for offside after I'd knocked the ball across just before the interval. It was a diabolical decision. I could see from where I was close to the byline that Cliff was on.

I missed an easy chance after starting a move which led to Bobby nodding a cross from John to me. I was underneath it close to goal but headed over. But I managed to help create the goal which put us in front 21 minutes from time.

It was a brilliant move. Ron began it by giving the ball to John who found Bobby. The ball moved on to me and I worked a one-two with Les and floated it to Bobby who beat his man to smash it in.

We relaxed and found our trademark form and then my moment came with just 15 minutes left. Bobby had the ball wide. I gave him a signal to cross. I timed my run to spring up high to meet his ball and head home beyond the diving Gordon Banks.

Kenneth Wolstenholme was the commentator for the BBC television coverage. But it was the BBC radio commentator Raymond Glendenning who conjured up the most memorable phrase for me on the day when he described my goal excitedly. He shouted, 'It's in the net! It's in the net! That's a beautiful goal by Dyson.'

I went flying away, jumped up, smiling from ear to ear, lost in the moment as I celebrated. It was the goal which sealed the first Double in English football since the 19th century.

I've looked at the famous picture of it a few times. The caption says, 'Dyson's header flies past.' It did fly in as well. I've spoken to Gordon and he told me with a smile, 'I keep seeing that picture. I'm going to save it soon.'

It was unbelievable. I thought as I trotted back to the centre circle to restart the game, 'I've done it, I've scored at Wembley. I've actually done it. I'm a lucky lad.'

All those years of dreaming of such a moment from when I was a kid in the field close to the family home in Malton had come true. Many kids did the same, especially on cup final day, either listening to it on the radio or watching it on the TV and then trying and re-enact it with your mates, perhaps pretending to be the match-winner. I was quite emotional, there were tears of joy in my eyes as all these thoughts raced through my head.

It was the best moment of my career, even better than another goal I got which made sure we conquered Europe. I've seen the goal since and it went in like a bullet.

I should have got another one after that. I hit one with my right foot but Gordon, who went on to collect his World Cup winners' medal, saved it. I could have had a hat-trick!

It wasn't a great final. We had had a lot of possession without breaking them down too much. Part of it stemmed, I think, from Chalmers getting injured, and they went a bit defensive. They had to.

But that wasn't the only reason. I still to this day don't really know the reason for us not flowing the way we had done for so much of that unforgettable season. It certainly wasn't through lack of trying, I can tell you. I ran my socks off. And the whole team put in 100 per cent.

THE CELEBRATIONS were brilliant. We went up the 39 steps to the Royal Box. Danny accepted the FA Cup from the Duchess while we all collected our medals.

Then we took the cup around the edge of the pitch to show the supporters. There's a famous picture of me ducking underneath it, smiling widely as I look up, while Danny and Bobby hold the trophy high as we jog along. Perhaps I was joking about how I was so small I could run underneath it and between my team-mates.

We had a celebration dinner at the Savoy Hotel on The Strand in the West End that night. Eddie Baily, Ted Ditchburn, Les Bennett and others from the 1950s Push and Run team Bill had played with were there. There were even four players from our 1921 FA Cup-winning side. They were nice touches, recognising individuals who had done so much to make the club's name.

I remember the soup we had. It was cold – as it was meant to be. We teased Ted about it as he headed towards his table. 'Hurry up Ted, your soup will get cold,' we joked.

Then we had the speeches. Ernest Marples, the Government's Minister for Transport, was very complimentary. So was John Arlott, the famous sports writer. Bill said a few words, mainly about the support staff around the main XI.

There were a few celebrities there, such as Harry Secombe, the singer and comedian. I was pictured with him, with my quiff and a girl I used to go out with at the time, Sandra, who was a dancer. Funny lad, Harry. Entertainer Roy Castle was there too.

Shirley Bassey was due to sing for us but she'd lost her voice because of a bad throat so Harry stepped in. Yet Shirley presented us with a few mementos, such as a record that had been made by a group of showbiz types who supported us and called themselves the Totnamites. It was a 45rpm single – many born before the 1990s will remember those – called 'The Spurs Song' on Oriole's blue label.

The first lines are, 'Tip top Tottenham Hotspur, the greatest team of the year.' The lyrics went through the team and when it came to my mention they sang, 'The Jones boy and Dyson on the wings how they flew.' There was also a tribute to Bill, 'For making this year the Spurs happiest year of all.'

The flip side was, appropriately, 'Danny Boy', the Irish ballad in reference to our captain. We had a bit of a sing-song with assistant secretary Alan Leather on the piano. We were all clapping along. Bobby and our reserve John Smith were in good voice.

And we could do what we wanted afterwards! So a few of us went to another posh hotel just up the road, including Dave, Bobby, John and myself. There were two or three of our supporters who had plenty of money and were putting on their own celebration evening there. We had a very good night.

On the Sunday we had a coach parade along Tottenham High Road on a sunny afternoon. It was an open-topped double-decker and we travelled on the exposed top deck with the league trophy and the FA Cup.

I'd been a bit worried it might prove a bit of an anti-climax. I had picked up Dave in my Ford. And as we came down closer to the High Road I turned to him and said, 'There's nobody about. This could be embarrassing, this.' He said, 'I know.' We wondered where everyone was.

Then we got to the Edmonton Town Hall where the parade was due to start off from. The size of the crowd was absolutely incredible. We pulled up into its car park and went into the Town Hall to meet a few dignitaries. And we came back out and got on the bus with our wives and girlfriends for the three-mile trip to Tottenham Town Hall.

The police were in front guiding us through. The supporters were amazing all the way there – on both sides of the road. People were clustering on the pavements and hanging out of windows of flats and houses. We went by the ground on our left and the Royal, where we used to go for a dance or two, on the right. The dance band were on the roof playing and waving to us. I knew most of them. And we ended up, on schedule, at the Town Hall.

It was magic. We couldn't believe the extent of the reaction. Danny had told us before the parade, 'You haven't realised what you've done.' He was right.

At the Town Hall, we had a civic reception with the mayor and other bigwigs. All us players went out on the balcony to show the trophies to the thousands looking up at us.

It was fantastic to see at such close quarters just what our achievements had meant to the fans who'd been waiting hours to see us. We were waving away and they were waving back and cheering. It was quite moving to see the effect of what we had done on the community.

My mum came down from Yorkshire with her friend. They stayed at the Bell and Hare pub near the ground. I went there to see them after the parade. I was with Dave, Cliff and John. Dave was clearly in the mood as he found a bowler hat from somewhere and put it on. I think he was trying to copy our chairman Fred Bearman's choice of headgear.

My dad had come down with my brother John for the FA Cup Final but someone had to run the family pub back in Malton so they had dashed back home for the Saturday night session.

It meant I did not see them at all on the day, but when I went back home in the close-season my dad told me how what I had done was 'brilliant'. My brother told me he had enjoyed the whole thing.

It was wonderful to go back to my home town in such circumstances. I went to the grammar school where I first learned to play organised football and saw Bruce Rolls, my most influential teacher.

It was a sport day and I gave out the prizes then gave them a talk, saying that I was so proud of being part of the school. To achieve what I achieved, to play in the FA Cup Final and win the Double was a big thing.

I mentioned Vic Wilson, captain of the Yorkshire cricket team, and said how it was amazing two different sportsmen from the school had achieved what we'd achieved. I also thanked Mr Rolls for all his time and encouragement. And he thanked me afterwards, hoping I might have inspired a few of the current pupils.

I gave another talk at another 'do' in Malton. But there was no civic reception. My mum, who passed away in May 2002 aged 95, always thought there should have been.

16
Team Of The Century

THE MOMENT referee Jack Kelly blew the FA Cup Final whistle at Wembley I felt satisfaction in having risen to the challenge, the biggest challenge in English football.

It might not have been a great final but we had every right to stick our chests out because we'd created history as he first team to win the Double in the 20th century, a feat that had us dubbed the 'Team of the Century'. Author Ralph L Finn hailed it as the greatest soccer achievement of all time. He wrote in his book *Spurs Supreme*, 'This Spurs Double is not only the greatest soccer feat of the century. It is the greatest soccer achievement of all time.' He came to this conclusion after comparing it to Aston Villa's Double of 1897, which involved less games and, he thought, less fierce competition.

And more than 50 years later people are still talking about it. It remains relevant. A benchmark. The *61 Spurs Double* book was so popular when it came out in 2010 that it was voted the Best Illustrated Book at the National Sporting Club Awards, announced on 10 May 2011, the day after a 50th anniversary dinner for our achievement back at the Savoy.

Why? Well, people talk about Roger Bannister being the first to break the four-minute barrier in running the mile. Beating Chris Chataway and Chris Brasher, collapsing at the finish and doing what he did was unbelievable, especially when you consider what the track at Iffley Road in Oxford looks like in those old films. Many run inside four minutes now – comfortably, because of improved tracks, training methods, sports medicine and diet – but it is Roger Bannister people remember because he was the first to do it.

People talk about Edmund Hillary being the first to climb to the top of Everest. Again, he is known because he was the first. And we are remembered for the same reason as Bannister and Hillary will forever be recalled. It was big, big news, even to non-sporting people. So you can draw a comparison to the likes of Roger Bannister and Edmund Hillary,

Dad, a jockey, looks happy enough with his ride

With my brother on a day out

My brother John and I as kids

Looking smart in my shirt and tie with mum and dad and our pet dog

With mum and dad
in The Fleece pub
they ran in Malton

(Right): Lying on the
ground playing Bottom
the Weaver in a Malton
Grammar School
production of Shakespeare's
Midsummer Night's
Dream

(Far right): On the beach
in Whitby with a Frank
Sinatra-style hat

A smiling soldier

With my Army pals doing National Service aged 18

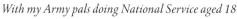

My original football boots dating back to the 1930s. Picture by Mike McNamara

Looking younger than the rest I pose on the far right of the front row with my Malton Grammar School team. Mr Rolls, a teacher who was such a big influence, is standing directly behind me

The Spurs Push and Run team who were so supportive

Leaping in for my Spurs debut in a 5-0 win over Sheffield United at White Hart Lane in 1955, an amateur on National Service

Warming up watched by a Spurs fan

Heads up against Arsenal at Highbury

On the ball

Coming out of the old corner pitch entrance with old Army pal Ron Henry (left) and Les Allen at White Hart Lane to the strains of McNamara's Band over the sound system

In action against Nottingham Forest

Arm aloft in the foreground, I have a splashing time in the bath with my Spurs team-mates as we celebrate sealing the title with victory over Sheffield Wednesday

With Bobby Smith and the trays we received to commemorate our winning run of 11 matches at the start of the Double season

My miss that upset Bill Nicholson in the 1961 FA Cup Final against Leicester at Wembley

I beat a diving Gordon Banks to score my goal in the 1961 FA Cup Final

I duck under the FA Cup as we take a lap of honour after the 1961 final

The Spurs Double squad: Back row (left to right): Ron Henry, Maurice Norman, Johnny Hollowbread, Bill Brown, Mel Hopkins, Ken Barton. Middle: Peter Baker, Tony Marchi, Cecil Poynton (trainer), Danny Blanchflower, Bill Nicholson (manager), Dave Mackay, John Smith. Front: Cliff Jones, Terry Medwin, John White, Bobby Smith, Les Allen, Frank Saul, Eddie Clayton and me

A 1961 Double team picture from a signing. Left to right, back row: Bill Brown, Peter Baker, Ron Henry, Danny Blanchflower, Maurice Norman and Dave Mackay. Front row: Cliff Jones, John White, Bobby Smith, Les Allen and myself

The cameras capture the Double-winning team at Spurs' training ground at Cheshunt

My invite to the Savoy Hotel for a dinner to celebrate the Double

Wembley triumph away from football. I look on as Spurs team-mate Tony Marchi receives the trophy on behalf of our Stamford Hill ten-pin bowling team with fellow Spurs team-mate Micky Dulin to Tony's right

(Right) On a camel in Egypt during a visit to play a friendly against Cairo club Zamalek in November 1962

Getting in some golf practice

Cliff Jones, Tony Marchi, Bobby Smith, Peter Baker and myself (left to right) with Danny Blanchflower holding the European Cup Winners' Cup on our lap of honour pitchside in Rotterdam

The 1963 European Cup Winners' Cup Final programme

The Spurs 1963 European Cup Winners' Cup-winning team inside a packed Rotterdam stadium before beating Atletico Madrid 5-1. Left to right (back row): Tony Marchi, Danny Blanchflower (bending), Maurice Norman, Ron Henry, Bobby Smith, Bill Brown. Front: Me, Cliff Jones, John White, Jimmy Greaves, Peter Baker

Jimmy Greaves and I step off the plane with the European Cup Winners' Cup following our flight from Rotterdam

In front of an amazing crowd in Tottenham with the European Cup Winners' Cup

Going past celebrating fans outside the White Hart pub at the top of the lane leading to the stadium in an open-topped bus with the European Cup Winners' Cup. I'm pointing skywards far right on the bus for some reason

The European Cup Winners' Cup squad

Larking around with Spurs team-mates Cliff Jones (right) and John Smith while on tour in South Africa in 1963

The Spurs 1964 team line-up: Back row (left to right): Laurie Brown, Eddie Clayton, Bill Brown, Alan Mullery, Cyril Knowles. Front row: Jimmy Robertson, Alan Gilzean, Ron Henry, Jimmy Greaves, Cliff Jones and yours truly

Challenging Burnley goalkeeper Adam Blacklaw

I'm in the front row far right in this Fulham team shot soon after arriving at Craven Cottage. Stan Brown, Tony Macedo, Bobby Keetch, Bobby Robson and George Cohen are in the back row from second left. Johnny Haynes is next to me with Graham Leggat to the captain's right

Smiling for the camera third from the left in the front row of my Colchester team of the late 1960s

Ball juggling with Colchester

Lining up, front row second right, with my Guildford City team-mates in the early 1970s

Lining up with Wealdstone in the 1970s, second from right in the front row. Johnny Haynes is fifth from the left in the back row

The Dagenham team which helped me enjoy a winning return to Wembley in 1980. I was assistant manager as Daggers lifted the FA Trophy

Boreham Wood FC manager in the 1980s

Winning a trophy as Boreham Wood FC manager in the 1980s with owner/founder Bill O'Neill to my right

Posing in the back row, far right, with the Kingsbury Town team I managed

(Far left): Reunion with Bill Nicholson to my right in the front row and Peter Baker to my left. Left to right in the back row are Mel Hopkins, Maurice Norman, Danny Blanchflower and Cliff Jones

(Left): With Cliff Jones

Dear Terry,

At last I have been able to enclose the photographs we had taken at the re-union of the 61-62 team last August.

They are not as good as I was hoping for but I do hope they will be a good reminder to you of a very nice evening together and of course many good times in the past.

Thanks very much for coming along and I do hope you really enjoyed the opportunity to discuss and possibly compare the old times in the game with the new.

Every Good Wish.

Yours sincerely

William Nicholson

A personal letter from 'Bill'

Dear Terry

At last I Have been able to enclose the photographs we had taken at the re-union of the 61 - 62 team last August.

They are not as good as I was hoping for but I do hope they will be a good reminder to you of a very nice evening together and of course many good times in the past.

Thanks very much for coming along and I do Hope you really enjoyed the opportunity to discuss and possibly compare the old times in the game with the new.

Every Good Wish.

Yours sincerely

William Nicholson

With the crystal decanter presented to me by Spurs chairman Daniel Levy as I became one of the first with my Double team-mates to be inducted into the club's Hall of Fame in 2004

Kay and I on the day we met in 1965

With Kay after our wedding at Holy Innocents Church in Kingsbury in 1966

Eldest son Neil and his daughter and my granddaughter Katie

Spurs pals Dave Mackay, Bill Brown and (far right) Micky Dulin at our wedding in 1966

My middle son Barry with daughter Lauren, partner Mandy and son Conner

My youngest son Mark with his children – and my grandkids – Jessica and Ben – and wife Liane

The family horse Miss Van Gogh, wearing Spurs colours white and navy blue, is ridden to her first win by Paul Hanagan in front of the family at Leicester in October 2014. What a magic day. Picture by Tony Knapton

Myself with the family, Paul Hanagan and Miss Van Gogh. Picture by Tony Knapton

Me at 80.
Picture by Mike
McNamara

and let's mention how Yuri Gagarin became the first human in outer space, travelling in his Vostok spacecraft, less than a week before we sealed the title and a month prior to the completion Double.

His and our feats caught the public imagination. They were massive happenings in 1961 and my Spurs had taken football to a wider audience.

To me it was more than just being the first to turn what seemed the impossible into a reality. It was the way we did it. We did it with a panache which attracted more than two million people to our league games and over half a million to our cup matches. We were reckoned to be the 'first superstars of the modern age', according to *The Spurs Double*.

'Their greatness lay in their ability to produce the unexpected,' wrote John Cottrell in *A Century of Great Soccer Drama*.

A few teams have won the Double since, including Arsenal, Liverpool, Manchester United and Chelsea, but ours will, I believe, always be rated the best one. Bob Wilson, the Arsenal goalkeeper when they completed the feat ten years after us, agrees. I was down at Arsenal watching an Academy game on behalf of the Premier League and spoke to Bob who said to me our side was the best to do it. Without a doubt. I thought that was good of Bob considering his side had also done it too.

Was our Double side the best of all time in this country? It's always difficult to compare eras. What we can say is that we were the best of our time. The club have always had a tradition for playing attractive, flowing, innovative football and our side was viewed in most quarters as being as close to a perfect version of that ideal as is possible. We tried our best to satisfy the perfectionist in our manager – and got as close as any is likely to in my opinion.

As *1961 The Spurs Double* viewed it, we had 'laid the foundations for the modern game' and 'played a large part in helping to define how the game's evolved' but 'the football they played belongs to a standard all its own'. That'll do me.

We had an attacking approach. There was no thought to a defensive outlook. We thought we'd win. Subconsciously we weren't frightened of anybody. Home and away it was the same – attack, attack, attack. It was an entertaining strategy that attracted full houses wherever we went. Why we managed 115 goals in the league.

Bill made sure we treated teams with respect. We were never going to just take the mickey. We thought we had to play well to beat teams – and we usually did, no matter what the pitch conditions, which were, as I've already mentioned, often pretty awful.

The supply was there from midfield and all five forward players took full advantage, reflected in all five of us reaching double figures with Cliff and I constantly getting in the box from our wide starting positions.

It was exhilarating to be a part of it all. We looked forward to every match. As we sat in our dressing room, we knew there would be a big crowd out there to watch us. We knew we'd trained well. Just to make totally sure everything was in place, Bill used to come around to each of us with practical advice on the opposition and reminders about our roles.

If we won and I scored and played well there was no better feeling for me. And the icing on the cake would be that 'well done' from Bill afterwards.

We were a unit, the perfect blend in many eyes. Like a chain without weak links. We had proved Push and Run could be tinkered with successfully and were a special team, the equal of which we are unlikely to ever see again in my humble opinion.

I felt – and still feel – proud to have been a part of it. But from one to 11 we had a team of special individuals with a special manager.

Bill Brown was a very good shot stopper, athletic and brave. He was a good organiser of the defence and tended to throw the ball out rather than boot it long. He was tall, over six feet, but a lightly-built lad.

Although not too good at coming out for crosses, he had the support of players like Maurice who was a big, strong, physical presence whenever the ball came over. It is funny to think he was an outside-left like me when he trialled for Scotland schoolboys.

Peter Baker and Ron Henry, our full-backs, did not attract much attention with so many big names in our team. But they were as vital as anybody to the success we had and were one of the best full-back partnerships. They shared an approach and abilities when they played; Peter on the right and Ron on the left. They were both quiet and just got on with it.

It was in the days when full-backs pretty much just defended and ours did just that to a high level. They were fantastic at it. Peter and Ron were such good tacklers and hard to get by. The pair of them kept it simple. Peter was calm and had good positional sense and helped cover Danny when our captain was in the attacking half.

My old Army pal Ron had been a half-back and centre-half as well as a winger but got his chance at left-back when Mel Hopkins broke his nose. Ron developed into an intelligent and cool performer. I was delighted for Ron when he claimed that man of the match award when we beat Leicester in the FA Cup Final.

Maurice was a tower of strength at centre-half. He was a big lad who was good in the air, tackled well and so quick off the mark with a long stride he rarely got done. Big and brave, he also had good positional sense. The Swede – nicknamed because of his rural background in East Anglia – was also a lovely lad.

He was quiet, no problem to anyone, and just got on with his game. He played deep behind Peter and Ron. That was an unusual tactic. So was his coming up for set pieces. He did well when called forward by Danny who dropped back to cover. His way of playing his position was certainly innovative.

Danny at right-half and Dave at left-half, linking up with John White at inside-right, was the team's axis.

Danny was key to us on and off the field and deserved his second Footballer of the Year award, which he received just a couple of days before the cup final. We each got a £100 bonus for winning the Double and Danny helped negotiate it. He acted as the middleman generally. If we ever had any gripes with the club we went to Dan. Dan would talk to Bill about it.

Danny was just right as our skipper because he was a very bright individual with lots of ideas, some controversial, and unafraid to employ them if needed. Sometimes he would give us talks and Cliffy used to turn to us and smile, 'I can't understand what he's talking about.'

He was full of good sayings. Danny told us, 'If you are a good player you need to have plenty of the ball because as a good player, although you will give the ball away and have some bad games, you will generally do good things with it.' Danny was a good player and so had plenty of the ball. Danny was a fantastic attacking wing half. A superb passer – short or long – and able to control the pace of a game.

His 'game's about glory' quote sums up what my Spurs team was all about and has remained the outlook of all the club's sides ever since. Part of it is even displayed in big bold letters along the side of the new West Stand at White Hart Lane. His personality left an indelible mark on the history of the club.

I can't overstate how important Dave was to the team. He wanted to win badly and loved it when we did, all the time. He did everything he could to make sure that happened, driving us on and on. Dave led by example and words as well as presence.

He put himself into tackles even if it meant getting hurt. That sort of thing never bothered him. He was unbelievable the way he used to throw himself in. He was forceful but not a bully and inspired us to do things, to raise our game. Dave formed a great half-back partnership with Danny. He made a good side a winning side with his mentality.

His approach was the same whatever he did. I remember playing him at snooker. He missed the black with the cue ball which went round the table and down a pocket. He went 'Damn' and smashed his cue. I asked him, knowing the answer, 'What's the matter with you, Dave?'

John was one of our Big Three with Dave and Danny. One of the nucleus. A fantastic athlete, he had continued to earn his nickname of

The Ghost with his wonderful knack of drifting around largely undetected by the opposition, and then pop up and provide a crucial link between the midfield and attack.

Bill liked to play with two wingers and, of course, I was on the left with Cliff on the right for much of the Double season. He was funny, Jonesy. He used to go on these long dribbles with his head down and Danny used to say to him, 'You are allowed to pass, Cliff.' And Cliffy used to reply with a smile, saying, 'Okay, Danny.'

He was great in the air and so brave. He used to get so many cuts and bruises, especially across the nose as it collided with either a defender's boot or head. And he could score goals. He scored plenty that season.

Everyone saw Bob as just this big bustling centre-forward. And he was very strong, but he also had good ball skills, a good first touch and he could pass the ball.

He was very brave. He would just go in with his head in dangerous situations. There was one game I remember against Wolves where he went in and I thought, 'He's going to get hurt.' But he got to the ball and headed a goal which helped us to a win while the keeper bottled it. It was the bravest thing I've seen on a football field.

Les worked hard and also got loads of goals. He got 20-odd and was superb. They brought in Greavsie the following season, which was understandable as he was the game's best goalscorer – and went on to prove himself the best of all time. But it was hard on Les who eventually had to make way.

There were a lot more glamorous names in the team than me – marquee signings that got most of the headlines, like Danny, Dave and John. But everyone's contribution was appreciated. I worked hard. Julie Welch, the lovely lady who wrote the film *Those Glory Glory Days*, described my contribution in *The Spurs Double 61* as like 'fat in a frying pan' because of my bursts of energy. I did my bit.

Bill was a superb manager. His vision was very much what Danny was talking about when he said the game was about glory and to achieve that we not only had to win but win in that manner I've spoken about.

All the players loved Bill. I was among them but I was in awe of him. If I had a bad game I spent most of the week sweating about whether he would select me the next week, or if I'd be relegated to 12th man, assisting the kitman or just playing back in the reserves. Fortunately I managed to do well enough to keep my place and only missed a couple of games through injury in the Double season.

Bill was very thorough and I enjoyed his employment of short, to-the-point phrases rather than long-winded tactical talks. He was serious but not distant and I must underline how his relationship with Danny was a big part of our success. I believe he even allowed our captain input into team selection. On a Friday before a Saturday match Dan used to go in to see Bill and I understand they used to sort out the side together.

A lot of the time it didn't need much sorting out. It was largely the team everyone knows. We only used 17 players in total for the whole season. That in itself is a remarkable stat. Can you imagine that happening today? I can't.

By the way, us players thanked Bill for his efforts in 1960/61 by clubbing together to buy him a Remington shaver. And, in their turn, Spurs gave us players each a set of suitcases.

THERE WERE a few behind the scenes who played their part in that fabled campaign. Harry Evans, Bill's assistant, was so popular among the players and was a lovely guy. Sadly he died of cancer the year after the Double and he was only 43.

On the training ground at Cheshunt there was Billy Watson. He was an Olympic weightlifter who was hired to get us fitter. As well as getting us to do weights, he used to get us to jump over these flipping ropes. Knackering it was.

In the office there was Alan Leather, who was a nice man. And a lovely woman called Barbara Wallace who was Bill's PA. I went to her funeral.

The players got on well with the backroom staff in general. It doesn't seem to be like that now. On the official tours I do at the ground, I spend some time chatting to the girls in reception and they tell me how refreshing it is that someone who was a player talks to them. That they don't even see the current players.

BILL MIGHT have made a big thing about 'doing it for the fans'. But all the players were always appreciative of our followers' support. We would get letters from them which were put on a big wooden table in the middle of the dressing room each morning at White Hart Lane.

Some had cuttings from papers which asked, 'Can you sign this?' which we did before sending them back. I remember one which said, 'Dear Terry, can I please have your autograph and could you get Dave's and Danny's for me too please?' Flipping hell, I thought. I bit cheeky, but I did and sent them back all the autographs they wanted.

As I've said, we were close to the supporters.

BEHIND EVERY good man there is a good woman, they say. And I, of course, have one in Kay.

But remember I was single when we won the Double, although many of my team-mates were married, and I've got a great picture of their partners together that season. Among those featured was Joanie Jones, who is still married to Cliff, and is a lovely lady. She hasn't changed a bit.

There was Betty Blanchflower. Danny had a few marriages. He was with Betty, a nice girl with a rich Birmingham accent, at the time. They eventually split up. He said there was no point in both of us being unhappy. One of us might as well be happy and it might as well be me.

Mavis Smith's another. She eventually left Bobby because he was messing about. She got together with Cliff's cousin, who died. Bobby married again.

Jacqui Norman's there. She was nice too and is not very well now. She suffers with arthritis and Maurice looks after her.

Isobel Mackay isn't in the picture, but Sandra White, Pat Allen and Vera Hollowbread are. So is Terry Medwin's wife Joyce. Five kids she had. Med joked, 'I had a pack of three when I got married and I've still got two left!'

Alma Evans, John White's mother-in-law, is in it too. I knew all of them and they were a great bunch.

WE HAD a good relationship with the press. They used to come away with us. We got to know them quite well. We used to tell them things, but they never took liberties. If things were said in confidence they would not disclose what we said. We trusted them and it was justified.

The following season, when we got into Europe we travelled and socialised with the press guys. Whatever we did, they did. It isn't like it is now with teams coming straight back the same day as the game. Then the teams and the press stayed overnight and mixed. The media never appear to see players outside of press conferences these days.

17
Historic Hat-Trick

THE BUZZ was brilliant as we reported back for pre-season in July 1961. I had a short break back in Yorkshire – when I went racing with the Classic-winning jockey Eddie Hide, who lodged with mum and dad – and was raring to go. I had been part of a team which had become one of legend and was ready to pull off back-to-back Doubles.

I was still, thankfully, very much a part of the Team of the Century, as we had been dubbed. I was on cloud nine and now knew dreams could become reality.

A unique consequence of Spurs winning the Double is that it posed a problem as to who would play each other in the FA Charity Shield (now known at the Community Shield), the annual curtain-raiser to the season between the league champions and the FA Cup winners. Talented as our team was, we weren't able to play ourselves.

So the governing body put together an FA XI, which was, basically, an England team minus our members of it with national manager Walter Winterbottom as their manager.

They lined up as: Ron Springett (Sheffield Wednesday), Jimmy Armfield (Blackpool), Michael McNeil (Middlesbrough), Bobby Robson (West Bromwich Albion), Peter Swan (Sheffield Wednesday), Ron Flowers (Wolverhampton Wanderers), Bryan Douglas (Blackburn Rovers), Jimmy Robson (Burnley), Johnny Byrne (Crystal Palace), Johnny Haynes (Fulham) and Bobby Charlton (Manchester United).

It was a strong team, but not as strong as our one which fielded our famous 11. Johnny Haynes, the England captain, put our guests to White Hart Lane in front but Bobby equalised and Les hit a couple after the interval to seal our win before Johnny Byrne, the Crystal Palace striker who joined West Ham the following year, bagged a consolation. So Spurs were capable of beating 'England'.

It was fun, raised a few bob, with a good-sized 36,000 crowd at the Lane, and showed we would still be more than half-decent. That our Double success wouldn't be a one-hit wonder.

It would have been almost impossible to have emulated the start we had made to the previous season of 11 wins on the spin. Well we managed six from the same number in 1961/62. I enjoyed myself and was among the goals once more. I managed a couple in a 2-2 home draw with West Ham and hit the only goal of the game as we overcame another team in claret and blue, Aston Villa.

But there was one game in that period which stands head and shoulders above the rest for me. That was on Saturday 26 August 1961 when we entertained Arsenal.

It already looked, thankfully, like we hadn't lost our tag as the biggest crowd-pullers in the English game. More than 50,000 had seen that deadlock against the Hammers in what was our opening game of the season at White Hart Lane.

But the Gunners at our place? Well, that proved our rivalry against West Ham was not quite as great as it was against the side from Highbury.

Nearly 60,000 squeezed into White Hart Lane that Saturday afternoon. It was the 66th showdown since the clubs first locked horns on a football pitch in 1896. It was wonderful. I can remember everything.

Mel Charles, the player Bill had pursued before signing Dave, was in their side. They were a decent outfit and also included Terry Neill and Laurie Brown, a future Spurs manager and player respectively, along with George Eastham, the same George Eastham who was to bring a case against his old club Newcastle which ended the retain-and-transfer system.

We went 2-0 up. I nodded one of them in off the bar and Les Allen got the other. But we went 3-2 down when Mel scored twice and winger Alan Skirton once. Then the ball came through a crowd of players to me from a corner and hit me on the arm and I lashed it in with my right foot. The ref gave it and Arsenal went flipping mad. Next I did a one-two with Danny Blanchflower and we'd won the game 4-3.

The Spurs supporters celebrated! There was one we knew who was especially over the moon. Johnny 'The Stick' Goldstein, the ticket spiv – reckoned to be so good he could get you into the Queen's garden party at Buckingham Palace – who so hated Arsenal.

It followed up another satisfying goalscoring day for me when we beat Arsenal on their own patch the previous season. And it is a goal I am constantly reminded of as I've got a framed picture of it hanging in our hallway at home.

Any result against the Gunners means so much to the fans. Even the players on occasion. The rivalry wasn't as intense between the players in 1961 as it was between the fans. Both sets wanted to win and we had some good games against them. Yet there was no animosity amongst the players. We got on quite well together. But I recall Alan Mullery later putting everything he had in one north London derby PURELY because it was Arsenal.

It was and remains THE London derby for Spurs followers. And that it why I'm very honoured I went into the Spurs history books as the only player to score a hat-trick against the Gunners. It is also a rare event for an Arsenal player to do likewise in the derby with only Ted Drake and Alan Sunderland – in 1934 and 1978 for you fact fiends – having managed it.

It's surprising there's just me who has done it considering the amount of times we've played Arsenal, marching on to 200. And the great goalscorers Spurs have had down the years like Jimmy Greaves and Gary Lineker? They got twos and ones but not threes.

Would I like to hang on to the record? Well, somebody will break it eventually. If and when that happens mine would have stood for a long time. Could any of the current Spurs squad emulate it? Perhaps.

The north London tussle has always been a hard result to call. I'd give Spurs the edge at home but there's not usually a lot in it generally.

Modern-day Gunners boss Arsene Wenger always gets Arsenal ready against Spurs even if they've had a disappointing result in the Champions League, like they had when they came to White Hart Lane and won 1-0 in 2013/14 just five days after holders Bayern Munich had knocked them out of Europe.

Win, lose or draw I don't think the derby – or indeed any match – means as much to the Spurs players of the current era as it did in ours. Part of the reason I feel that is there are too many who, because they are from abroad, do not appreciate the club's culture and history as much as we did. When we played, we were all from either England, Scotland, Wales or Northern Ireland. We did it for ourselves but we also loved the club so much we wanted to do it for everyone associated with it. That's the sort of attitude which is, I believe, less than common at Tottenham and many other leading clubs these days.

THE NEXT big thing for Spurs after the Double was success in Europe. Spurs were reckoned to be the team to beat in the 1961/62 European Cup. The media had made comparisons about how we would be a match for Real Madrid as we marched on to the Double. Now we had the chance to prove it.

A few months before we kicked off our unforgettable season, Real, with the original Galacticos of Alfredo Di Stefano and Ferenc Puskas, had won the European Cup in one of the great performances, defeating

Germany's Eintracht Frankfurt 7-3 at Hampden Park in front of nearly 128,000 spectators; Di Stefano scoring three and Puskas four. It meant they had won the then straight knockout competition in each of its first five years.

And Real had clinched their seventh Spanish crown to join us in our debut season in Europe, with Portugal's Benfica, who had become the first to succeed the Bernabeu giants as we sealed the Double.

But expectations were high for us given the way we had created domestic history. The fact Real were no longer invincible and Benfica were a decent rather than great side increased the speculation that we would conquer Europe.

We had confidence in our ability but, of course, were going into the unknown. And it was our biggest test. Bill said to the press, 'There's no doubt about it, playing in Europe puts you on a stage higher than just the Football League.'

But even Bill reckoned we'd win our first game in our first venture into the European Cup

We had drawn Polish champions Gornik Zabrze in the preliminary round. The first leg on 13 September 1961 was away in the coal-mining town of Katowice. It was a drab place behind the Iron Curtain, and was quite a culture shock for us.

We saw prisoners digging up roads with guards carrying machine guns and women on their hands and knees cutting the grass in a park close to the Slaski Stadium, where we were due to play.

Bill had tried to be as thorough as he could and went on a scouting trip to watch Gornik in action as well as finding out about the standard of the training facilities and accommodation, thinking the best hotel in town was terrible. We had a team talk and Bill told us, 'I'll be disappointed if we don't win.' As a further boost, we were at full strength. We fielded the Double team of Brown, Baker, Henry, Blanchflower, Norman, Mackay, Jones, White, Smith, Allen, Dyson.

We were 3-0 down at half-time when Bill said, 'For goodness sake, don't let them get another. If we do it gives us a chance for the second leg back home.' Straight from the restart they went and got another to make it 4-0. Cliffy scored and I got one, so at 4-2 we felt we had a chance. Without those goals our European dream might well have been over before it had properly begun. We might not have had the chance to experience a run of European Glory Glory Nights which have become so synonymous with Spurs' history.

I remember Dave upset the Gornik fans out there – they had 70,000 while we had just the one, a travelling student called David Mummery, I'm told. They thought we – Dave in particular – were a bit too robust. And Bill did question our discipline in the media.

Gornik gave us a memento of the trip – a lump of coal sculpted to look like a coal truck – but little else. It was certainly a rude awakening in a new world!

But the second leg seven days later proved to be the first of the Glory Glory Nights at White Hart Lane. We ran out wearing all white – I can't remember who made the decision to adopt Real's famed kit for our European matches – for the first time into an atmosphere I'd never experienced.

It was absolutely electric. The expectation of the 57,000 in there was high. The big three-tier East Stand was packed and they closed the gates well before kick-off, so lots were locked out. There were so many people who wanted to be there.

Their centre-forward – a good player he was – got a great goal after we'd taken the lead. He lashed his goal in. But then we murdered them. The crowd got on top of our visitors, who were frightened to death of us, and we won 8-1. I managed to get one of our goals. Cliffy got a hat-trick – a perfect one with his left foot, right foot and head – and many believed it to be our team's greatest single-match performance. We did play well that night.

We loved it – and so did our supporters, who went home happy, which of course pleased Bill. It would leave people forming long queues for tickets every time we played our home European ties.

I kept scoring in the first round proper against Dutch side Feyenoord. In fact I netted in both legs, ensuring my name was on the scoresheet for our opening four games in Europe.

I put Spurs in front in the Feyenoord Stadium in Rotterdam which was to become the scene of my greatest football triumph two years later before Frank Saul bagged a couple to make the home leg a lot easier, although the second-leg performance in front of another full house at the Lane didn't please Bill too much. He said, 'We muddled through.'

The Dutch certainly dished it out in the second leg. Dave suffered a hairline fracture of the skull – with blood spotted trickling out of his ear as Cecil treated him – after a collision and was carried off, although he insisted on coming back on! And they took the lead but I managed to nod in an equaliser.

But I was in for a shock when we took on Czech champions Dukla Prague in the first leg of our quarter-final in the Czech capital the following February. I was out. Even though I'd scored in every game up to then. Terry Medwin replaced me and Bill lined the team up more defensively with Tony Marchi as a sweeper.

When I spoke to Bill and asked him why he was leaving me out, he said, 'I think we've got to play this way.' I believe the fact we had gone 4-0 down in Poland had played on Bill's mind. He might have felt that he'd made mistakes in not considering the defence enough in a new competition for us.

I was choked. The Double side had been about all-out attack and I didn't agree with Bill on this negative approach. I'll admit the fact I hadn't been chosen may well have been one reason for my viewpoint.

I watched from the stands as we got through against Dukla Prague. We limited them to a 1-0 win in their country and cruised through the second leg.

But then we suffered frustration in the semi-finals against Benfica. They were a good team and included at least half the Portuguese international team, with Eusebio one of the best players in the world.

Yet we were so unlucky. Jimmy Greaves had signed for us by then and him and Bobby got goals chalked off for offside as we lost 3-1 in Lisbon. And we were out of luck in the second. We gave them a battering and won 2-1 on another amazing Glory Glory Night but another disallowed goal from Jimmy proved crucial – as well as Dave hitting the bar. Eusebio, a striker and a good lad, ended up in defence as we threw the kitchen sink at Benfica in that second leg. The decisions to disallow goals for offside were diabolical. We got done there.

I still believe that if substitutes had been allowed back then I would have made an impact coming off the bench with my knack of being able to find a goal in big games. People were saying I should have started for that very reason.

We fancied our chances in the final against Real, because we felt they weren't the power they once were. We were convinced the winners of our semi-final would lift the trophy – and that is how it proved.

Looking back I've often thought we should have gone at these teams a bit more rather than adopt a greater defensive approach.

AS WELL as losing my place in our European Cup side, I'd been dropped from the league and FA Cup side too with Bill wanting to try something different again.

I had lost my spot in late November having played in all of our first 18 games. Yes, they had included my hat-trick, but all told the team had won just nine, drawn three and lost SIX. They were unthinkable stats in comparison to the year before.

Bill decided a change was needed after we lost 2-1 at home to Leicester, of all teams, at White Hart Lane, our second defeat in four and third in six.

It was the Double team bar Johnny Hollowbread for Bill Brown, but somehow the Foxes managed to take a small revenge for their defeat in the FA Cup Final a few months earlier.

Bill restored Terry Medwin on the right and switched Cliff back to the left, with me back in the reserves as there was no substitutes' bench to keep warm.

I wished Terry well, but I was upset. Having played what I considered a big part in the club's most momentous season after years of struggling to make the first team, it was hard to take that I was no longer a part of it.

I did not play in the first team again until Spurs drew 2-2 with Manchester United at White Hart Lane in late January 1962, with Terry Medwin out. Jimmy Greaves scored both our goals. Jimmy had arrived from AC Milan the previous month, with Les switched to number 9 in place of Bobby (before being left out himself).

And I was back on the sidelines when Terry Medwin returned for the next game, an FA Cup fourth round tie at Plymouth. Terry scored one and Jimmy two in a 5-1 win.

Jimmy had hit the ground running. It brought his total to five in his first three games in the competition for the Lilywhites, having bagged three against Birmingham in a draw and a replay as we began the defence of the cup. Frustratingly for me I was not involved. A cup hero had become surplus to requirements in this defence it seemed.

I deputised for Cliff in league draws against Aston Villa at Villa Park and Bolton at home. And I figured in a 3-1 home win over Everton with Terry Medwin absent before Eddie Clayton came in to occupy his shirt for three straight league games as I returned to reserve duty. The only other appearance I made that season was in the last game, again stepping in for Jonesy as we turned the tables on Leicester.

I was saddened to be a bit-part player but the first team had a good season in the league and it was generally agreed that we would have completed a second successive Double but for two defeats against Ipswich Town, managed by our boss's former team-mate Alf Ramsey. Alf had deployed Jimmy Leadbetter and Roy Stephenson as deep-lying wingers and the tactic worked well against us and the rest of the league.

I read Bill knew how to negate this tactic by getting a half-back instead of a full-back to mark each winger, but that his players had persuaded him not to adapt our usual set-up to cope. It meant their two strikers Ray Crawford and Ted Phillips had lots of space because our full-backs were drawn out of position by Leadbetter and Stephenson.

But there were no regrets in the FA Cup for Bill. Terry and Cliff were ever present on the wing throughout as they completed their road to Wembley with wins over West Bromwich Albion, Aston Villa and Manchester United.

And I was pleased for everyone – particularly Bobby Smith, who had got his place back and scored – as Spurs lifted the cup for a second year, beating Burnley 3-1 with Jimmy and Danny also scoring for us. I'd loved to have got my opportunity to play a role but there was still no bitterness at the fact Terry had taken my place. I couldn't have been more delighted for him.

We've been in touch occasionally in recent years, although Terry lives in south Wales and I'm in Hertfordshire.

We should have made it a double Double. That might well have ended any debate about whether or not we were the greatest team of any era.

Bill insisted on HIS tactics to deal with Ipswich's deep-lying wingers in the FA Charity Shield match at Portman Road before the start of the 1962/63 season and Spurs won 5-1 – with Terry and Cliffy on our wings. It was such a shame he didn't put his foot down during the previous season.

18
Big Freeze Thaws

BEING A FOOTBALLER isn't just about football. It's also about giving you a few life experiences. In the early 1960s, holiday breaks abroad were far from common. The effects of the Second World War were still being felt in the 1950s, with rationing still going on. There was not much in the way of spare money for most and anyone who took a holiday in this country did so at home, often at seaside resorts like Blackpool in the north-west, Scarborough near my home town on the Yorkshire coast, and Margate, Brighton and Southend in the south.

Cheap air flights out of Britain weren't available until entrepreneur Freddie Laker in the 1970s. He led the way for firms like Easyjet and Ryanair.

So the summer tours abroad we had at Tottenham were special. I've told you about the contrasting trips to North America and the USSR we had. My third one, in the close-season in 1962, was different again. The Middle East was our destination, Israel specifically. It was, literally, a religious experience.

We booked into our hotel in Tel Aviv for a short tour which included just two matches. Our guide took us up on the roof of it. He wanted to give us a view over the walls into the Old City. It was incredible.

We were looking down at one of the oldest cities in the world – built in 3,000 BC and considered holy by several religions. We were looking at a place written about in the Bible. As a believer, it meant a lot to me. And the historical significance of the city did too.

We were taken to the Wailing Wall. It is the Western Wall of the old city where people come to 'wail', and bemoan the destruction of a temple it is said. We saw people actually 'wailing' and praying and the people who took us there said they were 'useless to the country', and they didn't contribute to it.

It is a desert area but the Israelis had turned a lot of land into green fields through irrigation and seeded them to grow food.

It wasn't all about culture and learning about the country. One hotel we stayed in just outside Tel Aviv, about 50km from Jerusalem, had a nice swimming pool and we used it a lot. Bobby and I spent time in it practising our diving techniques. We were in and out of the pool a lot and suffered with blisters because we didn't put any sun protection on.

The sun affected me during our first match against a Tel Aviv Select side. I got sunstroke and had to come off. It was in the middle of the afternoon and hot. They dosed me up with water and I recovered.

Our second game was in the evening a few days later and I was fine. I came on as a sub for Terry Medwin as we beat Haifa Select 5-0.

I WAS frustrated and disappointed to largely be out of the side for most of the 1961/62 season after I had helped it create football history by winning the Double in the previous campaign.

But that didn't mean to say I was sulking or feeling sorry for myself because the world was against me. I had reason to, I suppose, because I had more than paid my dues by playing reserve football for my first five years at the club after leaving the Army to become a professional footballer.

I had an early taste of playing alongside the Spurs big boys when I made my Football League debut as an amateur against Sheffield United. But initially it proved a false dawn, a tempting *hors d'oeuvre* without the main course of a regular run.

Now, it could be argued, I faced an even bigger task. When I helped the Lilywhites cut apart the Blades from Sheffield, the team was in transition. The jigsaw was incomplete so most pretenders were being given a decent opportunity to convince the management they were worth an established spot.

But the team was no longer in transition. It was considered the finished article, the Team of the Century, and I had been a part of it. So I knew first hand just how good this team was from the inside.

But Bill had deemed I no longer fitted and, generally, Terry Medwin did. So how was I supposed to get back in a team which was that good? To my mind, there was only one way. Hard work. I gave it 100 per cent. Every second of every minute of every training session and reserve match I played.

I did get the occasional run out in the league team in the first half of the 1962/63 season. My first appearances came back-to-back in September, helping the team beat Blackburn comfortably and draw against Wolves up at Molineux where Jimmy Greaves bagged a couple, moving towards breaking the club goalscoring record in one campaign (he ended up with 37).

I had got back in with Cliff out but after the 2-2 draw with Wolves I was back in the reserves.

Two games later the way back for me looked tough with Jimmy firing four to chop down Nottingham Forest 9-2. Their player, the now late Trevor Hockey, joked how Forest had scored first and last while Spurs scored nine lucky goals in between!

And the team continued to underline its scoring prowess, banging in four against Arsenal, six against Manchester United – Jimmy getting three of them – and five against Leyton Orient, with a mere two in a victory at West Brom.

Cliffy being sidelined saw me deputise for him in a 4-0 home win against Leicester to ensure the side had scored an amazing 30 in six games. Five goals a game is some average, although it dropped a fraction as I was dropped in the next match with the Lilywhites managing just a 2-0 home win against Fulham.

THE FANTASTIC run of results for the team saw a bubbly party fly off for a brief sunshine trip to Egypt for a midweek friendly against one of the African country's top teams.

Zamalek was a Cairo club managed to the national title by Dave Mackay in the 1990s, and the club that future Spurs striker Mido has played for and coached.

I had a great time and got a couple of goals as a substitute in a 7-3 win in front of 60,000. The Cairo press said they bought their best players on near the finish. I agree! I also got to ride a camel in the desert and visit the pyramids. Awesome. We saw someone run up and down one for money – so we gave him a few Egyptian pounds as a reward as sweat poured off him.

MY PERFORMANCE at the Cairo International Stadium seemed to do me a favour because I was back in the league team three days later.

My return came on 17 November against Sheffield Wednesday at White Hart Lane, the same fixture that had secured us the title the previous season. It ended in a draw and was the last of an eight-match unbeaten run.

But my appearance in Cliff's place was my last in the league for FIVE months. I did get a chance to make my mark again in the FA Cup after being left out for the entire winning run the previous season.

It came in the middle of an infamous British winter which has gone down in history as the Big Freeze. It broke all sorts of meteorological records. Temperatures were at their lowest since the 17th and 18th centuries in certain parts of the country. And it went on and on.

Spurs had not had a game since Boxing Day because of the weather when I was called into the team for the start of our defence of the cup.

It took a while for us to be able to get the tie against, ironically, Burnley, played. Our ground staff – and a few fans – got the White Hart Lane pitch ready for the Wednesday afternoon of 16 January after the tie had been originally scheduled for the fifth. In fact, the FA didn't get all the third round completed until 7 March.

The whole pitch was covered in snow and the only visible signs of grass were the touchlines and centre circle and we played with a bright orange ball to help with visibility. But Bill made a mistake because the conditions proved a leveller. The ball wouldn't run, forever sticking in the snow. It shouldn't have been played.

And unfortunately our two-year unbeaten run in the competition came to an end with Burnley gaining a small revenge for what we did to them the previous May. It certainly did little for my hopes of re-establishing my place in the side.

IN THE meantime, I remained frozen out of our second successive venture into Europe. It followed our run to the semi-finals of the European Cup in which I had at least played a part.

The side had gained qualification for the European Cup Winners' Cup by beating Burnley in the FA Cup Final, minus your disappointed Yorkshireman.

It was the third year of what was another knockout competition set up by Europe's governing body, UEFA. And it did what it said on the tin – invite purely the cup winners of each affiliated country besides the holders. It was a simpler, welcome format in my eyes given how criteria has changed for UEFA's major club competitions these days.

We were drawn against Glasgow Rangers in the first round. Rangers had been beaten finalists in the first year of the competition, 1961, suffering a two-legged defeat against Italy's Fiorentina.

And the extra incentive for them to go one better in this campaign – in which the final would be a one-off – was the fact they were up against a team hailing from south of the border, from a country considered the 'auld enemy'.

They were dying to beat us and were gutted when the lads overcame them. I watched from the stands as John White, a Scot, put one over his countrymen in the first leg on a Hallowe'en evening on which we produced a bag of tricks to treat the near 60,000 at White Hart Lane.

It was almost forgotten that it was a continental competition. There seemed more emphasis in some quarters about it being a domestic dust-up. But we played very well to win 5-2 with John getting a couple of goals he certainly deserved with Maurice, Les and an own goal from Bobby Shearer securing our nap hand.

It left the second leg at Ibrox a formality in most objective eyes, if not those of the hosts. We got the impression Rangers wanted us to allow them to win the second leg by enough to save face. That was never going to happen. We completed the victory with a 3-2 win – with Bobby bagging two and Jimmy one – in front of a vociferous and partisan 80,000 but unfortunately Danny got injured.

A couple of Rangers players got him and the joint challenge damaged his cartilage and all but wrecked his season and he went on to miss 22 games of it as a result. After all he was no spring chicken at 37 years of age. But he was still a massive influence.

Danny was still recovering when it came to playing the second round against Slovan Bratislava the following March. It was a tie that had been delayed by the Big Freeze which also covered Europe.

It was a third trip behind the Iron Curtain in European competition. The first one, in Poland against Gornik in the European Cup the previous season, had been a sobering experience as we have discovered. I was able to get that goal which helped limit the damage there.

The second was the loss, against Czech outfit Dukla Prague, later in the competition. And it would not be a case of third time lucky as we put on a performance against a second Czech side which was considered our worst in Europe to date. As the nearby Danube froze, so did we because the boys were defeated 2-0 and but for Bill Brown it could have been a whole lot worse.

I could do nothing personally as Bill Nick left me out, as he did in Prague. And there was no recall for the second leg. He had preferred Cliff to be partnered on the wing by young Frank Saul, with Terry Medwin, who had played in both games against Rangers, stood down. Bill was messing about with the team and I didn't know why.

And, as far as the second leg against Slovan Bratislava was concerned, I could not argue. As against Gornik and Dukla Prague, there was an emphatic home victory, six of the best without reply. A Glory Glory Night with close to 62,000 roaring and singing 'Glory Glory Hallelujah'. Jimmy got a couple while Bobby, Jonesy, John and Dave made up the scoreline.

Bill was particularly impressed with our half-backs. Tony Marchi had stepped in for Danny and he and Dave dominated. Bill said it reminded him of the way Danny and Dave performed as a partnership en route to the Double.

Danny, as always, summed up our Jekyll and Hyde characters either side of the Iron Curtain. He told author Phil Soar in *And The Spurs Go Marching On*, 'We were never happy over there, but they couldn't believe their eyes when they came to London. We rarely had any trouble at home.'

Spurs had made the semi-finals of a major UEFA club tournament for a second successive year, but we had made the last four of this one without any contribution from me.

I DID get into one first team during this time – and it led me to another Wembley final. It was The Cockerels ten-pin bowling side based at Stamford Hill.

The London district where it was based is known for its Jewish population, some of whom support the club, which has been known for being popular with East End immigrant families of the faith since the late 19th century. Lord Alan Sugar, the businessman, government advisor and television personality with his show *The Apprentice*, is one. He was even chairman of the club in the 1990s.

I sided with Spurs team-mates, Peter Baker, Tony Marchi, Micky Dulin and Johnny Hollowbread to beat one from Brighton. The only downside was having to wear the shoes supplied by the bowling alley as they were used by any number of bowlers who visited it.

I FINALLY got my chance to wear football footwear for the Spurs first team on a memorable Easter weekend which saw three games in four days. I wonder what the likes of leading managers Arsene Wenger, Jose Mourinho or Louis van Gaal would think of that kind of schedule these days!

The first, my return, took place on Good Friday, 12 April, against Liverpool at Anfield. Bill had decided to pick me in place of Frank and perhaps he might have been regretting the decision when the final whistle blew even though we had faced a strong Reds line-up. They included the Scotland international Ian St John, Ian Callaghan, who was in Alf Ramsey's World Cup-winning squad, and Roger Hunt, who played in the global final in that famous year for English football.

What might have played a part in me keeping my spot for the following day's home game against Fulham and the reverse fixture against the Saint and Co on the Monday is that I had managed to have a part in both our two consolation goals in a 5-2 defeat. I scored with a great volley. It bounced out after smashing the stanchion! And I crossed for Les to bag our other goal. Those efforts put us 2-0 up but Ian St John was in great form for them and it all went downhill for us.

We were held to a 1-1 draw by Fulham, and almost inevitably it was Jimmy, who had shown red-hot form in front of goal, who netted for us.

On the Monday, and with more or less the same line-ups as four days earlier, we locked horns again with Liverpool. It was at White Hart Lane and we won 7-2! Jimmy got four goals in a game again. He was totally on fire that season while beating the club record held jointly by my pal

Bobby and Ted Harper. And we certainly had the bit between our teeth as far as scoring goals was concerned. We scored in our first 19 games of the season.

Unfortunately, for the second season in a row, a disappointing finish cost us the crown. We only got eight points from our last ten league games – and I played in the final nine!

But that period more than had its compensation. For the fans, for Bill, for the players. For everyone at Spurs. And that is probably the biggest of understatements. It was a time in which European glory came to the club – and I gratefully was at the centre of it.

MY STARRING role began on Wednesday 24 April 1963, just 12 days after my return to the first team at Anfield. In the day, much of the nation was glued to the box watching Princess Alexandra, the Queen's cousin, marry Sir Angus Ogilvy at Westminster Abbey on a royal occasion oozing class. Meanwhile, I was in the Spurs party which had travelled to Belgrade for a contrasting occasion for tin helmets rather than robes and bridal gowns.

It was in the Red Army Stadium in Belgrade, home to OFK Belgrade. There were 60,000 partisan home fans creating a hostile atmosphere for the outsiders – us. It was the first leg of our European Cup Winners' Cup semi-final against the then Yugoslavian capital's third team behind Red Star and Partizan.

I must have done enough over Easter and perhaps even in a 1-0 defeat at Everton, who ended up winning the league, to convince Bill I was at last worth including in Spurs' bid for European success at the second attempt.

But another trip behind the Iron Curtain was a whole world away from getting stuck against the Toffees at the other end of Stanley Park to Anfield inside Goodison Park.

Our Yugoslavian hosts adopted roughhouse tactics. Some described them as an attempt to bully and intimidate. I guess OFK thought they would be unable to match us in quality. But, as I have said, we were no shrinking violets. We could mix it while still being able to show our class – and this is what we did as we gave every last ounce of effort.

There were certainly a few flashpoints in the volatile atmosphere. There was one which illustrated our ability to balance physicality with technique – and it led to us taking the lead.

Bobby was almost cut in two by a challenge from their right-half Dragoljub Maric and Hungarian ref Lajo Aranjosi awarded us a free kick. Before it could be taken, Maric was lying flat out in the area. Bobby was the prime suspect and their players surrounded the ref to point him out as the guilty party.

When the kick from Tony Marchi, our captain with Danny sidelined, was finally taken, Bobby superbly laid the ball on for John to volley into the net.

Their equaliser caused more controversy. It came just before the interval from a penalty though Milorad Popov. The award seemed harsh with the ref adjudging Dave to have handled even though the ball had deflected off his boot. Perhaps the official was trying to balance things up, or concerned that members of the emotional crowd might seek him out afterwards.

The third flashpoint came just after half-time when Jimmy was sent off. He had taken plenty of stick and this geezer Srboljub Krivokuca tried to thump him – believing he had just clattered him when in fact it had been Bobby. Jimmy got out the way and lashed out himself – and completely missed him. Yet the ref gave him his marching orders. The official told journalist Peter Lorenzo, who went on to present football on the TV, 'I sent off Greaves for taking a kick at number 5 when he hadn't got the ball.

'I told Greaves that this wasn't gentlemanly. In fact, Tottenham were a more gentlemanly side when they were down to ten men. This was not a rough game, but Spurs were physically strong.'

Bill was fuming. He thought the ref had got it wrong. So did I. There's no way Jimmy should have become the first Spurs player to get sent off since Cecil Poynton, who had become our trainer, 35 years before!

OFK certainly provoked. They were right so-and-sos! One of their geezers spat right in my face. I wanted to smack him but couldn't get at him with players having got in the way. Eventually I checked myself.

By then, I'd marked my return to Europe with what proved the winning goal! One of their players tried to knock it back to his goalkeeper. But it was too short and I got there before the keeper could get it. I'd helped myself to another big goal in a big match for Spurs. It was described as a 'brilliant opportunist winning goal'. I'll not dispute that.

I might have been tempted to thump the player who spat at me if we had been losing 2-1 instead of winning by the same score!

The guy came up to me and apologised afterwards. He'd been out of order but I accepted his gesture, saying to him, 'It's all right.' Again, having sealed the win, his disgusting action didn't bother me as much as it might have done. I felt a bit for the lad anyway as the crowd had turned on their own players.

I kept my place for the second leg the following Wednesday. Jimmy, of course, was suspended. Danny returned and was superb, along with Dave.

It was a tense evening with OFK putting in a few body-blocks to try and wind us up. Cliff had to be dragged away by Danny from one flare-up, although the game as a whole never boiled over.

I got spoken to a few times by the ref. He thought I was being too aggressive in my challenges, but it was just me being tenacious.

The game had such a big reward at the end of it. If we could nail a positive result it would mean us becoming the first English side to make a final of a major European competition.

OFK did threaten our defence but Peter, Ron and Maurice were solid apart from one moment when the visitors levelled after Dave put us in front.

Danny calmed us and we retook the lead. Esteemed writer Desmond Hackett gave the goal to me in his report for the *Daily Express*. Unfortunately, I can't claim it. John and Dave set it up for Cliff! I'll let him have that one. Bobby, who had a superb game, headed the third and the dream had become a reality.

Atletico Madrid, the holders, would be our opponents in the final in Rotterdam 13 days later. The Spaniards had overcome Nuremberg from Germany over their two-legged semi-final.

19

Eu-phoria

THE PROFUMO Affair, involving the relationship of our government's Secretary of State with model and showgirl Christine Keeler, the Great Train Robbery and Beatlemania dominated the domestic headlines in 1963 along with a few other stories…like Spurs creating more football history.

It was all very well being the first English team to reach a European final, but once in it we just had to win it. I was among 11 players who had gratefully been perceived by experts as having legendary status by being part of the Double-winning team. But even legends can break new ground to enhance their status.

We still had a couple of league games to play before our date with destiny against holders Atletico Madrid in the European Cup Winners' Cup Final at the Feyenoord Stadium in Rotterdam on Wednesday 15 May 1963.

There was the visit of Sheffield United to White Hart Lane, the fixture in which I had made my first team debut as an amateur eight years before.

No one wanted to get injured and miss the big one, but we all wanted to show Bill we were worthy of lining up in our all-white kits in Rotterdam. We managed a 4-2 win – and I found the net.

But four days before the biggest game in the club's history in terms of global status any momentum was lost as already-relegated Manchester City – two years before the start of the Joe Mercer–Malcolm Allison reign which brought Second and First Division titles in 1966 and 1968 – defeated us 1-0 at Maine Road as Everton sealed the First Division title.

The moment the final whistle blew our undivided attention was on our date with Atletico Madrid. We were buzzing at the prospect. We stuck to our regular regime of training and bantering in the days leading up. We were trying to keep things as normal as possible, but it was hard to rid yourself of the thought that we were attempting what no other British team had ever done – becoming the first to lift a European trophy. There wasn't any chance of it escaping our attention because of the big reaction following our 5-2 aggregate win over OFK.

We flew to Holland the day before the match. It only took about an hour to Rotterdam and we were soon flying over the shipyards of Europe's biggest port before landing at its airport. Then we checked in to the seaside hotel in the village of Scheveningen close by. It was lovely. Like always, it was a first class hotel. It was part of Bill's preparation to ensure we were rested mentally and physically.

We didn't need to worry about anything that was going on around us. The club sorted our the hotel booking – as well as organising our tickets for family and friends – as we hung around the lobby.

I was handed a key with my room number on it. I still remember what it was – 261. Les Allen was given the same number. We were sharing a room. The two full-backs, Ron and Peter, were together. Maurice and Bobby shared. Cliffy was in with John. Danny had a room on his own. It is funny how you remember such details, but it was a time to remember.

Bill had everything planned down to the last detail and he had found a place for us to train nearby and we had a session just as soon as we'd checked in.

When we got back, Bill left us to ourselves largely because he knew he could trust us; that we knew what we were doing and wouldn't do anything to upset the preparation. It did get a bit boring, though, because we just sat around the hotel, had a bite to eat and then trooped off to bed around 10pm.

The mood was fine. We weren't really nervous about the game. After all there was plenty of time to get like that the following day. Les is a good lad, good company. And he didn't snore. That helped me. I didn't sleep too badly.

Then came the morning of the day in which I produced the best performance of my career. I'd hoped it would be an 'out-of-this-world' kind of day. It seemed appropriate as an astronaut, Gordon Cooper, was becoming the first American to spend more than 24 hours in space.

We all met up in the dining room for breakfast, tea and toast and cereal, and relaxed before a light lunch. I opted for egg on toast. The Egg Marketing Board had encouraged us to 'go to work on an egg', so I guess I took them up on the idea. These days I might have earned a few bob with a commercial sponsorship deal in the view of how things turned out for me later in the day.

Bill got us together for a team talk in a spare room. He went through their team. I wasn't familiar with their players at all and neither were any of us, really. It is not like today when you have the likes of satellite channels, such as Sky providing 24/7 sports news, and the internet keeping us up to date on footballers all over the world.

Remember there was still little football on television bar the FA Cup Final. *Match of the Day* was still a year away from appearing on our screens for a weekly dose of highlights from the English league.

I thought it was probably good we didn't know too much about them. I was only interested in what we did. About how well we'd done to get to the final and hoping we would perform like we should.

I don't know which players had listened to what Bill was saying but the information was useful in that we got to know who their key players were, their weaknesses and how they could be exploited. Bill had scouted them and was very thorough. I hadn't realised just how good they were.

THE COMPETITION involved cup winners from UEFA-affiliated countries, plus the holders. It meant Spain was represented by two teams. One was Sevilla, in place of Real Madrid who beat them in the domestic cup final but were otherwise engaged in the European Cup as Spanish champions. The second was Atletico, attempting to retain the trophy.

Democracy has been restored in their country with the help of King Juan Carlos, who abdicated in 2014, but when we faced Atletico it was a time of dictatorship in Spain. Fascist Francisco Franco had established himself as dictator in 1939 following the Spanish Civil War, in which he was supported by Hitler and Mussolini.

And in football it led to the Spanish Cup being named after him: the Copa del Generalisimo. From what I've read, Franco developed a state which was described as 'totalitarian', repressing opposition.

So it was ironic the country dominating European football did so by playing football with freedom, largely through Real Madrid, although the Bernabeu giants had achieved five successive European Cup wins with a few foreign-born stars, like Di Stefano – a hero of Bobby Smith's by the way – and Puskas.

But Atletico also played their part in establishing Spain as a force in the game in the early 1960s. Domestically the club based in what was considered the more working-class part of town gave Real a bloody nose in the first two Spanish Cup finals of the 1960s.

They had been edged out by their neighbours in the semi-finals of the 1959 European Cup after a replay following two even legs. And they did it with the help of Brazilian Vava, fresh from helping his country lift the World Cup in 1962.

Atletico lifted the 1962 European Cup Winners' Cup in only its second year by beating holders Fiorentina 3-0 after a replay in Stuttgart following a 1-1 draw at Hampden Park in the first one-off final.

They were highly regarded opposition as Bill Nick was to re-emphasise in our dressing room at the Feyenoord Stadium before kick-off.

Atletico had eight survivors from their European triumph a year earlier. That meant they had Jesus on their side! Jesus Glaria that is. He was in midfield with Miguel Jones – not related to our Cliffy, by the way – who had netted in the 3-0 second leg cup-clinching win over Fiorentina 12 months earlier.

Star striker Enrique Collar, who had played with the now departed Vava, had been central to their continental successes. And he was joined up front by a couple of other useful forwards, Jorge Mendonca, who had also scored in the crucial victory over the Italians, deep-lying Adelardo Rodriguez, a playmaker, and Chuzo, converted from playing at the back.

Their defence included the previous year's medal-winning goalkeeper Edgardo Madinabeytia, Feliciano Rivilla and Ramiro. Rivilla was of particular interest to me as he was at right-back and I would be up against him in the final.

Spanish international Joaquin Peiro, who scored in both games against Fiorentina, had relocated to Italy with Torino, while cup-winning manager Jose Villalonga Llorente had been succeeded by Rafael Garcia on being appointed Spain's national boss.

Under Garcia, they would end up runners-up to Real Madrid in La Liga that season. It seemed they might have almost rivalled Diego Simeone's 2013/14 side which, with the help of Diego Costa's goals, won La Liga but lost the Champions League Final to Real.

Garcia's red-and-white-striped army were no mugs. And I'm told they were on a bonus of £360 each to beat us, quite a sum when you consider my weekly wage of £40. We had to be at our best.

FOLLOWING OUR team talk in the hotel, we went to our rooms for an afternoon nap. The wives of my team-mates had arrived that day and been sent off on a tour of the tulip fields nearby. Bill wanted no distractions to the task in hand.

The wives weren't too happy about that. But the sleeping arrangements for that night changed from the previous one. Myself and Frank Saul – the only single players – shared a room while the other lads moved in with their other halves.

THERE WAS concern we might be without Danny, John and Dave when we stepped out on to the field at the stadium, the three key players in everything the club had achieved in the 1960s.

Danny was struggling with the cartilage problem which he had sustained during the second leg of our opening-round tie against Glasgow Rangers. He might have managed 90 minutes against OFK at White Hart Lane but at his advanced age – in terms of football – injuries such as the one he was enduring didn't vanish as quickly as they once did. They had to be nursed.

Danny told Bill he would have to choose between either himself on one leg or reserve John Smith on two. Bill decided he needed his 'one-legged' captain and Danny took a painkiller to get him through the game.

There was a suggestion Bill was considering dropping Danny anyway, and replacing him with the more defensive-minded Tony Marchi, although I never believed that rumour.

But Bill never had to make that decision because, as we were told before we set out for Holland, Dave, our talisman, was out injured. It was a massive, massive blow. Dave's swashbuckling performances had been the main reason we had made the final. He was my mate and I know just how shocking it was for him to miss out. The only role he could play was one of supporter.

It added to another disappointment for him that week, being pipped to the Footballer Writers' Association Footballer of the Year award by Stanley Matthews (although he would manage to share the trophy with Manchester City's Tony Book in 1969).

Dave should have won it this year, in my opinion, for the performances he put in for us, although it seems the FWA was keen to ensure Matthews's illustrious career was recognised a second time before he retired. After all the great man was 48.

So Danny and Tony made up the half-back partnership. In the meantime, thankfully, John passed a late fitness test to enable him to pull on his number 8 shirt.

WE SET off from our hotel in a team coach about two hours before the evening kick-off – 7.15pm UK time – and drove through the streets of a town rebuilt after being bombed in the war.

It had been raining and was damp. It was a bit different to my coach journey with the team to Wembley two years before as there were no fans lining the way. Those who saw our vehicle didn't know us from Adam.

Then the stadium came into view. We were already familiar with it, of course, having played Feyenoord in the European Cup there. And you also might remember I had scored that night in front of more than 60,000 home fans in a decent team performance and win. It was already a lucky ground for me.

The stadium had been built before the war. And it had a nickname, the locals called it De Kuip, which translated means The Tub, due to its shape. It was a big venue with a capacity of 69,000. Impressive, although given the fact both sides were from foreign fields, a decent rather than packed crowd was expected. As it was, 40,000 turned out.

When we got inside we sought out the dressing room, then we chatted. We were excited and confident. Some of us had a quick leaf through the official match programme. On the front of it was a cartoon depicting us as the bull and Atletico the matador.

It didn't take long to read as inside the notes were all written in Dutch bar one paragraph penned by Gustav Wiederkehr, the Michel Platini of his time, the president of UEFA. He wrote, 'I'm sure both teams will do their utmost at Feyenoord in order to conquer this much-wanted trophy and I'm also sure they'll make their effort in a good and fair match.'

Bill gave us all a few final words of encouragement. And he had a special few just for Cliffy and myself who were on either wing. He told us that this would be our night and that we should take the full-backs on as often as we could.

He underlined the strength of Atletico to the group, which is when Danny pointed out we weren't half bad and that our opponents would be worried about us. And we thought Danny definitely had a point.

Then we got word: it was game on.

THE STADIUM was a little like Wembley in that our dressing rooms were below the level of the pitch. Kitted out all in white, we walked up concrete steps alongside the Atletico players looking out at the crowd as we emerged in the stadium. When our 4,000 fans caught sight of us they roared 'Glory Glory Hallelujuh'. It give us a real lift. But I wasn't thinking about anything, really. I just want to get the match started.

There wasn't as much pomp and ceremony as there is now. None of all this rubbish where you shake hands with every one of your opponents. We just ran out on to the field, lined up briefly alongside Atletico and the officials at right angles to the centre circle before a knockabout with the ball. There was a quick coin toss between Danny and the opposing captain Enrique Collar and we kicked off. The pitch did not look much, a bit muddy and worn from a season's play, but it played all right.

We did fine in the first half but the quality of play was patchy, bitty. We were praised in the media. Donald Saunders reported in the *Daily Telegraph*, 'During the nervous opening stages they [Spurs] kept their heads and by half-time had moved, methodically and calmly, into a two-goal lead.'

At the time I thought we were the better team in the first half. But Atletico, on watching a video re-run recently, had about the same amount of the play as we had and 2-0 flattered us. The only difference was that we managed to score those couple of goals. Jimmy got the first and it was a good one.

Bobby was being clattered by them. He had got brought down by their big centre-half Jorge Griffa early on. Griffa also seemed to stamp on

Bobby as well. I thought Bob would retaliate like he did when the guy from OFK caught him and ended up on the deck. But he didn't. He showed his football intelligence by dropping deeper away from his marker and using his technical skills while we stepped up the pace of our passing.

After about a quarter of an hour, Bobby picked up the ball after Danny and John had broken up an Atletico move and put a lovely ball inside their Brazilian left-back Ramiro for Cliff down the right. Cliffy knocked it across on the run and Jimmy turned it in.

It had become gloomy and Danny and Ron asked the Dutch ref Andries van Leeuwen if he could get the floodlights put on. It wasn't like today when the lights might well be on even when the match is played on a sunny afternoon.

Danny, John, Cliff and myself went close to a second before I helped us double our lead just after the half-hour. Jimmy controlled a return ball from Tony after we'd won a throw-in over on the right. He crossed, Bobby dummied a defender and the ball reached me. I looked and saw John in a decent position so I pulled it back to him just inside the box. John got a beautiful touch on the ball with his right foot and lashed it into the top of the net. As we went in for the interval, I noticed that some of the press photographers shook the hands of the referee, a strange occurrence you couldn't imagine these days.

It was a happy dressing room at the interval and we sat there sipping tea. Bill told us to keep going as we were. That we had played well and were better than them. But even at 2-0 nothing is guaranteed and we were forced to produce a few battling qualities after half-time.

They came forward straight away and Ron had to handle a shot which had beaten Bill Brown on the line to prevent it going in. These days that action would have seen Ron get a straight red for preventing a goalscoring opportunity. Fortunately for us that rule didn't apply back in 1963. The ref didn't even talk to Ron, concentrating on retrieving the ball so he could put it on the spot.

But we still suffered when Collar beat Bill with the resultant penalty, unfortunately for us.

As I've said, Atletico were no mugs and weren't going to give up either their trophy or the huge win bonus without a fight. They slaughtered us for about 20 minutes.

I thought, 'We are going to get beat here.' But Danny kept us calm by example and word of mouth and our defence was superb, particularly big Maurice. They got their tackles in and put their bodies on the line. I don't think they got the credit they deserved.

Shots were raining in, with Ramiro and Chuzo going close as our opponents forced four corners in quick succession. Ron had injured himself

– suffering strained ligaments in his left leg – but he managed to head an effort by Mendonca off the line.

Rivilla joined in the onslaught from right-back. He belted in a shot that was goalbound. As the ball left his boot I thought, 'What would Dave do here? He'd put body and soul into somehow getting in the way. And perhaps injure himself in doing so.' It inspired me. So I launched myself straight at the ball knowing I would get hurt because of the power of the shot. And bloody hell it did as it hit me right across the shins. I went down like a sack of potatoes. But I'd saved a goal. It was just the lift we needed. Who knows what would have happened if Rivilla's shot had gone in and made it 2-2?

Shortly afterwards, though, came THE turning point which, I believe, won the cup for Spurs. It changed the game completely, ending Atletico's barrage and putting us on the front foot.

I collected a quick throw down the left-hand touchline by Danny, drew Rivilla, flicked it over his head, and ran round the other side of him. I could feel Rivilla's breath down my neck. But I controlled the ball after it bounced with my right knee before crossing first time with my left towards the near post. I watched as it curved in and thought, 'Blimey, that's a bad cross.'

The keeper came to get it and pushed it into the net. He was crying afterwards, the poor lad. I told him after I'd deliberately put a swerve on it to fool him to make him feel better but, to be honest, it was a fluke. Although I felt for him, for me it was the most important goal of my entire career. The celebration? I just jumped in the air and thought, 'Blimey, I've scored in a European final.' And all the lads came over to congratulate me with hugs and encouraging words.

I then made Jimmy's second goal to secure us a 4-1 advantage. A free-kick routine by Danny didn't work out but Tony Marchi picked up the loose ball and fed it out to me on the left. I did the full-back Rivilla on the outside and crossed it over for Jimmy to stroke in on the volley. Jimmy appreciated my contribution and showed it by running across as I stood there with my arms up and wide with a big smile on my face and he lifted me high in the air.

It was game over but, thankfully, I had time to score a second goal. I worked a one-two with Tony in defence. Tony passed it out to the left to John who knocked it inside as I continued my run inside our own half. I ran diagonally left to right across the middle of the pitch and, as Atletico backed off, I carried on, switching the ball on to my left about 20 yards out. I couldn't see where the goalkeeper was but just hit it.

You always have players say they aim for the corner. You don't. You just get the ball down and shoot. And if it is on target then brilliant. If it is in the corner then it is a lovely bonus. That was how it was against Atletico – and the ball flew into the top corner like a rocket!

The referee blew his whistle before Atletico could take a corner after Bill Brown saved from Miguel Jones. The cup was ours. We'd won 5-1, still the joint biggest winning margin in a one-off major European final.

It was a cue for a friendly invasion of fans. Including a group who called themselves 'The Angels', and dressed up as such! They were formed, I'm told, after someone dubbed us a bunch of hard men in Poland a couple of years before when we played Gornik in the European Cup. The group preferred us to be known as 'angels' rather than tough guys, I suppose. Bobby hoisted one of them up as the newspaper photographers took pictures.

We jogged over to wave at our supporters, many with rattles, rosettes and banners, as some ran on the pitch and closed in on us, cheering. The fans had been joined by 2,000 British soldiers who were stationed on the continent and also roaring their approval. That was special as I'd been a soldier myself, of course. It was an amazing atmosphere.

The lack of ceremony at the start was reflected at the finish. There was no big platform in the middle of the pitch with deafening fireworks crackling around as dignitaries handed out the medals and trophy. There were steps up to a box high in the main stand for the same purpose. There were just a few UEFA execs shuffling around by the touchline waiting for us to come across from where we were surrounded by snappers, fans and even angels.

The head dignitary – I cannot remember who – quickly gave Danny the cup and us our medals. We posed for a few seconds as the morning newspapers got their pictures. Then Bobby and Tony lifted Danny, clutching the trophy, on to their shoulders as us others gathered either side before parading around the pitch.

The fans in general were fantastic. One of them even got his hands on the cup as we paraded it around the pitch. No one threw him off. We had a special bond with those supporters. We knew many of them personally and were delighted they could share the moment with us. And the moments which I described earlier in that bar next to our hotel.

Those scenarios could no longer be played out these days in such big games with the players so distant from their followers.

WE WERE buzzing on the flight back the following morning, chatting excitedly to each other about what we'd done. I don't remember there being a big reception for us as we got off the plane. The press were there, though, and I posed with Jimmy on the steps of the plane as we got off.

But there was a huge, emotional reception from the fans on the Sunday when we had another open-topped bus parade up Tottenham High Road. Those parades symbolised so much of the Glory Glory Years at Spurs for me. You could see how much it meant to so many. There were thousands there after we had made British football history in Rotterdam. The reaction was huge and positive. They were in raptures. It was the proudest I've ever felt apart from my marriage and the birth of my children.

20

Remember Rotterdam

OUR PERFORMANCE in Rotterdam left a legacy not only for Spurs but for the whole of British football. We were all good players with different strengths and it all came together on the day. We played our natural game, showed what we could do and coasted to victory.

We could have felt sorry for ourselves after what had happened against Benfica in the European Cup the previous season. Nine members of the team which were in the first-choice Double side donned all-white kits that unforgettable night at De Kuip.

What makes it so special is what made the Double special – it was a first. British teams had been trying to win on the continent since the European Cup – now more commonly called the Champions League – began in the mid-1950s. Manchester United, Wolverhampton Wanderers, Burnley, and Ipswich Town, besides ourselves, had had a bash at lifting the champion of champions prize.

United made the semi-finals in the first two of three consecutive appearances. Tragically, the Munich air disaster – which Danny's brother Jackie survived – claimed the lives of several of the side known as the Busby Babes on the way back from sealing their place a second time.

Wolves had two campaigns, making the quarters in one as did Burnley. Alf Ramsey's Ipswich were knocked out in the first round in 1962/63. And Wolves made the semi-finals of the first European Cup Winners' Cup in 1960/61, losing it to beaten finalists Glasgow Rangers, who included several of the players who faced us in our winning year like the legendary Jim Baxter.

And the following year the likes of Swansea Town, Leicester City and Dunfermline Athletic flew the Union Jack.

I felt so proud my side had led the way once more and laid the foundations for all British sides which have followed and achieved. Everyone in the team that tub-thumped in The Tub, to a man, was magnificent. As was Bill.

I will always feel privileged to have been a part of it and want to pay tribute to all involved.

Bill Brown did his job in goal. He made two or three good saves and dealt with any corners, and the defence in front of him was superb.

The two full-backs, Peter and Ron, did well. They did not go bombing forward. There was no point in Ron running past me or Peter doing the same to Jonesy with the way we played with FIVE forwards. Ron did not have a choice when he gave away the penalty. It was either handling the ball or them scoring, although, of course, he was fortunate the laws did not punish him for the offence with at least a finger wagging.

Maurice was a colossus at the back, assisted by Tony and Danny who dealt well with their defensive responsibilities.

Tony had big boots to fill with Dave out. No one could replace Dave, with the way Dave was. But Tony slotted in superbly. He had the experience, having been Spurs captain in the 1950s before Bill brought him back from Italy. He was a good defender and was helped by his long stride. He also had a good touch, which he showed when I worked that one-two with him before my second goal.

Danny, of course, carried out his roles in midfield and as captain immaculately. Although he had that knee problem, there was no sign he was struggling with it. He always wanted the ball. He was bloody brilliant – the best. People didn't realise just how good he was to be performing at that level at the age of 37.

Our captain always said he wanted to be with a successful team which played great football while winning trophies. And that is what he found with us when he joined beyond the first flush of youth, having been with Barnsley and Aston Villa after leaving his native Northern Ireland. Age was never a problem when he played for us. Without doubt he stood for what my Spurs side was all about with the way he played and conducted himself.

John had an understanding with Danny to get us motoring. It was said he got a knock early on, which I don't remember, yet he would have struggled through it anyway. He was such a fit lad. John floated over the Feyenoord pitch in inimitable style and deserved his goal. Showed his wealth of abilities.

The centre of our strike force was in form too. Jimmy showed why I think he's the best goalscorer I've ever seen. The best player overall was Pele, because he had everything. He didn't have a weakness. But Jimmy was a better goalscorer. He could just knock them in from anywhere.

How would he do today? Fine. No one would be able to afford him, he was that good. The nearest I've seen to him in recent times was that kid from Liverpool, Robbie Fowler. He was good and, like Jimmy, a poacher of goals.

It was all about anticipation and making those runs with Jim. Someone said to me, 'He was lucky.' I said, 'Lucky? He wasn't lucky.' Jim would make a run 12 times and always be in a position to score if the ball came to him, no matter if it was a tap-in. He was always there either at the end of a cross or a through ball. He showed those qualities in the European Cup Winners' Cup Final when he bagged his two.

Bobby was his usual self. He showed the skill he had in the control and passing departments. All I have to do is refer you to the ball he put out to Cliff which led to our first goal. It also showed how quick his thinking was, that he could be delicate and accurate. He also showed his toughness and courage, while taking stick.

He kept his cool in the final but was certainly able to dish out retribution. Bob certainly did in the first leg of our semi against OFK. Flipping heck did he do the geezer.

Bobby used to tell some stories. He was a regular Hans Christian Andersen. He told one about a centre-half. This geezer kept kicking Bob so Bob said to him, 'If you keep kicking me I will do you. You'd better pack it in.' The bloke kept doing it. Bobby told me, 'I did wait, Terry, but then I really clattered him. As they carried him off I said to the guy, "I told you, but you wouldn't listen".' But, as I said, he behaved himself against Atletico.

Cliff had a good game on the right wing. He has not had the credit he deserved for his performance that day. He slaughtered their left-back, most notably when he laid on Jimmy's first goal.

I have to mention Dave again. It must have been so hard for him watching. He had done so much to get us there and yet wouldn't even get a medal. These days every player in a trophy-winning squad seems to be collecting a medal. Back in 1963 there were just 11 winners' medals minted. Should we get together and get one for him done now?

Our manager deserved nothing less than such a triumph. Bill had always wanted us to prove ourselves in Europe. Domestic success was all very well, but glory in international competition was – to him – a true yardstick of just how good his team was.

He had still felt bitterly disappointed we had gone so close in the European Cup the previous season and missed out. Success in that competition would have been the ultimate achievement for him.

We players redoubled our efforts when we were given a second opportunity to triumph in a continental tournament in part for Bill. We wanted to make sure all the planning and general effort Bill put into our European Cup Winners' Cup campaign would not go to waste.

We were all so delighted for him. When he joined in the celebrations – a rare event, let me tell you – in that bar next to our hotel, I never saw him more pleased. And I was grateful to have been able to help him feel that way.

He told the press a few years later in reference to my second goal, 'My greatest recollection of that night was young Dyson's shot.' I can't tell you how proud and humble that made me feel when I read that. And I still feel the same way, as I do about the performance of my life in the European Cup Winners' Cup Final.

Jonesy and I are still in touch and we banter with each other – good-naturedly – about our time together in the Glory Glory Years.

And if it gets to comparisons between our careers – he had a fantastic one, by the way – and there's a suggestion mine might have fallen short of his own, I throw in the line, 'Remember Rotterdam.'

I WAS generally fortunate as far as injuries were concerned but I copped one just five days after the final.

We had two league fixtures left after Rotterdam before a two-week trip to South Africa. I came through the first, a draw at Nottingham Forest, but wasn't so lucky in the final one. It was another on the road against Blackburn Rovers at Ewood Park.

This Blackburn geezer smacked into my back as I knocked the ball back. I tried to run it off but couldn't. The pain was terrible and I couldn't sleep that night. I saw a specialist the following day and had an X-ray which showed I'd displaced a bone in my back. I was given a painkiller in my arm – Pentathol – and the bone was manipulated and put back in place. I was told I'd be all right to train the next morning. I woke up, went in, changed and went jogging round the track at White Hart Lane in front of our trainer Cecil Poynton.

I went about ten yards and pulled up and told Cec it was hurting. He told me the specialist said it would be all right. I told him I didn't give a damn what the specialist said, it hurt. I needed more time to get it right.

Cec, assisted by Johnny Wallis, was our trainer AND our physio in so far as he had read a manual about injuries which meant he knew a bit more than you or me.

These days sports science in football is so sophisticated with its qualified physios, nutritionists, psychologists and conditioning coaches. In my day it seemed it was more what 'magic' the magic sponge – a sponge soaked in a bucket of water – could conjure up to help players with physical ailments.

It is amazing to think that as players have always been a club's prized assets! With what they know now, I'm sure Danny, for instance, would have played even longer.

IT WAS decided I would still go to South Africa for the tour that had been arranged that close-season. And I managed to play in all our games there with my back problem, sustained just a week or two earlier, not playing me up.

We enjoyed the football. We played in front of some big crowds and won all of our three games. I got on the scoresheet in a 5-2 win over an NFL Select XI in Durban with Cliff and Jimmy getting a couple of goals each.

I liked Durban and enjoyed a day at the races while we were there. Peter was so taken with Durban he moved out there a couple years later with his wife Linda. He played for Durban United and became their manager before setting himself up in a stationery business, although he has returned to north London in more recent years.

And I started as Jimmy, Bobby and Eddie Clayton scored in a 3-1 victory against a South African XI in Jo'burg to finish off the tour.

But it was not all good news on the pitch. In our opening match against an NSAFL Invitation, I came on for Terry Medwin who had sustained a broken leg. I felt so bad for Terry. We all did. And he was sadly unable to come back from it fully.

For me the tour was a brilliant experience, the best I went on with Spurs. The hospitality was fantastic. It is an amazing-looking country and we saw a few sights.

We went up Table Mountain in a cable car. One player who didn't travel by cable car was Frank Saul. He was a fun lad but frightened of the mode of transport which saw us go up to about 3,500 feet and offered amazing views. Some have said they are among the most epic in Africa and I saw what they meant. People might think the mountain was flat because of its name, but it certainly was not. It was made up of jagged rocks.

I am a big film fan and I was delighted our party bumped into actors and crew filming *Zulu* while we were in Durban. I remember the actor Stanley Baker, who played a starring role alongside Michael Caine in the historical tale of the Battle of Rorke's Drift during the Anglo-Zulu War.

The people working on *Zulu* sent us a big goodwill message and Stanley even joined us for a drink. Stanley spent a long time chatting to his fellow Welshman, our full-back Mel Hopkins.

There was another trip we had around this time that involved movies. It was in what was then Yugoslavia. We must have been there to play a friendly, although I can't honestly remember. What I do recall was seeing a movie being filmed in Montenegro.

It was called *The Long Ships*, about Vikings in search of a golden bell and coming into conflict with the Moors. I saw one scene in which actor Richard Widmark was staggering up a beach after he and his crew had been shipwrecked before the director Jack Cardiff shouted, 'That's fine,

Dick. Cut.' Then all the extras got their fags out from their boots and lit up. Coincidently I met a former jockey my family were familiar with while we were there. He told me he had given up racing because of failing sight and had decided to become a film extra.

MY ARMY past became my present when I received a letter postmarked 19 August 1963. Any glories achieved on the football field just three months earlier were of no consideration.

It was from a Col M.A. Runacres who wrote, 'You will of course know that you are liable on mobilisation to recall to Army service... the instructions in this letter will take effect only in the gravest emergency necessitating general mobilisation when the recall of reservists would be notified.'

I'd have to report to the Royal Artillery regiment at Stamford, Lincolnshire. I could be whisked off to fight for my country at a time of glories on the football battlefields, a dose of perspective and reality. Thankfully nothing came of it.

21

The Break-Up

THE SPURS team which kicked off the 1963/64 season was the same one that lifted the European Cup Winners' Cup, apart from Dave returning to replace Tony.

We had a successful retention of the continental trophy in our minds, but we had to wait until December before we began our defence.

Instead we had an inglorious start in comparison to the glorious experience of Rotterdam. We went up to Stoke City's Victoria Ground on the season's opening day and came away licking our wounds, with Bobby getting a consolation goal in a 2-1 defeat.

But we soon got going with three wins on the bounce. And I managed a couple in the third at home to Wolves. And after a freak 7-2 reverse at Blackburn, we scored five victories in a row and I got a couple more against Aston Villa and Birmingham City in that run, although it was Jimmy, naturally, who was our main target man, netting 14 including two hat-tricks.

I MANAGED a third for the campaign – and Jimmy a 15th – in a draw with Sheffield United as we stuttered on a winless run of four. We ended it by pipping Fulham – with Jim the match-winner.

But the next game, against Manchester United at Old Trafford on 9 November, proved much more than just a defeat. It was a symbolic day which witnessed the last time Danny put on a Spurs shirt in first-team competition, although he did not announce his retirement as a player until 5 April 1964.

The knee problem – no cartilage to prevent bones rubbing together and flaking and floating – he had sustained against Rangers, and battled through the European Cup Winners' Cup Final with, was just too much. I've always felt he tried to come back too quickly and paid the price.

He decided to write about football rather than play it, becoming a journalist for the *Sunday Express*.

Danny was considered the greatest player in Spurs history by *The Times* in 2009. You could certainly argue the case. He was an attacking midfielder, with fantastic technical skills and unerring ability to pick a pass, while also possessing defensive abilities which enabled him to jockey rather than tackle. As a team-mate, I found his captaincy his greatest asset on the field, using his intelligence. He led by example and knew how to motivate us, how to get us to play the way Bill wanted us to. And his influence went beyond the playing field, as I've mentioned. Danny's departure sparked the break-up of the glory team.

A second body blow came on 10 December 1963. Coincidently and ironically, Old Trafford set the scene. And it cost us the most swashbuckling of our Big Three as my mate Dave suffered a broken left leg.

We had managed to maintain decent form in the league. I'd enjoyed myself with a couple of goals in a 3-2 win against Ipswich Town – with new manager Jackie Milburn, Newcastle's 'Wor Jackie', having taken over from Alf Ramsey who had become England manager – at Portman Road. But after a home draw with Sheffield Wednesday it was time to begin our defence of the European Cup Winners' Cup.

We were drawn to play an all-English tie against Manchester United, who had qualified by lifting the FA Cup against Leicester in May.

The first leg under the White Hart Lane floodlights in front of 58,000 went okay, if not perfectly. We beat them 2-0. United put up a red wall and were difficult to break down. Eventually Dave got a great goal. But we needed more than a 1-0 lead to take into the second leg. Fortunately, the opportunity fell to me to double our advantage just three minutes from time. Their defender Tony Dunne tried to pass back to goalkeeper David Gaskell. But I don't think he realised I was about, as I nipped up on his blind side to lash it in.

I could – and should – have had two that night. I had already had the ball in the net, but the ref ruled it out for offside. If we had finished 3-0 winners that night who knows what might have happened.

Bill said he was not entirely happy with the advantage we took into the second leg the following week but that it would take a lot for United to beat us by three goals.

It didn't look good when David Herd gave them a sixth-minute lead to the natural delight of a noisy 49,000 home crowd.

And it got worse when Dave lay on the ground with his broken leg a minute later after a collision with Noel Cantwell. Dave knew straight away he'd broken it. In his autobiography he wrote, 'My foot had twisted round by 90 degrees.'

He heard it break. I don't think Noel did it deliberately but I don't think Dave was too happy with him, insisting that he didn't break his leg, it was broken. In his book he adds, 'Intentionally or unintentionally, Noel Cantwell broke my leg. I don't think Cant (as I preferred to call him after that night) was anywhere near the ball. He may not have set out to break a bone, but that was the end result. I had a reputation as a "hard man" but I was never a dirty player and I would not have been able to live with myself if the situation had been reversed.'

Dave had played the ball but unfortunately Cantwell's boot hit his shin as they both went in. To see Dave lying there was gut-wrenching.

But our ten men – still no subs in competitive games, remember – defended for our lives. Dave had instilled that spirit in all of us. I tried to do my bit in defence, just like I had in Rotterdam.

Noel Cantwell kindly praised my efforts in the *Manchester Evening News*, saying, 'Outstanding of the Spurs ten fighting men was the smallest of them all – wee Terry Dyson, who stands only 5ft 4in. He dropped back to an extra centre-half position where he displayed the heart of a lion. He looked like a pocket Dave Mackay – and you cannot hand out bigger praise than that.'

And Bernard Joy, despite the fact he was a former Arsenal player, wrote in the *Evening Standard*, 'That amazing little man Dyson rose to the occasion as he always does.'

Herd got his second to level the aggregate but Jimmy pulled one back before Bobby Charlton scored twice, the second sealing the tie just two minutes from time.

In the meantime, Dave had his operation and came back to our hotel. Myself, Bill Brown, Jimmy and a few others went up to his room as did United's Denis Law, a Scotland team-mate of my pal. I was feeling a bit tearful as I tried to lighten the mood by joking how Dave had just lost his left-half spot to me!

Dave travelled back with us the following day and Bobby and I got him on a wheelchair when we arrived back on the train in London and wheeled him to a cab. We all travelled together back to Southgate. Nine months later Dave broke the same leg in a reserve game at White Hart Lane against Shrewsbury in a collision with the visiting centre-half Peter Dolby.

Dolby told the *Sunday Express*, 'He called for the ball, then rushed past me lunging out his leg. The next thing I knew he was on the ground. I don't think I even tackled him. Dave shook his head and murmured, "I think it has gone again." He rolled down his socks and I could see he had broken his leg. I patted his shoulder and said, "I'm sorry, Dave." He looked up with tears in his eyes and said, "It can't be helped. It is not your fault. I can move my toes but not the rest of my leg. It seems numb."'

I read that Dave, even with the distress he must have been feeling, told those in charge of the reserves not to tell Bill because he knew how bad his manager would feel about it for the sake of the team and, of course, Dave. But word did reach Bill who was quoted saying, 'This is terrible luck for Dave.'

I was playing for the first team in a derby against West Ham at the Boleyn Ground that day. They had pipped us and Danny, well into his new career, reported in typically articulate and forthright fashion that we were not good enough to win any honours.

But Danny's summation was relegated to second lead story on the back page by the *Sunday Express* when it was published the following morning. The lead was about what had happened to poor Dave. I went round to see him the following day at the Prince of Wales Hospital to see how he was. He was still his old self and seemed to be taking it well. But deep down he must have been gutted.

Players struggle to get back from one broken leg, let alone two, but Dave was no ordinary individual. He wasn't known as an Iron Man for nothing. He came back for the start of the 1965/66 season – after I'd just left the club – and went on to captain Spurs to the FA Cup in the following campaign.

JOHN WHITE, the third member of our Big Three, was struck by lightning and killed on a golf course on Tuesday 21 July 1964. It was an absolute tragedy beyond belief.

I was just about to return for pre-season from Malton when I got a call from the Adcock family at my digs telling me they'd heard John had been killed. I returned down south and reported for training at White Hart Lane in the morning and Bill confirmed it as we all met up in the changing room.

Bill was so upset he had to dash away to the toilet. It was unlike him to show that sort of emotion, but he had had to identify the body with Cecil. He came back out and told us we wouldn't be training. That instead we would go out on the training pitch and stand for a three-minute silence for John. All the staff were out there taking part. John was so popular. We were all crying, especially Dave Mackay. It was the strangest, eeriest experience. John's death will always be with me.

All the players at Spurs were member of Crews Hill Golf Club near Enfield, north London. Danny had played off six. Dave, Bill and Peter were good players while I just tried to knock the ball down the fairway and hope. We used to go down there during the season on a day off.

John had decided to visit the golf club in the afternoon after spending the morning at White Hart Lane and helping Terry Medwin with his rehab from the leg he broke in South Africa the previous year. Cliff popped in on their session.

John wanted someone to partner him for golf. Rob White said in his book about his dad, written with Julie Welch, that John tried Cliff who didn't want to play that day, Terry declined because of another commitment and that he seemed to extract a 'half-promise' from Jimmy Robertson. Jimmy, Rob says, decided not to go down to the club because the weather was looking bad. John, though, went down there. He knocked a few balls down the fairway and went to walk down after them. It started to lash it down and I was told he had been crouched under this tree, the tallest on the fairway, when the lightning struck, coming through his studs.

It doesn't seem like half a century has passed. The funeral was so sad. He was only 27. Loads of people were unable to get in because it was absolutely packed. My memories of him flood back every time his name is mentioned. He was such a fun person to be with.

John had a few tricks up his sleeve. If we were either in a hotel before an away game and had got bored waiting for the coach or all together the night before a home game, John would entertain us – at our request. He was able to juggle coins with his feet and flick them up on to his forehead. He would also try keepy-uppy with an orange, which is so hard because the fruit gets mushier and mushier as you juggle it.

He used to catch it on his instep, head and shoulder and keep it up until the orange was totally squashed. We all used to have a go. We found it almost impossible. I was useless. Four or five flicks and that was it. Try it. There's just no bounce in an orange!

John was a practical joker too. Dave recalled in his autobiography how John used to sit next to strangers in a pub and rest his head on their shoulders, or how he'd take a flower out of a vase and eat it.

He was good mates with Cliff and they used to share a room on away trips and enjoy a lark. There was one tale I was told about when they were in a room in a Manchester hotel and John rushed to he window and shouted 'help', attracting the attention of people in the street.

It was a bit too much for Bill Nick so he got me to share with John, while Jonesy went in with Jimmy, who had become my room-mate.

Rob and Julie told us in *The Ghost* how he and Cliffy put pebbles in the wheel hubs of Bobby Smith's motor and Bob wondered what the rattling was. They also recalled how the pair did a little Errol Flynn-style swashbuckling after finding a couple of swords hung on the wall of the reception venue following the Benfica game in Lisbon. And they burst into a party hosted by Spurs fan Sid Brickman on ice-cream bikes.

I told the story in that book of how the pair once served up the bird food Trill to Ron Henry as he bred budgies.

In his more serious moments, John offered me some good advice which stood me in good stead. He said to me, 'Never stop running. Make sure you're ready to move into whatever position is appropriate.' I worked that into my game and it improved me as a player. Thank you, John.

I was personally sad to see Bobby Smith leave in May 1964 – he joined Fourth Division Brighton – leaving a trail of anecdotes largely connected with his gambling such as the time he supposedly ran up a massive hotel phone bill on a European trip. I can believe that.

Myself, Peter and Les Allen were to leave the following year, when Maurice's career was cut short by a broken leg sustained during a friendly against a Hungarian XI.

In October 1966, Bill Brown departed for Northampton Town, the season after Ron had made his final first-team appearance. And the remaining two of our super side departed in 1968; Cliffy leaving for Fulham and Dave signing for Derby after being targeted by Brian Clough.

The special team might not have been at White Hart Lane in body, but it has remained in the mind at Tottenham's home – and beyond.

My Spurs side in the Glory Glory times has been turned into a millstone around the necks of the teams which have followed them at White Hart Lane by those with perhaps unrealistic expectations. The fact Spurs have not won the league – as I write – since our Double feat has been used as a stick to beat our successors.

It is true we set a certain standard and created a modern-day tradition for the club to be known as one which plays good, open, attractive and entertaining football, and of producing individuals which excite with the likes of Dave, Danny, John, Cliff and Jimmy.

It is good for Tottenham that the players who have followed us should be striving to follow in our footsteps. But it is unfair to keep comparing us and them in a negative way.

The game today is different. It is played at a higher tempo because the ball and boots are lighter and the players fitter due to improved regimes and technologies. They are able to perform on much improved pitches thanks to scientific developments.

Our slower brand of football was played on less robust surfaces. Pitches were 100 per cent grass, rather than the mix of artificial and the real thing with a sand base they have now. They used to break up early in the season as the weather worsened towards and during winter. The pitch could be bog-like or rock-like dependent on the prevailing conditions.

Someone asked Jonesy, 'How well do you think your side would have played today? Would you have coped?' He replied, 'Never mind that, how would the modern-day players have coped with what we had to put up with?'

You wonder how much better we would have been had we been able to play given the advantages they have now!

You could say it was all masterminded by Bill. He took all the training. We worked hard for him and he got us to play to our potential. And it is true that without what he did we would not have done what we did.

But a lot of it was luck. It just happened. We just gelled as pals and team-mates to reproduce what we practised when it mattered.

21

Cottage Industry

S PURS FINISHED the 1963/64 season a respectable fourth and I played in all but three league games, scoring 11 goals.

But we were knocked out of the FA Cup in our opening round for a second successive year following on from winning it two years on the bounce. I managed a goal in a drawn home tie against Chelsea in front of nearly 50,000 before 20,000 more saw us lose 2-0 in the replay at Stamford Bridge.

But Bill, of course, had been forced to rebuild his side quicker than he might have wanted as the Double team's core crumbled. Alan Mullery had moved from Fulham to take over the number 4 shirt from Danny after Tony Marchi and Phil Beal kept it warm.

Mullers was a good, good player. And a lovely bloke. We used to play squash together up at this court in Finchley, which wasn't too far away from Tottenham.

He might have been taking over Danny's shirt, but was a lot different in style. He was more physical and robust, although possessing undoubted skill. He took time to settle and the crowd were on his back but he came good.

With Terry Medwin out, Bill had also signed winger Jimmy Robertson from St Mirren. Boy, was Jimmy quick, I'd have backed him to beat any player over 100m and he was also a good crosser and scorer of a few goals, including one which was to help Spurs claim the 1967 FA Cup.

I WAS still enjoying my pop music and the 1960s was a fantastic time for it. And I certainly got into the scene at Spurs.

I loved the Dave Clark Five and enjoyed their singles 'Glad All Over' – the same version they play at every Crystal Palace home game these days – and 'Bits And Pieces' which were big hits in 1964. I can reel them off! They were local lads and I got friendly with them.

Mike Smith was a good singer and Dave, the drummer, was a good lad. They were all just down-to-earth, ordinary lads. They were part of what was called The Tottenham Sound in answer to the Mersey Sound with The Beatles and the like.

The boys were Spurs fans and invited me, along with Jimmy Greaves and Johnny Hollowbread, to see them play at the London Palladium in the West End, close to Oxford Circus. It was for the popular TV show *Sunday Night At The London Palladium*.

We got to go backstage afterwards and had a good chat with the band. It had gone well and we told them so. I know they were well pleased to be there. The Palladium was the pinnacle in those days.

I remember doing a photo-shoot with them. They dressed up in our football kits and we put on their trendy 1960s gear and posed with their instruments. There was Jimmy and others including myself. I posed with the guitar of one of the group's members, Lenny Davidson.

I also went to gigs. I saw the Rolling Stones at a small local club at the junction of Tottenham High Road and Seven Sisters Road, a former cinema and bingo hall. It was called the Noreik – Kieron spelt backwards and named after the owner's son.

This guy used to have shows on a Saturday night and there would be quite a few people there, dancers and then the main act. Englebert Humperdinck performed on its stage. Or, to give him his real name, Gerry Dorsey from Leicester (I'm unsure whether he was a Foxes fan!). It was before he made his name, particularly with 'Please Release Me' and his other singles. He was quite good. And Dusty Springfield performed there too. They started to put on bands like The Who and, of course, the Stones.

And I saw Mick Jagger, Keith Richards and the others at the Noreik in the early hours of Sunday 9 February 1964, a few hours after we had been hammered by West Ham 4-0 at their place.

The Stones had performed two shows that evening at the Regal Theatre just up the road from our ground in Edmonton. They had become big news since playing the theatre early on in their first British tour the previous October. And on their return to the Regal they were already on their third, performing their first big hit 'I Wanna Be Your Man' – written by John Lennon and Paul McCartney – along with lots of rhythm 'n' blues numbers, like 'Talkin' 'Bout You', 'Road Runner', 'Roll Over Beethoven' and 'Walking The Dog'.

And they were due to travel up to Leicester the following night, but accepted an invite to squeeze in a visit to the Noriek. Mick Jagger and the rest of the band had got to know the Noriek having done an all-night rave down there the previous December.

I've been told John Lennon, with his wife Cynthia, and Paul McCartney came to see them there for a social chat that night before the Stones went on stage; the Beatles having done a Christmas show at the Finsbury Park Odeon just a mile or two up the Seven Sisters Road earlier in the evening.

I felt fortunate for me and the rest of the crowd that the Stones wanted to entertain us at this 'extra curricular gig'. They were great, playing the sort of stuff they'd just done in Edmonton. Dave Clark was also there and we had a natter.

It was packed with 16- to 17-year-old kids upwards. I don't remember screaming from teeny-boppers, a feature of the new pop sensations such as the Stones, probably because there were 'older' types like me around. I still love the Stones.

IN WHAT was to prove my last season at Spurs, 1964/65, Bill stepped up his rebuilding programme, buying in goalkeeper Pat Jennings, full-back Cyril Knowles and striker Alan Gilzean from Watford, Middlesbrough and Dundee respectively.

Ron, Maurice and myself were the only survivors of the Double team as Pat and Cyril debuted on the opening day, a 2-0 win against Sheffield United at White Hart Lane.

Pat was only young and raw. I remember a 4-1 home defeat against Manchester United in his second month when he was terrible. We got murdered and he let in a few goals he should have stopped – one through his legs – but he learned. Bill Nick kept faith and he became a world-class goalkeeper for Spurs, as well as a legend for club and his country Northern Ireland.

It was difficult for Bill Nick because Bill Brown was still there and in that season he alternated between the two. Who was better? How do you compare Gordon Banks and Peter Shilton? They are both good keepers. It was just that Pat and Bill were different. Bill was still a good shot-stopper and Pat liked to come out and get crosses, sometimes one-handed. Pat left for Arsenal but told me he would have stayed had Spurs given him a two-year contract. He went on for years with the Gunners.

Cyril was a bit wild when he first came. He used to go smashing into tackles, getting himself booked. He was even like that in practice matches. Bill had to calm him down, telling him, 'You don't have to go in like that.' And he settled down to become another club legend, prompting the record 'Nice One Cyril' by the Cockerel Chorus.

Cyril was known for the two goals he got against Leeds which helped keep Spurs in the top flight in 1975.

He suffered so much tragedy. His son was killed in a freak accident when a stone flicked up by a lorry came through Cyril's car window and struck his child's head. And he was only 47 when he himself died, struck down by cancer. Like John White, very much before his time.

I figured in Gillie's debut in a 2-2 home draw with Everton in the December. Gillie was such a good player. He was superb in the air, with a good touch on the ground, an eye for goal and was a team player with an excellent ability to link up.

He liked a drink after a game. Gillie had a quiet Scottish accent which I couldn't understand much when he was sober never mind drunk (only joking, Gillie). He went missing for ages after he left the club. I know Jimmy was after him to signs some photographs for a while. But he'd gone to ground, although he finally re-emerged in recent years.

Bill was getting a second good team together which eventually won the FA Cup in 1967. Joe Kinnear. a full-back, came through the youth system. I remember playing with him for the reserves at Portsmouth and this geezer was kicking him all over the place. I went over to the guy and said, 'Give him a break, he's a kid. What's the matter with you? I'll kick you if you don't stop.' He told me to clear off but he stopped kicking Joe. Joe was a confident lad and did well.

Bill signed Mike England in 1966 with Maurice's career brought to its premature end through that broken leg against the Hungarian Select just a few months after I'd left the club. As you know I'd played against Mike when he was a rookie full-back with Blackburn and he turned into a good centre-half for Spurs.

Terry Venables came from Chelsea in the same year. I heard he was a bit of a Jack the Lad with plenty of chat. There was a story I heard that he got into a training bust-up with Dave, jutting his backside out and knocking Dave over during a five-a-side. Dave was not amused.

Frank Saul turned out to be a good player too once he'd sorted out his terrible dress sense and long hair and smartened up! And he started to keep Cliffy out when Bill Nick moved him to a wide position.

Jimmy Greaves still continued playing for the Lilywhites, banging in the goals. Although there's no doubt Jimmy was the best finisher there's ever been, he was a terrible trainer. He was always at the back when we ran around the gym. If he felt like putting it in he would. If not he just ambled around. Who knows how good he would have been if he had trained better – but then look what he did.

Still, Cliff got to be part of FA Cup history when he and Chelsea's Joe Kirkup became the first subs to be named for the final as Spurs overcame the Blues at Wembley in 1967.

I PRETTY much remained a regular in 1964/65, my final season, but it wasn't easy to hold down my place.

As Lou Margetts wrote in *Team (Incorporating Lilywhite)*, the journal of the Spurs Supporters' Club, in January 1965, 'Give me two Jimmy Greaveses and nine Terry Dysons and I'll guarantee the Double every year. When it comes to hard work, Terry Dyson is without peer.

'Terry Dyson does not have to play well to hold his place – he has to fight like hell. So much so that it is now second nature. Nothing seems to blunt his appetite for hard work; his enthusiasm appears to be endless.'

I had been in the reserve side defeated by one goal by the first XI in the last public pre-season trial in front of 10,870 at White Hart Lane that pre-season. But I got my promotion for that opener against Sheffield United and managed 32 league appearances.

I also helped Spurs get beyond their opening round of the FA Cup – the third – for the first time since winning the trophy in 1962 before we went out to Chelsea in the fifth. I managed a few goals. More than 50,000 at White Hart Lane witnessed my last one in a 3-2 win over West Ham who went on to emulate our European Cup Winners' Cup triumph that season. And the Hammers included Geoff Hurst and Martin Peters, two of England's 1966 World Cup-winning team.

MY FINAL 90 minutes in a Tottenham first-team shirt was up at Roker Park in front of over 44,000 fans on Saturday 20 March 1965. It had been the scene of that astonishing FA Cup tie in the season we won the Double.

Sunderland might have come close, with their incredible fans, to upsetting us that day. But on my swansong, the Mackems actually succeeded in getting the win. I lined up with Double team-mates Bill Brown, Ron and Cliffy. Jimmy was still firing in the goals and managed one of the 35 he got that season against the Wearsiders, but they got one more.

Bill experimented with the likes of Keith Weller and Derek Possee on the wing for the remaining fixtures as Spurs ended up sixth. I remember Derek did not best please Bill by ringing his manager's home trying to get a date with one of his two daughters.

Anyway Bill pulled me in one day and said, 'Look, Terry. I want to put you on the list – but I want to be certain you get a good deal wherever you go. And if you don't get one you will be a Tottenham player next season.' I thought to myself, 'It is time to go now.'

I was still fit enough – and young enough at 30 – to carry on so I agreed to go along with what Bill said.

You never know how you might feel in these situations. Some might think it was heartbreaking after what I'd experienced with the club for a decade. But it wasn't that much of a wrench.

Yes, it had been a life-changing experience after coming out of the Army, which I guess is obvious. But the current team wasn't as good as it was in the Glory Glory Years and I felt ready for a new challenge. And, besides, I'd already been a part of so much history-making at the club. Nobody could ever take all that away from me. Bill put me on for £5,000, a cheap fee to help me get some extra money from a deal. He was very fair about it all. Also, because I'd served for a decade, I got a taxed £1,000 benefit from the club. It wasn't much really, but it was better than nothing.

Charlton Athletic were the first club to come in for me. I had a cup of tea with their chairman. They wanted to give me a four-year contract, but the money wasn't good and I said, 'Thanks very much, but no thanks.'

Wolves were keen. Very keen. Their assistant manager came down and told me it was nice up there in the Black Country. That they were still a big club.

But by this time Fulham had shown interest. I had met manager Vic Buckingham, who played for Spurs in the 1940s. He had just taken over at Craven Cottage that summer after coaching Ajax in Amsterdam where he was credited with starting up the famous Total Football concept while spotting legend Johan Cruyff who developed his boss's ideas.

Vic, who went on to manage Barcelona, told me, 'We're looking to do well this year. You'll slot in easily and have a successful season.'

He didn't have to try too hard to convince me. I didn't want to trot up to Wolverhampton and leave London. I'd not long known a lady called Kay – who was to become my wife – and that was a big factor in why I wanted to stay in the capital. Another was that Fulham had the former England captain Johnny Haynes playing for them. I phoned back Wolves to tell them I'd chosen Fulham.

I discussed the deal directly with Vic. There were no agents involved. I think agents these days are ruining the game. What they are doing is for themselves. I was happy with the money offered and the two-year contract with a two-year option. What I agreed with Vic was based on trust and Vic was a man of his word. I was settled.

I'D MET Kay through this chap I knew, a bit of an East End character who had minders, Jackie Doris, and he invited me along to his daughter's 21st birthday party. He expressly told me not to bring anyone along so I agreed. He was match-making, setting me up with a blind date. That date was Kay. She worked in the used car trading department of Henlys where Jackie got his vehicles from.

We got introduced. Poor Kay had just had her tonsils removed but was well enough for us to have a good chat to get to know each other. We started dating, going for nice meals and the pictures. She even came along to the dogs. My friends got to know her. For the first couple of weeks she had no idea I was a professional footballer.

She came up to York with me to meet mum and dad and the rest of the family after a few months. Kay thought they treated her lovely. She got on well with all of them, especially my brother's girlfriend and the pair became pen pals.

She didn't know anything about football at all. We never talked football. Footballers, as I've said, weren't as high profile as they are now. When she found out what I did for a living she viewed me and my colleagues as ordinary people doing their job like everybody else. She reckons our going out was no big thing but the relationship progressed.

Kay first started to watch me play as I was leaving Spurs and signing for Fulham. There was no preferential treatment when the switch was completed and I started playing at Craven Cottage. She made her own way there with her dad on matchdays. Her dad – who died prematurely at 55 – loved it. I drove to the ground earlier and was lucky to get a parking spot, even though I was playing.

THE MOVE provided me with an opportunity of staying in the top flight, but at a club which had been more used to life at the lower end of the table while I'd been enjoying Glory Glory Nights with Spurs. Relegation fights as opposed to title challenges were the order of the day at Fulham.

When Spurs claimed the Double, the Cottagers were sixth off the bottom. Fulham missed relegation by one point as Tottenham secured the FA Cup the following season before moving up to seventh off the foot of the table as the Lilywhites claimed the European Cup Winners' Cup.

It was different and fun. I got on all right with Vic. It was no surprise he wanted to play a good, passing game given his background at Ajax, where he'd set up a youth system, influenced, I guess, by the ideas of Arthur Rowe, who'd managed him at White Hart Lane. He knew his football and knew what he wanted. He could be a strange fellow, though. When I went to sign, he completely changed the subject to something irrelevant. Like his golf. He said, 'Look at this golf swing' as he swung his arms. I said, 'Very good, but what about the deal?' That's how he was.

Vic's training could be mad. He used to make us run up and down Epsom Downs by the racecourse. From the mile-and-a-half start, we ran all the way round the edge of the Derby course. I've got a picture of me coming round Tattenham Corner in front – although I faded up the hill! The human replacing the racehorse. Bizarre.

FULHAM WAS a bit of a showbiz club reflected by the fact chairman Tommy Trinder was an entertainer; an actor and comedian on stage and screen. He even proved Bruce Forsyth didn't have exclusive rights to famous catchphrases as he had one of his own, 'You lucky people.'

I remember we went up to Nottingham Forest in a bus and got a good point and Tommy returned with the team. It was a long journey, about two and a half hours. But it went by so quickly because he kept us entertained all the way.

He was unbelievable, telling us stories of when he was on the club circuit up north trying to make a name for himself, or how he was booed off and had things thrown at him. He was good fun.

Lots of showbiz types used to come along to Craven Cottage to watch us play at a time when London was central to the Swinging Sixties; perhaps the fact we weren't too far away from Theatreland in the West End was part of the attraction.

I met them in a pub near the ground. There was the famous late and great actor Peter O'Toole, who appeared in Shakespeare and some fantastic films like *Lawrence of Arabia*. He was later also known for playing the part of a hard-drinking journalist in a comedy play called *Jeffrey Bernard Is Unwell*. And I saw him for real while chatting to friends in this pub. He was paralytic. I've no idea how he managed to get home.

I think actors used to go in to the pub because it might help them get a part, hoping either the scriptwriters who drank in there or the landlord, who also wrote, might pen a role for them.

One of the scriptwriters who got in there was Johnny Speight, a nice bloke with a terrible stutter. He wrote the TV sitcom *Till Death Us Do Part*, about a working-class East End family headed by Alf Garnett who spouted racist and anti-socialist viewpoints and supported West Ham.

Some of the cast used to get in, like Warren Mitchell, who played Alf. He liked Fulham but was in fact a lifelong Spurs fan.

Tony Booth was another customer. He used to play Alf's socialist son-in-law Mike and is the real-life dad of Cherie Blair, the wife of former British Prime Minister Tony Blair. He would get plastered and was a horrible so-and-so in my eyes. He used to moan to Johnny that he didn't get enough storylines.

Johnny, who sadly passed away in 1998, told him, 'You are not the main character. That is Alf Garnett. If you don't like it you can leave the cast and we can put someone else in your place.'

FULHAM HAD a mix of good players, big characters and promising youngsters when I joined. And they were all great lads. You usually found that at whatever club you played for. They had top-class performers who were to remain loyal one-club men.

George Cohen was terrific. He went on to win the World Cup with England at the end of my first season. Very athletic, was George. He used to get up and down the field from full-back.

I was also fortunate to play alongside the late, great Johnny Haynes. We got on well and had a drink or two together outside of work. He lived in Epsom and had a flat not far from the ground. Pele reckoned he was the best passer of the ball he'd ever seen. He was also a great reader of the game and, of course, skippered England.

But he could be horrible to play with. He'd soon let you know if you didn't give the ball straight to him or take up a good position. He still holds the record for the number of first-team appearances for Fulham (657).

Johnny is rated as the best player ever to play for the club. I wouldn't argue with that – and he fully deserves the statue of him they've put outside Craven Cottage.

That figure is certainly more appropriate than the one of the late pop singer Michael Jackson erected near the ground by the former owner Mohamed Al Fayed in recent years.

He could have gone anywhere, Johnny. I know Spurs wanted to sign him. But he was always happy to play for Fulham. It didn't affect his England career. He earned getting on for half his England caps playing for them in the Second Division.

Stan Brown and young Les Barrett, who also both came through the system, were decent players and proved to be loyal servants too.

And there was goalkeeper Tony Macedo, who spent 13 years at the Cottage and would eventually link up with me again at Colchester United. Tony was from Gibraltar and would probably have turned out for the country's national side now it has been given full UEFA membership which entitles the team to compete in the European Championships.

He was an excellent goalkeeper and reckoned to have been good enough to play for England had he been eligible. He got his ribs broken by a backpass from Tosh Chamberlain once.

His dad played for Real Madrid. I remember his son got done for murder after the family moved to South Africa. It was devastating for Tony.

Bobby Robson had come back to the club after an England international playing career with West Bromwich Albion, where he had been managed by Vic and had scored THAT goal which stopped my Spurs Double side securing a record number of points for the season.

He had started his career with Fulham when manager Bill Dodgin Senior went to Bobby's native north-east and offered him a pro deal when Bobby was an electrician's apprentice. And he was still a quality wing-half when I came to the club.

Another top player there in my time was Graham Leggat, a former Scotland international, who played on the opposite wing to me in my first season. And he finished top scorer for the fifth time.

Vic also brought in Mark Pearson, a former Busby Babe, from his one of his previous clubs Sheffield Wednesday.

Fulham had established the tradition for attracting characters before I arrived like Jimmy Hill, who had done so much to break the maximum wage for players in 1961, and Rodney Marsh. I arrived as one of the biggest of them was leaving, Tosh Chamberlain, like me a number 11.

I heard how Tosh had scored three or four goals in one game and yet Fulham were being beaten, so he spread his arms out to the crowd as if to say, 'What more can I do?'

There is another story about Tosh that old Spurs team-mate Alan Mullery tells. Mullers was 15 and joining the Cottagers and had been invited along to a game at Craven Cottage. He was given a pitchside seat with the next one to him empty. Suddenly Tosh came off the field and occupied the vacant seat – and began smoking a ciggy handed to him by a supporter. Johnny Haynes hit a ball across to where he should have been standing before noticing Tosh was sitting down. Johnny and Tosh got into a right old barney about it. And Mullers insists the incident helped convince him Fulham was the place for him, saying, 'If it is that much fun in the first team I want to be involved.'

Defender Bobby Keetch was another larger than life figure. He was a bit of a ladies' man and a good-looking lad, Bob. He told me a tale about how Fulham were playing West Ham and that he had got booed off the field because he had been clogging a few Hammers opponents.

But he had good reason not to let it affect him too badly. He was going out with a woman with plenty of money and she had organised a weekend trip to France for them both. A cab was waiting for him as he came out of the West Ham ground to take him to the airport and he told the fans who were giving him stuck, 'I'm off to flipping France, now. Where are you going?'

And Jim Langley, an experienced left-back, was a funny lad, although we weren't together at the club for long. I arrived in June 1965 and he was gone the following month. But I remember he told me a story about a player bonding session he had had on an away trip on the train. He and a few of the other Fulham lads were playing cards and he dressed up like a croupier with a green visor! A good laugh, Jim went on to lift the League Cup with Queens Park Rangers.

I DID not play too badly for Fulham. I made my debut – lining up with Johnny Haynes, George Cohen and Bobby Robson – in a 2-2 draw against Blackpool at Bloomfield Road on 21 August 1965.

It was an historic match which saw Rodney Marsh, a flamboyant player who went on to have quite a career, become the first Fulham player to be named as a substitute. The rules had changed so sides who had an injury could have someone replace the stricken player.

I was also in the Cottagers team as Graham Leggat became the first used Fulham sub, coming on for Johnny Haynes, in a 3-0 defeat entertaining Chelsea.

In between I scored on my home debut with a penalty in a 5-2 home win over Blackburn Rovers at Craven Cottage. The press said I sent the goalkeeper the wrong way but I just hit the ball down the middle of the goal. I also managed to net in two successive games in a 2-1 reverse at Arsenal and a 3-2 victory over Everton at the Cottage. But results weren't that brilliant, generally.

22
Another Layer

DAVE SEXTON came in halfway through the season as Fulham coach for Ron Burgess, who had played with Bill Nick in Spurs' Push and Run team.

Dave had quit his first job in management at Leyton Orient in the December. He loved developing young footballers, did Dave. He had done that when he began coaching under Tommy Docherty at Chelsea. And when he took over at Brisbane Road, he threw out many of the experienced lads and threw in youngsters, although unfortunately when he left Orient were bottom of the Second Division.

But he kept faith in the kids at Fulham. He got the likes of Les Barrett and Stevie Earle into the first team whenever he could. The older heads were under threat. If Haynesy hadn't have been who he was he'd have tried to get him replaced by one of the kids, I reckon. Dave, I believe, wasn't keen on the older players.

He didn't include me in what he was doing. I didn't dislike him. He was nice enough but he was a strange guy and not one I could get on with.

Dave went on to have a successful career in coaching and management with the likes of Manchester United and QPR, and he's dead now, poor lad, but he wasn't my cup of tea as far as working together was concerned.

Eventually, Fulham managed to survive the 1965/66 season in the First Division; finishing just two points off the relegation zone with Northampton and Blackburn Rovers going down.

THE SUMMER of 1966 is famous in English football for England winning the World Cup. It is also a famous one in our household because that is when Kay and I were married.

There had been no getting down on one knee. No engagement. One of us must have proposed to the other but neither of us can remember.

The wedding at Holy Innocents Church in Kingsbury went well. Kay's mum Louise was a dressmaker from Nottingham, where they specialise in that sort of thing. So that sorted what Kay wore. My brother John was best man.

We had a great reception at the Victoria Sporting Club near Marble Arch in London. I used to go down there for the boxing shows and snooker matches it staged. Kay, who preferred swimming and dancing as leisure activities, came with me a few times.

We had originally booked up at Hendon Hall, our FA Cup Final hotel. Then I told the Victoria how Kay and I were getting married and the staff asked if we wouldn't mind if they held our reception there as their guests. I said yes a bit sharpish.

A few of my old Spurs team-mates attended. Dave Mackay was there along with Bill Brown and Micky Dulin.

Jimmy Greaves couldn't come because he was otherwise engaged in helping England prepare for the World Cup. He sent a telegram as did Bobby Robson to congratulate us.

It was a good do. The day went by in a blur. There were 150 there and I dug out the menu recently. The guests sipped sweet or dry sherries before sitting down for the meal of minestrone, cold salmon mayonnaise, roast turkey, chipolatas, stuffing, veg, roast potatoes, and strawberries and cream before a coffee. The drinks flowed: 47 carafes of white and red wine, 19 bottles of champers, four bottles of vodka, six of gin. Also consumed was brandy, rum, Martini, Scotch, Double Diamond bitter, Skol lager, squash, tonic water, bitter lemon, Pepsi, orange juice and lemonade. Our bill for the food and drink? £142.64, plus £23.15 for the champagne and £23.10 for the vino. Prices have gone up since, all right.

We spent the night at a hotel near the airport and went back to Kay's mum and dad's for Sunday lunch. Then we flew off to Jersey for our honeymoon.

I DIDN'T get involved much with the social scene at Fulham compared to Spurs when I was a single young man. I didn't see my old Spurs pals either. But I was very happy setting up home with my new wife. Life was good.

I'd enjoyed playing in the 1961 FA Cup Final at Wembley, but didn't know I'd end up living in the area. But Kay had grown up nearby with her parents and we found a nice place to rent. It was nothing fancy – we didn't have the money. It was in Ealing Road and a lovely little area back then. Henry Cooper, the boxing legend, had a shop on the corner close to the flat where we lived. We did it up nicely with the help of people who could get furniture and whatnot cheap. The first of our three boys, Neil, was born two years after we moved in.

We were there for 30 months before taking on a mortgage at a house in Kenton, not far from Wembley.

THE 1966/67 campaign was another one of struggle for Fulham. Vic brought in Allan Clarke from Walsall. It was a good bit of business considering Allan banged in plenty of goals to finish our top scorer in successive seasons (29 and 27) before going on to a stellar career with Leeds United, managed by Don Revie, and England.

It was also a season of struggle for me. I spent most of it surplus to requirements as far as the first team was concerned. I was an unused sub three times in defeats at Arsenal and Manchester City and a home draw with Aston Villa. The only time I got on I helped us force a goalless home draw with the Gunners. Otherwise it was reserve team football for me.

Fulham's position got even worse in the 1967/68 season. At the turn of the year we were rock bottom and the board replaced Vic with Bobby Robson who had left for Vancouver Whitecaps as a player a few months earlier.

Bobby had done his coaching badges but it looked a poisoned chalice as it seemed as though the club was heading for relegation.

He was a good manager. I liked him and the way he spoke to you. He clearly knew the game and how he wanted it played. The training was superb with so much variety and lots of ball work.

Unfortunately I wasn't in his team. He had players in it who I felt I was as good as. But we never fell out. He was a lovely man.

His trouble was that he had played with many of the players he was now managing. It made for a difficult transition. It was different to when Bill Nick took over the Spurs team. He hadn't played with most of us, apart from the likes of Danny Blanchflower and Peter Baker in the first team and Ron Henry and myself in the odd reserve game.

Bobby wasn't able to assert his authority. Those Fulham players took liberties because of that. They showed a lack of respect and helped get him the sack. I understand he only discovered he had been fired by spotting a headline on an *Evening Standard* newspaper placard outside Putney station.

If Fulham had persevered they could have done well. They were idiots for doing what they did. They got rid of him too quickly. Just look at what he went on to achieve at Ipswich, Porto, PSV Eindhoven, Barcelona and Newcastle.

He didn't mess about when he went to Ipswich. There's one story he had a fight with one player who kicked up rough. But that's where he proved himself.

Bobby also went close to emulating Sir Alf getting England to the semi-finals of the 1990 World Cup, with Gary Lineker's goals and Gazza's tears.

Bobby ended up so revered and I was saddened at his passing in 2009. But Fulham didn't have a clue. They didn't realise just what a good manager they had.

It's often still the same today with chairmen and owners who think they know more than their manager. So many of the foreign owners who come in with money and buy clubs haven't got a clue. The manager might as well not be there for the decisions he gets to make. There's one, Vincent Tan, who brought in a 23-year-old friend of his son at Cardiff City to help recruit players.

Bobby and I got to talking about my future at the club. He asked about the possibility of paying up my contract. I was earning a lot more than players in the first team even in the reserves. I asked him how much he would give me. I think it was £5,000. I said I'd accept it as long as Fulham paid the tax on it. He agreed. They gave it to me in two lump sums.

A FRIEND phoned up a couple of non-league clubs to see if they wanted me but I was too expensive. I was without a club for the first time in 13 and a half years. I tried to keep myself fit by going over the park close to my home for a run.

Eventually, just after the 1968/69 season had started, I got a call from Colchester United. They were in the Fourth Division. It was Dick Graham, their new manager. Dick had taken Crystal Palace up from the Fourth to the Second and wanted to do something similar at Layer Road, which was then the home of the U's before they moved into Colchester Community Stadium in 2008.

He wanted me to come along for a trial, something perhaps I shouldn't need to have done, I suppose, given that what I could do was well known. I agreed and went up by train.

When I arrived I was told by Dick I would be playing against Leyton Orient reserves in a friendly at Layer Road. I warned him I hadn't done that much training in pre-season. Dick told me I'd be all right. We beat them 2-0 – and I headed a goal. I'd impressed and eventually got a contract from 1 October 1968 to June 1969 with a one-year option. Dick dropped me back at the station and told me in the car, 'I want you to play in our league game at Chester on Saturday.' I said all right. We got beat 5-1. Dick went mad.

I didn't escape the stick everyone got. He told me, 'You should have been back. Why didn't you get up there.' I replied, 'You can't be in two positions at the same time!'

Dick told us all to report to training in the morning. But, to be fair to him, he did, on this occasion phone me up in the evening and say, 'Don't bother coming in tomorrow. I threw you in too early. See you Monday.'

I got to know that if we won it would be, 'Get the bottle of sherry down from the shelf and have a glass each' from Dick. But if we got beat it was, 'You are in flipping training tomorrow.'

It was quite a trek from Wembley to Layer Road for me via the London Underground, overland train and two buses. And the more limited Sunday service made travelling in the morning after a Saturday game even more difficult.

When we had to come in on the 'day of rest' after a performance which disappointed Dick, we'd get to the ground and get changed, jog around the pitch, increase and decrease the pace for ten laps and be told, 'Right off you go.' That was it. The limited service meant I wouldn't get back until 4pm. But we had to be punished for losing. Dick treated us like kids.

He was the same at Palace, according to my old Army pal Eddie Presland, who worked with Dick there. Eddie told me Dick once got a big board out which said 'keep on running' during a game they were losing at Selhurst Park.

Dick's training was a nightmare. We used to have a drill in this big field where we had to pick up and run with these weights. It got us fit. But it was hard. Dick, who looked a little like a sergeant major with his crew cut, concentrated more on fitness than ball work.

He had some good ideas at times. Tactically he could be astute. He would do his homework on the opposition. He once told us our next opponents would push up and that our quick left-back could get in behind them and provide chances for our forwards providing they could stay onside. We got two goals from doing that in that game.

I got fitter, Tony Macedo joined a month after me and we began to get some decent results after a poor start. After just one point in the first five, we managed 33 from the next 42 available to climb up to fourth place. But we stumbled around Easter and missed out on promotion by just four points.

I managed to hit the target. I netted a couple of penalties, which helped us beat Southend United and Bradford Park Avenue 4-0 and 3-0 at Layer Road.

I also managed one in open play – the winner right on time in a 2-1 victory against Aldershot in the Army town. I beat the full-back to the ball and headed it in. Vic Buckingham was there, he was a mate of Dick's, and remarked on how late I'd left it! I also bumped into the full-back who told me he had got a right rollicking for letting me get in.

I got smacked in the mouth against Port Vale for carrying out a tactic Dick had asked me to employ. Vale had this big centre-half called Roy Sproson. It was my job to try and block him off at corners. I did it twice and it worked. Sproson was clearly not best pleased and it was third time unlucky for me when I tried it again. Sproson's whack left me hurting and I turned round to Dick on the sidelines to tell him I would not continue to carry out the tactic.

There seems to be a lot of shenanigans at corners these days which has become an issue. It's got ridiculous in comparison to my attempts to stop Sproson who has become such a legend at Vale Park an adjacent street has been named after him and a statue of the defender erected outside the main reception. Little did I know who I was mixing it with back then!

First to Fourth Division was some jump but I adapted all right. The major differences were the attendances, single figure thousands as opposed to tens of thousands, and, unsurprisingly, the standard of football. Clubs didn't have the individual players to make the difference. At Spurs we had those players, like Danny, Dave and John. If I made a run I'd be picked out.

I'd banter with opponents. If one tried to prove a point by kicking this Double and European Cup Winners' Cup winner I'd smile, 'Who the flip are you. Do I know you? I'll look in the programme to find out.' Then I'd underline that it really was a joke rather than a wind-up by adding tongue-in-cheek, 'Do you know who I am?'

I played at a lot of grounds I didn't think I'd get to play at. Travelling remained tricky for me especially when we played at Layer Road on a Friday night. The last train to London was 10.10pm so we had to change quickly so they could get us to the station in time. It was a bit of a 'milk train' and used to stop at every station and lumber into Liverpool Street at 11.55pm – and the last Tube to my home was around midnight!

I played another season with Colchester. Tony Macedo had left for South Africa and Dick brought in Bobby Cram, the old West Brom player and uncle to the former Olympic athlete and commentator Steve, who had left The Hawthorns to play in Canada. Again we did okay, although injuries hampered our promotion chances.

But my contract was up and it wasn't renewed.

24
Digger Dagger Oi! Oi! Oi!

I WAS COMING up 36 and still quite fit and free of injury. I wanted to get another club after Colchester released me. Some players say they want to go out at the top. These days they can afford to, of course.

But I did enjoy playing and wanted to continue as long as I could, something I'd still advise professional footballers to do – you are a long time retired.

It was a tricky time. Football can be ageist and probably people thought that at my age I was past it. I knew I still had something to offer. But I wondered if and when the phone would ring. I decided to put myself about a bit and be seen at matches to make sure I would not be forgotten while impressing on the football world that I was not finished as a player.

Out of the blue, this guy – Bill Cauldwell – rang up and told me, 'I didn't know you were available.' So much for my self-promotion!

Anyway, Bill was manager of Guildford City of the Southern League and keen to sign me. I had not heard from any league clubs, so I thought I'd give it a go in non-league.

Their league was a feeder for the Football League and, wryly, I thought it must be a decent league as Spurs had been in it early in their history, winning the FA Cup while members in 1901 and lifting its title before that!

Also, Guildford had been Jim Langley's last non-league club before he kicked off his Football League career at Leeds United.

They had financial problems, resulting in the club eventually falling apart in 1974 before being reborn in 1996.

But it wasn't all doom and gloom during my couple of seasons there in the early 1970s. The club nicknamed The Sweeney had had one or two flying squads as far as cup competitions were concerned.

They'd won the Southern League Cup a couple of times and, two years before I turned up at their Joseph's Road headquarters, had a run in the FA Cup itself which included a famous win over Brentford.

And I helped them into the second round proper in the 1971/72 campaign, my second in Surrey. Having played in each of their qualifying round ties that season, it meant I had played in EVERY round of the FA Cup, bar the prelims, which is something not many can say.

From the first qualifying round that term – 'quacking' the resistance of the Ducks of Aylesbury, then in the Athenian League – to scoring in and winning the final by outfoxing the Foxes of Leicester City from the Football League First Division, I had covered them all.

But when I took the field against the Ducks at Joseph's Road I wasn't thinking it was a long way from playing the final at Wembley, I just wanted to do my best for the team.

I felt the same when I scored the winning goal in the last minute of extra time of a second replay against Bishop's Stortford at Joseph's Road to get my side into the fourth and final qualifying round.

To make it through to the second round proper in the oldest and greatest domestic competition for a veteran turning 37 was more than satisfying. There was life in the old dog. It proved the magic of the cup was very much in evidence. They were magical moments for Guildford – and me.

NEXT, I went to Wealdstone, another Southern League club. They were based in Middlesex and local for me. They were managed by a coach I knew at Fulham. He asked me whether I'd come down. And I was happy to.

I scored in my first game as we beat Stevenage 4-1, ironic as I now live in the Hertfordshire new town. We won the next game 3-1 and the following one 1-0 away and the manager went. He came into the changing room after our third win and said to us, 'That's me finished. I've just had a row with the board.' I told him, 'You flipping got me here.' He said, 'I know but I can't handle the board.' They brought in Sid Prosser, who was quite successful on the non-league scene.

The training facilities at Wealdstone were rubbish. We had to either run around the pitch or use this little indoor place where Prosser put this absolutely hopeless session on one time.

Team-mate Eddie Presland, a good player who'd played for West Ham, and I looked at each other, both thinking the same. Prosser then asked us what we thought of the session. I said, 'To be honest Sid, and I'm not being disrespectful, but I thought it was terrible.' Eddie said the same. It was dull, uninteresting and had no fun in it. So static. He was gutted. He had spent a lot of time working it out.

Eddie and I ended up educating him. We suggested he used the indoor hall to get a five-a-side going because the players would love it.

But it still wasn't smooth sailing with Sid. We lost this particular game one evening – with our wives at it – and Sid did something that we had heard he'd done at other clubs. When we got back to the dressing room he said, 'Right, what do you want to drink?' We put in our orders – I asked for a half of lager – and got in the bath before getting changed as Sid went off to sort out the order.

We got our drinks in the dressing room and then he started to talk about the game and all that. I thought, 'flipping hell, this is a night game and our wives are waiting for us.' And I told Sid what I thought, adding we'd come in tomorrow if he wanted to have a chat. Anyway, he finally let us go.

I said to Eddie, 'This is rubbish, this. I'm not having it.' Eddie and I told Sid, 'This is not the way. You'll get players' backs up.' He said: 'Sorry, but I've done it at every club.' We told him we already knew that and that all the players feel the way we did about it. He was very keen and wanted you to play right, but he didn't hold us back again like that.

Wealdstone played all over. We'd sometimes not get back until midnight from away games. There were some long journeys. But we enjoyed it. I had a laugh with all the lads. The standard wasn't bad. There were some good players around. Besides Eddie and myself, there was George Duck who went on to become the club's all-time record goalscorer.

I managed to pick up the supporters' player of the year award in 1972/73. It seemed the fans liked me. Even a recent internet posting thankfully underlined that.

Tim Parks wrote about all-time favourite Wealdstone wingers and concluded, 'The best of all...Terry Dyson, former Double-winner with Tottenham and could land the ball in a dustbin at training, on the run, from 25 yards. Deadly when he was picking out legends like G Duck and Billy Byrne.' Flattering.

I got to pick up a championship medal with Wealdstone. It was for helping the Stones lift the Southern League First Division South crown in 1973/74. But it felt almost as good as when I was in the Spurs side which took the country's premier crown in 1961. I'd achieved once more.

I managed to get a goal here and there – one I remember I got against Basingstoke Town, who cheekily offered Brazilian legend Ronaldinho the chance to play for them in 2014. It helped us to a crucial victory in the run-in. George Duck scored for fun in that campaign.

Wealdstone also provided me with the opportunity of linking up with Johnny Haynes, my old Fulham team-mate. It must have been a long haul for Johnny who had settled across the River Thames. We might have been in our twilight years as players but we could still do a bit. It must have been quite something for Wealdstone to have the former England captain turning out for them.

Another character I remember at the Stones – who went on to sign two more in Stuart Pearce and Vinnie Jones in more modern times – was a player called John. I can't recall his surname but he was a cabbie and told a funny story one time. He had cut up another car and its driver was angry and gave John a verbal volley. John replied, 'OK, let's settle this with our fists.' The other guy got out of his car and was ready for a punch-up – but John just drove off and left him there.

Sid left and I went in for the manager's job with Eddie and Eddie got it while I was his assistant. I combined it with playing. Yes, it was different to be part of the management team but it was all right. I got on with the players. Eddie wanted to play a certain way and I agreed with his outlook.

I SPENT at least three seasons around this time coaching Wingate in the Hendon Sunday League – and guess who was my assistant? George Graham, who went on to a trophy-laden reign as Arsenal manager. George was still a player, with Crystal Palace, and was only too happy to help. We worked well together and I liked George. It is nice to see that my protégé went on to do so well! I got involved through my Spurs team-mate Micky Dulin who was linked with the club. They were looking for someone to take over from Tommy Harmer, another pal and colleague at Spurs.

I remember some great social occasions with Wingate. The club was very much a part of the Jewish community in the area and I lost count of how many bar mitzvah parties Kay and I went to.

LITTLE DID I know by this time that I would experience Wembley glory once again during my rollercoaster adventures in non-league football. My next move to a major non-league club provided it.

Eddie moved on to Isthmian League Dagenham and I joined him as his assistant in the late 1970s. I'd decided to hang up my boots, thinking, 'I'm over 40. I've had enough of this,' and threw myself fully into my managerial role. Dagenham was better than it had been at Guildford and Wealdstone. There was more money available and they were more organised. On cold training nights there was always hot soup waiting for us when we arrived.

They had some good players who had been associated with league clubs. The captain was Dennis Moore, a sweeper and a good lad. And his dad used to help out.

We had some good years and then the Wembley moment arrived on Saturday 17 May 1980. It was the FA Trophy Final when the Daggers became the first southern club to win it.

They beat Mossley, a team from Manchester, 2-1 with George Duck getting the winner. George, who had joined from Wealdstone, was a terrible trainer, always moaning, 'It's too hard,' but he knew where the net was.

We got in front and this fellow equalised and then George got a good connection on a cross to head home. All the fans went mad, chanting, 'Digger dagger digger dagger! Oi! Oi! Oi!'

Cliff's son Stevie also played well for us that day. Like his dad, he performed on the wing. And I was delighted he also followed his dad in being part of a winning team in a final at the home of football. Steve was a fine player and got some good goals down the years for us.

The build-up had been fantastic. Eddie and I had been up to Mossley to see them play. We noticed they had a big centre-forward who was good in the air. But I thought we could beat them.

There was no overnight stay in a plush hotel like there had been with Spurs in 1961. We all met up at our ground in Victoria Road – which wasn't a very good one as far as parking was concerned. Even the staff used to have to park up the road from it if they turned up late.

But we managed to get a coach in there and we all hopped on it to get to Wembley. The spirit was good. They really enjoyed the journey, like they enjoyed the whole experience. It was all great for them.

They'd never played at Wembley before – not a lot of players do – and made the most of it. I wasn't going on about my own experiences about playing in the FA Cup Final. It was their day, not mine. I just told them, 'You are going to enjoy this, lads.' And they did. We all did.

We had a parade of the trophy afterwards through Dagenham to the Town Hall. There were big crowds there. It took me back to when I was doing the same thing with Spurs. It was great for the Dagenham players to experience something like that too.

SHORTLY BEFORE our Wembley triumph, though, I suffered personal sadness when my dad passed away aged 72 in the February. He had helped give me and my family a wonderful upbringing. He and my mum were proud of what I did as a footballer and put memorabilia all around the pub that they ran. The *Yorkshire Evening Express* of Friday 22 February 1980 reported how dad had been 'one of Malton's best known personalities for over half a century'.

He moved to Malton from his birthplace of Liverpool when he was 15 and became a jockey, riding in Sweden and Calcutta, retired as a pilot in 1959 and was licensee of The Fleece for 23 years. He then quit and became vice-president of the Licensed Victuallers Association. Rest in peace, dad.

EDDIE AND I got the sack halfway through the following season. We were doing all right in the league – third – and still in all the cups. But the committee wanted us out and didn't give us a reason. We'd guided the club to a Wembley final victory – and then that. We couldn't even defend our trophy. Terrible it was, very unfair. We told the players – they were absolutely gutted.

Eddie and I went back to the club to meet some people and no member of the committee would face us. I looked at one and he walked away.

They got someone in who was a friend of someone on the committee. It was Ted Hardy, the old successful Enfield manager, who had built his success on going to clubs where there was money available. And the Daggers had some. If Eddie and I hadn't have done well over a few years we'd have expected the sack. Yet it seems to be the same at all levels.

25
Call Me Terry

B ILL NICK was the perfect manager and I learned a lot from him
about how to play the game, entertain and respect the fans, pay
attention to detail and motivate, communicate, organise and treat
players. His insistence that everyone called him by his christian name
rather than his title told you how he went about his job.

He was a big influence. And I hoped as my playing career wound down
that what he taught me would come in useful should I become a manager.
It would always be 'call me Terry, not gaffer' if I did.

I saw management mainly as dealing with people. I would say to players
when they came in after a game following a loss, 'Honestly ask yourselves,
like I did myself, whether you gave everything – everything – to win. And
if you tell yourselves "yes" then there is nothing else you could have done
about it.' I also told them to feel proud if they had achieved a victory by
giving their all. I eventually got the opportunity to put what I'd picked up
from Bill and my own personal experiences into practice.

I got my first job as manager after meeting someone in a friend's pub,
The Wellington, in Borehamwood. He was on the local club's committee.
Boreham Wood were a Hertfordshire non-league side and this bloke asked
whether I would like to come up to interview for the vacant hotseat.

The chairman, Bill O'Neill, had helped found the club. He had even
helped dig the foundations for the pitch. Bill ruled it and had a lot of 'yes
men' with him. I told him that when I got the sack!

At first it was good and we did all right for a couple of years. The
Wood were in the Isthmian League Division One when I took over in the
mid-1980s. The team were playing well and doing well. We finished sixth
and fifth – and then the chairman cut the wage bill for my third season.

It meant players who were getting £40 to £50 a week were now to get
about a tenner. I should have gone as soon as Bill slashed the budget. I
knew it meant we wouldn't have a chance of doing much.

It was ridiculous. I told the players what had happened and added that if they wanted to go I would understand, so quite a few left.

Results took a turn for the worse and a 4-0 defeat made me think, 'What am I doing here? This is terrible.' Bill wanted to see me in the boardroom later. I knew what about. I said to him, 'How about now? I'm in a rush.' He agreed.

When I arrived he said, 'Well, that's it then.' Acting dumb, I said, 'What's it? Are you sacking me?' He said, 'Yeah.' I told him I couldn't believe he was doing that. If you cut the wage bill you can't expect the same results. Five of our players who had left because of the pay cut were now in a side top of the league. You can't get players as good as we had with less money. His decision to pay less had caused the problem.

One player we were left with was on just a fiver a week. He was, though, a bit of a deluded individual this one. After we'd lost a game 5-0, he asked me, 'Can I have a rise?' I told him not to be so stupid and only ask something like that if we won 5-0! The Wood ended up 17th by the end of the season.

Borehamwood is famous for its Elstree Studios which records TV's *EastEnders* and there was bit of a soap opera going on over at the town's football club. There's rarely a happy ending in the BBC programme – and there certainly wasn't one for me at Meadow Park.

I MOVED on to Kingsbury Town, of the Isthmian League, and we did all right to start with. A double-glazing sales manager, Mark Hart, ran the club. He had plenty of chat! He did well after going in there when they had no money. The first thing he did was take ALL the keys – for the tills and everything else – and the club started making a profit. It seemed people had been dipping into the tills.

He gave me a wage budget that I stuck to. It was fair enough, although I do remember Johnny Still, who later became manager of Dagenham and Redbridge, Barnet and Luton Town among others, paying fortunes at rivals Dartford. One time we were able to draw 0-0 against his side and Johnny went berserk in their dressing room with his more expensive group of players. Presumably he felt they weren't giving him and the club value for money.

We got promotion and made the semis of a cup in the first season, but then all of a sudden Mark Hart started interfering. We had a lad called Desmond Dennis, a centre-forward. He was a good player. Des had this bad knee but still battled away for us. It was so bad for one game he just couldn't play. So Mark said, 'We're not paying him.' I said, 'That player played on one leg for us last week, he's getting paid.' We gave Des his £30 but Mark didn't like it.

We started having more rows. There was one time our keeper got clattered and our opposition scored. Mark blamed the keeper in front of everybody in the boardroom. I said, 'Don't say that in front of all these people. How can you blame the keeper?' Our relationship continued to go downhill and he sacked me in the end.

My youngest, Mark, used to come around with me when I managed at Kingsbury and the lads at the club did like to get hold of him and dump him in puddles. But he loved going.

He also earned an extra few bob by finding loose balls if they were kicked over the wall of the ground and into the adjacent park during evening games. He was a bit frightened because it was dark but used to get a fiver a session. The owner wouldn't give it to him – I did.

I WAS invited along to non-league Ruislip Town. The board were good and keen for me to become manager so I agreed.

I watched a game with us being beaten by eight and I turned to my assistant manager Ray Brandon and said, 'This is going to be 12 or 14!' I discovered from the board after the whistle that the players didn't train. So I went in to the dressing room and told them it was an embarrassment, that we are training Tuesday and if they didn't turn up, not to bother coming back. I wasn't bothered if some of them didn't and didn't want some of them at the club.

I knew the ones who wouldn't show – and I was right. Just FOUR turned up. So now I had to get players, which I did, and we started winning two or three games. All of a sudden the board came to me and told me, 'Things have happened. We've all had to quit.' So I asked, 'Where does this leave me?'

I got an answer from the fellow who was taking over. He told me, 'I'll pay you and Ray until the end of the season but I can only give you £100 for players' wages.'

I was told they didn't have enough money to keep going beyond that. So I said all right. I told the players they were getting tenners and some of them could get more at another club, but that if they wanted to stay that was fine by me. With three games left of the season, they wouldn't have to train, just turn up for the games. Who wants to stay?

I had enough to put a team out in our next game – with one or two 'ringers' who said they'd play under assumed names. My youngest son Mark, who was only about 14, was a sub! And he was gutted I didn't put him on.

We finished the season. I was paid up, the club folded and that was it. My last job as a manager was over. I'd had enough of being one.

I NEVER wanted to become a Football League manager. Not one bit. The Premier League would be brilliant but the lower leagues? Definitely not.

The managers there all seem to get the sack and then do the rounds, dressed to the eyeballs, trying to get another gaffer's job even at the expense of an erstwhile colleague – often for peanuts. That's rubbish.

I didn't want my living to depend on 11 players or to have to deal with directors with similar attitudes to the ones I'd experienced. I didn't want to cause disruption to the family by joining a club miles and miles away for a job that might only last for six months. These boards are all right when you are winning but when you aren't they change their tune – and you are left to face the consequences. And it is getting worse these days. It was not for me, especially as I had a wife and three kids.

Playing was always better than management for me. As a boss I thought I had a good rapport with the lads but the politics soured it a bit for me. Also I never had the facilities the likes of Bill Nick and Arthur Rowe before him had to work in. We had to train the players behind the back of a stand at Wealdstone. When I was there I went on a coaching course at Lilleshall. The facilities were wonderful and the session was a good one, but I said to the bloke, 'Can you tell me what I can do when it is tipping down with rain at the back of our stand?' He couldn't answer me. That's the difference.

As a player, there was no responsibility on my shoulders for things like that. I could just go out and enjoy playing.

26
Paying The Bills

FOOTBALL WAS no longer a part of my life for the first time since I could remember, since I'd been old enough to either join in games on the street or over the neighbouring field in Malton before the Second World War.

I'd gone from the top and down to the bottom. I had enjoyed the football side, being with the players and feeling the buzz when the team you played for or managed won. It was full of ups and downs, like the wonder goal or the one time a ref gave a goal against my team even though the ball had hit the side-netting!

Now I had no new season to prepare for. It was a big change. I thought I might miss it, particularly the banter in the dressing room. But, as a manager, I'd been losing my enthusiasm.

I could have gone back a couple of times. Jackie Price, my Tottenham pal who was involved in non-league football, asked me to team up with him to run Cheshunt United, who were based where I used to train with Spurs.

But I was sick and tired of trying to make things happen as a gaffer. I didn't like not being able to get the players I wanted, or making the tough decisions like letting people go I wanted to stay. Likewise dealing with directors who were often egotists thinking they knew everything, wanting their say and making the manager the scapegoat if it went pear-shaped.

And it's still the same at all levels. You'll get Dave Whelan, a former player who put his money in and has spent years being generally brilliant for his club, Wigan Athletic. But for one Dave Whelan there are a lot of Bill O'Neills. Bill knew nothing in comparison to what I knew when we were together at Boreham Wood.

You get nice people who do a lot of good for clubs whose directors, players and supporters are all close and get together in the bar after matches. They go through thick and thin together. But for a lot of directors with a lot of money it is a big ego trip. I wouldn't put any money into a football club. It's money you have to write off, especially on the non-league scene.

As I no longer earned anything out of the game, I had to find enough work to live on. I'd decided against joining my parents in the pub trade. Instead, I had got a role in education, in the PE departments of London schools. I had been building up my new career since retiring as a player. Professional football – particularly at Spurs – paid a reasonable wage in comparison to most, but not enough to keep me in clover for the rest of my life like it is for top players these days. And management roles in semi-pro football were never going to earn me enough to fully support myself, my wife and three kids.

I got a job with the Inner London Education Authority through Jackie Price, who was on the schools as well as being a pal. It was in physical education. I used to work as an unqualified teacher in the PE departments at two primary schools and at a secondary school in Hampstead before concentrating just on Hampstead.

I used to set up for football in the playgrounds and the kids loved it. We had lots of balls and did skills work, and finished up each session with a game. The heads were delighted because the kids expended a lot of energy and behaved themselves in class afterwards.

We had some good footballers at Hampstead. All the Stein brothers – Brian, Ed, Mark, Bert and Hughie, from a South African family – went through us and were all good players. The oldest, Brian, went on to score the winning goal for Luton Town when they beat Arsenal in the 1988 League Cup Final. He got capped by England.

Ed Stein was at Barnet and the youngest, Mark, who was the best player out of all of them, played for Chelsea, where he set a Premier League record by scoring in seven successive games and played in the 1994 FA Cup Final. He was also at QPR, Stoke and in the Hatters' team at Wembley with Brian.

Brian was a good lad. They all were. But Mark could be a little bit of a pain. He used to get the needle if team-mates didn't pass it to him. I sent him off so many times for losing it!

One of them – I can't remember which – was a good tennis player and came back to the school after leaving and I bumped into him. He had two tennis racquets and challenged me to a game, saying I couldn't beat him. I did! I did him 6-2 6-2. I played a lot those days – but he was a good player. I joked with him: 'When you are ready, come again.'

I used to take my age group to matches against other schools on a Saturday morning. Unpaid. We played our home games at Chase Lodge, where Spurs were to train. I used to advise them to get the posts out because then the other team would have to put them back, something our lot might not wish to do if they lost.

I remember a goalkeeper we had – a good one, a kid I liked – turned up one day with a Mohican hairdo. I wouldn't play him because of his hairstyle and told him so. Other teachers had a go at me for it. I told them that I was proud of the school and the team was representing it and me and that the image the kid gave was not the one I wanted for us. I might have been wrong, but I didn't think so. He shaved it off the next week and I played him.

I did the Saturday morning stint until some of our older players stopped turning up and a teachers' strike made it difficult to get regular fixtures.

I thought it was ridiculous. I was busy enough already with work and wasn't seeing much of Kay and the kids, and stopped doing it.

Sadly, Saturday morning football for the students largely faded away after the strike, which was over pay and hours. It was agreed Saturdays were a day off for staff and only the really keen teachers carried on.

It was Jackie again who got me into another school – Highbury Grove, where he had become head of PE. Right in the middle of the Arsenal heartland! He wanted me to do a couple of afternoons a week, which I did.

And that is where I got back in regular touch with Cliff. We hadn't come across each other since I'd left Spurs. It was good to see him again.

We used to organise games with the kids, each of us on opposite sides and each of us making sure all the players got plenty of touches of the ball. Each session took up the whole of the afternoon.

The kids realised who we were, but there was no idol worship – maybe because they were all Gunners fans. We had a decent rapport with the kids.

I retired from working for ILEA after 14 years. The people I knew had left and the new head was useless and discipline in the school got worse. Ironically, she went on and got an important role running education in this country. But I soon resurrected my teaching career in Hertfordshire. A pal of mine, Dave Starkey, who had been head of PE at Hampstead, phoned me up. He was off to a private school and wanted me to take over from him at a school in Watford. Soon after I arrived I was told the school was closing.

The Hertfordshire Education Authority wanted me to carry on with them and wondered if I'd be interested in this school in Bushey called Falconer.

It was a school for kids with emotional and behavioural difficulties, who had been thrown out of their old schools. My first day was an eye-opener. I saw teachers at the top and bottom of the building each holding on to pupils to restrain them. One of the kids shouted to the other, 'Don't let them grind you down, Harry.' And I thought, 'Blimey, what have I got involved in here?'

But I thought I'd give it a spin. The discipline was tight to keep the kids under control. The youngsters knew where they stood. If they acted up by effing and blinding and/or being disruptive, they had to be removed from lessons and assistance sought to keep them company until they'd calmed down.

And when they'd calmed down they went back in. There were kids who had Tourette's. We had all sorts. We also had threats of physical attacks on us by some of the pupils. The head told us not to take any notice and always warned the students how actions had consequences.

It was a tough job but I had empathy with these kids. They had no chance, many coming from dysfunctional families. Some used to be out until two or three in the morning as there was no parental control.

Many hated the school closing down for the holidays because they preferred to be there than at home. It was stressful but rewarding as you could have a positive affect on them.

I knew a lot of these children had the potential to achieve. There was one who was great at football. But he hung around with a bad crowd at night. I advised him to stop mixing with them. I was concerned he might end up inside and I wanted him to try and make a good life for himself. I suggested him joining a club to see if he could realise his talents. I hope he took my advice.

I also assisted teachers during swimming lessons and taught cricket and basketball. I did all sports as a member of the PE staff.

They were short of academic staff one time and needed someone to teach Maths. So I performed the role. I was quite good at the subject. The head gave me these old exam papers that I went through with the pupils so they could get to grips with the sort of questions they would face when they had to sit their exams. I used to mark their answers and explain any they had got wrong. And we finished up doing a quiz with numbers.

I loved helping the kids despite the stress. I just wanted to be a positive influence. But a good, well-structured, achieving school is dependent on a good head and we had one in John Page. That is what I said in a speech when he retired.

I retired three times but they kept ringing up asking me to go back because my replacements kept leaving as they were unable to deal with all the pressures of the job. The people at the school knew I had the right temperament, being tolerant and empathetic but disciplined. The children, I believe, understood what I was about. I wanted to help them. I ended up being at Falconer for years.

I got a lovely note from John Page when I left. He wrote: 'I couldn't have done without you. Ever willing, ever present. I hope I learned one thing from your recent years – how to say "no"! I'm glad you didn't do that to us. Your loyalty and friendship are outstanding qualities – much appreciated. Look after yourself. Best wishes, John.'

But I still wasn't finished with work. I got a call from someone in education who knew me and wanted my help with primary kids at Elms Sports School in Stanmore, Middlesex.

I used to do a bit of coaching for them with my son Mark during the school holidays. The people they had employed hadn't been able to handle these young kids. They were poor coaches who gave them poor drills. So we came in with our drills and the kids loved it. And the fellow then asked me to work for them through the week – so I did and thoroughly enjoyed it.

But the family moved from nearby Kenton to Stevenage which meant I was driving backwards and forwards to it through the week. I decided to enjoy my life in our new home, although I felt emotional about leaving. The kids and staff were wonderful.

So in July 2013 I retired properly. Aged 78!

I didn't get the thrill I got from football while in education, but a lot of satisfaction watching the kids I helped develop. I wanted to make sure they enjoyed the lessons because if they did they would look forward to coming back. It was work first and then mix in a little fun. Like that quiz or putting on a water polo session at the end of a swimming lesson.

Working in schools also gave me a perspective on life. As a professional footballer I had everything done for me. But in education I was able to cope in the real world outside the football 'bubble'.

FOR A few years I had a wonderful part-time job on the periphery of the game until the mid-to-late 2000s as a match observer for the FA Premier Academy League. I had to assess the academies at certain clubs. I used to go around to the likes of Arsenal, Chelsea, West Ham, Charlton, Watford, Reading and MK Dons to report on whether they were adhering to the standards laid down. I'd report on the match, the referee, the dressing room, whether the pitches were roped off. Even checking if the parents got a half-time cuppa. Most of them were quite good.

I got to see some good promising players. I remember one, Leon Britton, at West Ham. I enquired after him one day to the club's academy director Tony Carr, who has received plaudits like an MBE for helping to bring through the likes of Rio Ferdinand, Frank Lampard, Joe Cole, Michael Carrick, Jermain Defoe, Glen Johnson and John Terry.

I hadn't seen Leon that day and Tony told me West Ham had let him go. Well, the Hammers' loss became Swansea's gain because Leon joined the Welsh club to make a good impression in the Premier League. I think Tony made a rick there. Leon might be small – but so was I.

I also got to know Brendan Rodgers when he was academy director at Reading. It was before Jose Mourinho got him to join Chelsea as head youth coach and promoted him to take charge of the reserves. We got on. He even got me a cup of tea.

Brendan has gone on to do well for himself. Although I was rather surprised he bought the Italian striker Mario Balotelli for Liverpool before the 2014/15 season. Balotelli is very high maintenance! You never buy players who can be a problem. Brendan must have thought, 'I can change him.'

My job came about when I got a call from Arnie Warren, who I knew through Brian Ryder, a friend who worked for Charlton and had been taken on himself as a match observer. Arnie ran the set-up after a career as a respected scout who helped unearth home grown-talents for Crystal Palace and QPR.

He had it well organised and efficient. We were a good team. I used to know on a Thursday what match I had to go to on the Saturday when the club's under-16s and under-18s played and Sunday mornings for the eights to 11s. Arnie also used to arrange for me to go to a midweek game.

I remember one junior game, Charlton versus Chelsea. There was bad feeling between the two sides. The ref told me he had to send three off and abandon the game with players of both teams continually kicking each other. I told him all the players who got their marching orders deserved to see red.

I only got £25 per match, plus expenses, for doing it. But I didn't mind a bit. I loved it. It not only brought me in contact with the modern-day professionals, it also got me back in touch with some of my contemporaries.

But Arnie died and another guy took over and it wasn't as well sorted. I often had to contact the lad to find out what matches I would be doing. There was one time I phoned him and he told me to go down to Arsenal to watch one of their age group teams play. When I got there I was told the game had taken place the day before. It was embarrassing and I told the guy. He said, 'Well, you'll get paid.' What kind of attitude is that?

Eventually, I was told that the six-strong team we had was being cut to two for financial reasons. Ridiculous when you think of how the Premier has been awash with loads of money.

IN THE meantime, I decided to sell my Double medals like a lot of the lads did. There was only enough minted for me and the rest of the team. Kay and I had had them in the bank for ages and kept other memorabilia in the loft among the Christmas decorations. We got a good offer so we thought we might as well sell the medals and a few other bits.

The fellow who bought my stuff got quite a few of my team-mates to sell him their medals and such. He put on a Tottenham exhibition of them. Some were sold back to Tottenham. It was a shame to sell mine, but as myself and the family didn't see them anyway there seemed little point in keeping them.

I HAVEN'T been the only bread-winner for the family. Kay helped, with sons Mark and Neil, to run Terry Dyson Sports, selling sporting equipment and clothing. The shop opened in 1989 in Queensbury, near our Middlesex home at the time. Even an Arsenal strip was sold to help turn a profit. The place was all done out in Spurs' white and navy blue. We did well at first but the recession bit and we had to down tools in 1991. Kay also worked at a car sales place to help us put food on the table.

Kay managed to balance looking after our three boys – the middle one being Barry – and fitting in work. And I was able to help her out more in the school holidays. It enabled us to have a reasonable standard of living. Nothing extravagant but, for example, we were able to supply food and drink for friends to come over and play cards.

We spent holidays in Yorkshire – and had a great time. All the people up there made us feel welcome. We did all sorts up there. One thing was to go back to the football ground at Scarborough where I started. Kay thought it a funny little place! We've got a lot of fond memories of the five of us on those breaks.

Our children have been, naturally, our highest priority. We encouraged them if they found a positive interest they enjoyed.

All our boys played football with local football clubs. Neil, our eldest, played with Paul Merson at Belmont United in the Harrow Youth League. Paul is the former England and Arsenal player who has been a pundit on satellite television in recent years. I got to meet Paul's dad Fred as we watched our boys play. Paul played at centre-forward and looked a greedy so-and-so, but I found out later that that was just the way he played – rather than believing Neil and his other team-mates weren't up to it.

Neil got into his tennis and taking him to tournaments took up our lives at one point. Kay loved going to them and watching him. Even when it was cold, she'd wrap a blanket around herself in the outdoors rather than go inside to watch through the window.

There was one event she attended in Peterborough. Neil was playing Andrew Castle. You may know Andrew from either commentating on Wimbledon for the BBC, attempting a tango on the Corporation's *Strictly Come Dancing* television show or appearing on TV advertisements for lawyers. Back in the day, he was British number one, made the final of the Australian mixed doubles and took on tennis greats Mats Wilander and Goran Ivanisevic at Wimbledon. Well, our Neil took a set off Andrew. Not bad going.

Neil and I went in for a father and son tournament in 1990. We won our area tournament to qualify for the finals in La Manga – where the infamous pre-World Cup bust-up between Glenn Hoddle and Paul Gascoigne took place – and we reached the semis.

We were beaten by British Davis Cup left-hander Mark Cox and his son Stephen who in turn lost to Mark Petchey and his dad. Mark, who has coached Andy Murray and is a well-known tennis commentator these days, met his wife Michelle at the tournament.

Neil has kept his interest going. He is head coach at the David Lloyd Club in Bushey, but like me he is keen on horse racing and has his nose in the *Racing Post* a lot during his downtime at the club.

Neil, though, was a talented footballer as a youngster, a left-winger like me. Spurs wanted him to go along for trials when he was about ten and 12 but we didn't send him. Neil understands why.

He says, 'My dad had a clear idea of how it all worked and wanted to see if I was committed enough. I had natural talent but probably didn't work as hard as I should have done. I had other sports I could do like cricket. And by the time I was 14/15 the tennis had kicked in.'

Neil had a decent tennis-playing career, getting in the British top 20, and working with the British Davis Cup squad and British number one Samantha Smith.

And an understanding of what I did in my sport. He says, 'Growing up as his son, you don't appreciate what dad achieved. He is just your dad. A dad who instilled good manners and respect. But I've seen Spurs supporters treat him almost like a god. I'm immensely proud of what he's done.'

Barry enjoyed his football as a kid but became more interested in getting a regular job, which he did and is a manager for Tesco. He says, 'I wasn't as sporty as my other brothers. My dad was with Wealdstone when I was born and saw him play for them and in charity matches. He doesn't shove what he'd done in anyone's face. Doesn't boast, apart from in a jokey fashion. He was – and is – very humble. He only mentions what he'd done to the family if we ask him. He is just interested in us as his children and the family as a whole.'

Mark was the keenest of all of them about football. He was with me a lot when I was in non-league and was the most likely to have followed me into the professional game.

He didn't mind the training, but just wasn't dedicated enough. One time a West Ham scout, with Mark about nine or ten, was about to give us his card after watching him play. I told him to put it away. Eventually Mark followed me into full-time physical education at schools.

Mark says, 'I did have ambitions. I'm not being big-headed but when I was younger I had a lot of ability. I enjoyed central midfield or just in front.

I needed to be on the ball more rather than play wide like dad. Gazza was my big idol. But I found it easy and needed to be fitter.

'Dad's been a great dad and being with him while he was in non-league helped me mature massively because I was young and had to deal with adults.

'My first memory of dad's football was after his Dagenham side won the semi-final of the FA Trophy. My dad and the others were upstairs in the bar celebrating and I was crying, wanting to go home.'

Another member of the family who means a lot to me is my only brother John. He lives in York and we speak to each other on the phone at least once a day. We are close.

John was a useful football himself, a good little midfielder. He went down to Arsenal for a trial and they were good to him. He was also at Middlesbrough as a junior then moved to York City and Scarborough. He's now a retired bookie.

He has never been jealous of what I achieved. John kindly says, 'Terry was always better than me at any sport but he's the best brother anybody could have ever had. Always been the same. I've never seen him in a bad mood. A good person. My wife Ann and our two sons think the world of him.' Thanks, John.

He's known me longer than anyone, of course, dating back to sharing our childhood together in Malton.

There is an eight-year difference between us but he used to tag along with me to go over the farmer's field to play football. We never played serious football together I guess because of the age difference and life taking us off in different directions.

But he has always been a big supporter dating back to the days when he used to watch me play for the Malton Grammar School team.

27
Backwards And Forwards

I HAVEN'T a moment's regret as I look back on my time as a footballer. I squeezed every last drop out of the talent I had and it paid off big time. It enabled me to play against some of English football's most famous names, such as Stanley Matthews, Tom Finney and Bobby Charlton.

And the commitment and abilities I showed overall, more significantly, allowed me to be an integral part of Spurs' greatest and most successful team during the Glory Glory Years.

I felt privileged to be lining up with players such as Dave Mackay, Danny Blanchflower, John White and Jimmy Greaves. Of playing for such a team, for such a club, for such a manager as Bill. So, on the face of it, it would be greedy to wish for more. But human nature being what it is, I would have also liked to have represented my country.

I am a proud Yorkshireman with a down-to-earth, no-nonsense approach who blended well at a glamour club 'down south' in the capital full of Fancy Dans just as the likes of Bill Nick and Bobby Smith and – in more recent years – Tony Galvin, Paul Robinson and Michael Dawson from my home county managed.

But I am also a proud Englishman who played in a team of internationals without being a member of their exclusive club; the only other member of Double side to go unrecognised being Peter Baker.

Although England manager Walter Winterbottom saw me play, I was maybe too aggressive for him, even though I was never booked. I feel I should have got a cap but you can't re-write history. Overall, I'm more than pleased with what I got out of my career.

And I'm so happy Spurs teams which followed my own have achieved success despite the burden of comparison, and have produced outstanding individuals.

The second team Bill Nick built didn't do too badly by lifting the 1967 FA Cup and giving my mate Dave Mackay a fitting climax to his career at Spurs. And the third, with survivors of the second such as Pat Jennings, Joe Kinnear, Cyril Knowles, Alan Mullery and Alan Gilzean mixed with new signings and youth graduates, brought League Cup and more European glory, through lifting the UEFA Cup, in the early 1970s.

Phil Beal did well for himself as a sweeper, appearing in Spurs' three successive final wins, and Jimmy Pearce was a good winger who picked up a winners' medal in the 1973 League Cup Final against Norwich City. Jimmy Neighbour, who tragically died aged 58 in April 2009, helped the Lilywhites lift the same trophy two years before when they beat Aston Villa.

And Martin Chivers proved more than a decent signing. Chiv had big boots to fill because he had to replace Jimmy Greaves as the main Spurs goalscorer. And Bill Nick would, I was told, have to have a go at him for not using his strength enough. He was a big boy, Chiv. And that Bill's assistant Eddie Baily would slaughter him for being lazy.

No one could emulate what Jimmy Greaves did but Chiv managed to do well after coming in from Southampton for big money and got some big goals, netting two against Villa.

He also got a double as Spurs took a 2-1 advantage in the first leg of the 1972 UEFA Cup Final against Wolves at Molineux. Chiv got close to 50 goals in 1972/73. Perhaps he should have got more, but his record was more than respectable.

Martin Peters had joined by then. He came in from West Ham in exchange for Jimmy and cash after being part of the famous three Hammers, with Bobby Moore and Geoff Hurst, who had helped England lift the World Cup. Martin, of course, scored in the never-forgotten final against West Germany. Martin might have been a World Cup hero but my old mate Eddie Baily used to have a right go at him. He'd shout during games, 'C'mon, Peters, get your foot in.' Martin would turn to Eddie and tell him, 'I don't like people shouting at me Eddie. I'm not used to it.' And Eddie replied, 'You'd better had!'

But Martin did well. He'd ghost in like John White and get goals and was in all of Spurs' three successive early 1970s finals, finishing off with the League Cup win over the Canaries.

Ralph Coates, who sadly passed away in December 2010, got the winner against Norwich after coming on for John Pratt, another home product who did all right. Bill Nick signed Ralph on Eddie's recommendation. They had both gone to see him play for Burnley and Bill asked Eddie, 'What do you think of him?' Eddie told Bill, 'Sign him, we need him.'

Bill just wanted convincing. Ralph had a similar style to me in that we both put in plenty of effort, made lots of good runs and scored a few.

I met Ralph's widow at his funeral and asked her how she felt coming down from Burnley to live in the Big Smoke. She and Ralph told Hunter Davies, in his book *The Glory Game* about Spurs' 1971/72 season, that they were 'lost and abandoned', stuck in a flat on a busy road near Tottenham without a phone, TV or radio. And she told me, 'We just had to get on with it.' I told her about the conversation Bill and Eddie had had about bringing in Ralph.

Steve Perryman was another player Bill Nick brought in. He featured in all three of those finals in the 1970s and went on to captain Spurs to two FA Cup wins the following decade against Manchester City and Queens Park Rangers, while becoming the club's record appearance maker.

That team of the 1980s of course included Glenn Hoddle, who got the winner against Rangers. Glenn was spotted as a schoolboy by Chiv and Spurs defender Ray Evans. They obviously had a good eye.

Glenn has become a genuine club legend who would have stood comparison to the midfield players in my team, although he probably would have had to be fitted around Danny, Dave and John. Glenn was the most naturally gifted player of his era. He got a great goal on his full debut up at Stoke City – beating Peter Shilton from range. I'll remind him of that when I next see him. He might wonder how I'd remember that and I'd joke with him, 'I know everything!'

As a manager he was a good one with England and did okay when he took over at White Hart Lane in the early part of the 21st century but caused certain players to question some of his methods. I remember going down to Spurs in my role as observer covering academy matches one time and Teddy Sheringham and Les Ferdinand were saying to me, 'We've got to go and see that woman to tell us what we should be doing.' They were talking about Eileen Drewery, the faith healer Glenn recommended his England and Spurs players to see.

Glenn used to take part in five-a-side training sessions and was the best player in them. But I've also heard his man-management wasn't the best at times. He embarrassed David Beckham in training when they were together for England. He was trying to get Becks to flick the ball up and pass to Darren Anderton and Becks couldn't get the hang of it. So Glenn went over and showed him how. I can believe it. I remember Ron Henry could do a similar trick as he came out for games. I tried to emulate him but couldn't.

Bill Nick, who had become a consultant, took the first call which led to Spurs signing two 1978 World Cup winners – Ossie Ardiles and Ricky Villa – shortly after they had helped Argentina lift the Jules Rimet Trophy.

The caller was Harry Haslam, who had just taken over at Sheffield United. Harry had contacts in Argentina but knew his own club couldn't afford them and thought Spurs might be interested. Bill put him on to Keith Burkinshaw, who was then manager.

The two Argentinian lads were fantastic for Spurs. I met up with Ricky a couple of years ago and he told me how he couldn't speak a word of English when he first arrived at White Hart Lane.

When Keith told him he wanted him to play outside-left one game he spent the whole match at inside-left. When Keith picked him up about it after the game he told his new manager he didn't understand what he was saying. He said he played at inside-left because that was the position he normally played in. His goal in the 1981 FA Cup Final replay against Manchester City must rank as one of the greatest ever seen in the competition. It was a good team with two good strikers in Steve Archibald, an intelligent player, and Garth Crooks. The final was certainly one of the best I've seen.

Ossie was a good player. His passing, movement and balance were brilliant. I was with him at a 'do' one time with other Spurs players. We all had to sign these photos. Cliffy, Glenn Hoddle and John Pratt put their monikers on it. But as I signed I noticed Ossie's autograph. It was the best I've ever seen. Absolutely massive! Keith certainly got the Argentinian duo playing the Spurs way.

Bill also travelled to Weymouth to look at Graham Roberts and recommended him to Spurs. People have said Graham was a bit like Dave Mackay in style. His approach was physical but he was a bit cruder than Dave. He used to smack his opponents a bit. He was an important player for the Spurs team and captained them to a third European triumph, another UEFA Cup success.

It was a two-legged affair against Anderlecht in 1984 and reserve goalkeeper Tony Parks got all the headlines by saving the penalty which won the trophy a second time for Spurs. David Pleat produced a fine Spurs team in the late 1980s, one that should have won the 1987 FA Cup Final. It was a free-flowing, skilled team in the Spurs tradition with Hoddle, Waddle and Ardiles at its hub in front of top goalkeeper Ray Clemence and a predator in Clive Allen who got a club record 49 goals that season. Like father like son? Les certainly got his share.

I ENJOYED watching all these Spurs teams. Their outstanding individuals and the way they achieved successes, largely in the Spurs manner. I was pleased for them because they were Tottenham. I had spent ten years at the club. You maintain a certain affiliation. But I didn't get emotionally involved first hand, watching the big games on the TV.

Yet in 1991 I went to Wembley to watch Spurs in an FA Cup Final for the first time since I'd been in the one exactly 40 years earlier. I took my son Barry along with me.

I'd phoned up Bill Nick for tickets because when I played for Spurs he always sorted out that sort of thing – along with everything else, it seemed. He told me all that was too much for him and chairman Irving Scholar was dealing with it – and wishing he didn't have to. Irving, a nice lad, invited me up to his business offices in the West End and sold me two £65 tickets. I wasn't getting something for nothing.

People have said I shouldn't have had to pay considering what I'd done for the club but to my knowledge it has always been a bit like that at Spurs. Arsenal and Liverpool have always been good at giving tickets to ex-players. You still see their former players at games all the time. But Spurs are selective.

Jonesy got a ticket for me once in recent years but told me they wouldn't let me use the club car park. I said to him, 'Where am I going to park, a mile or two up the road at Bruce Grove?' Street parking has always been bad around White Hart Lane.

It was nice of Cliffy to try and sort something out but the way my knees are now I couldn't have done a long walk to the ground from wherever I'd have ended up. Ironically, though, I went to a game relatively recently and, with nobody about, drove straight into the main car park.

Anyway, Terry Venables had taken over as manager at Spurs and had got together a decent team. Gary Mabbutt was a good captain and they had a couple of superstars, Gary Lineker and Paul Gascoigne.

The pair of them had got the goals which had beaten Arsenal, of all teams, in the semi-final at Wembley.

Gary had been the top scorer in the 1986 World Cup for England and played under Terry when they were together at Barcelona. And he has gone on to carve a decent media career for himself, mainly presenting *Match of the Day*, as well as doing comic TV advertisements for crisps.

Gazza, though, was THE star. He was unbelievable for Spurs and great for England and could win games on his own. When he went on those jinking runs from deep no one could handle him.

He was the most famous player in the English game at the time and there was more attention on him than any other player. It is so sad he has become an alcoholic. It has happened before to top players – just look at George Best. It must be a terrible disease to be an alcoholic. Jimmy became one but got away with it.

Gazza has had all the help in the world. Gary Lineker and others put a lot of money in for treatment for him but, sadly, I don't think people like him can be helped. The final was his last game for Spurs before a multimillion-pound move to Italy with Lazio.

The atmosphere at Wembley was not much different from the one I experienced in 1961 – it was good and intense. I was pleased Spurs came out on top to win the trophy for the EIGHTH time, although it was a shame Gazza got himself injured. I must say the way he did it – a lunging tackle on Gary Charles – was idiotic.

A few of the Spurs players I'd played with, like Bobby Smith, Cliff, Ron Henry and Peter Baker, were invited to an evening celebration 'do' in the West End. They'd reserved a table for as many of the Double winners as could make it. I think Irving sorted it out.

Terry came over for a chat. We spoke about the game and how Gazza was. Terry is a real Spurs fan. He used to watch me and other Lilywhites before me from the terraces. He was a good manager for Spurs.

GERMAN WORLD Cup winner Jurgen Klinsmann became a favourite with the Spurs crowd when then-chairman Alan Sugar got him to the club to help front the Famous Five attack which also included Darren Anderton, Teddy Sheringham, Nicky Barmby and Ilie Dumitrescu under Ossie Ardiles.

David Ginola was another player the Tottenham fans loved. He was a real entertainer. I remember a goal he got in the FA Cup against Barnsley. He seemed to dribble through the entire Tykes team to get it and he was a part of the Spurs team – surprisingly managed by former Arsenal manager George Graham – which won the 1999 League Cup. He clearly had the ability to send Spurs supporters home happy.

Spurs under Juande Ramos produced another team good enough to win the 2008 League Cup, taking apart the Gunners 5-1 in the semis and beating a strong Chelsea team, largely put together by Jose Mourinho and managed by his successor Avram Grant, in the final.

Ledley King was a loyal and class defender and Robbie Keane gave it his all. Dimitar Berbatov was talented and got a goal in the final but I always felt with him that he only played when he wanted to.

I loved Harry Redknapp as Tottenham manager. He seemed an ideal fit for Spurs. He took over with the club bottom of the Premier League in 2008 and got us to safety. He was a perfect manager for my old club.

Harry is very different from Bill Nick in personality but he wanted the team to play. He got hold of players who you didn't think were all that and turned them into good ones. Harry also got us back into the European Cup for the first time since my day. He gave the club a couple of Glory Glory nights, most notably against holders Inter Milan, and took us into the quarter-finals against Real Madrid. In my book, he should have been given the England manager's job instead of Roy Hodgson.

Cliffy tells the story how Harry invited him and his wife Joan out to Lisbon when Spurs played Benfica – who Spurs played in the 1962 European Cup semis, of course – in a pre-season friendly. Harry got a courtesy car laid on for them too. Benfica's nickname is The Eagles and they had one hovering above their Stadium of Light ground before the kick-off. The music played and increased in volume as the bird circled before swooping and landing on the pitch. Harry turned to Cliffy and laughed, 'Can you imagine getting a pigeon doing that at White Hart Lane?'

I thought it a terrible decision to let him go after what he did for Spurs. I have wondered why it was made. Was it because there was so much talk of him taking over the national team? Who knows? Harry has gone on record as having no idea as to why. On the face of it, chairman Daniel Levy decided it was time for him to exit White Hart Lane. I like Harry a lot. He was a good manager and good for Tottenham. His teams played well and he was realistic in what he expected from them.

He was, though, certainly helped big time by the form of Gareth Bale. The Welshman – who I know is rated by my old mate and his compatriot, Cliff – was a freak of nature, so fast and strong. He carried the Spurs team on his own for long periods.

And who can forget his second-half hat-trick against Inter Milan at the San Siro in that 2010/11 Champions League campaign? It was a major highlight in our return to the competition.

He might have been a tour de force for the Lilywhites but he upped his level several notches when he joined Real Madrid for a world record £85.3m in September 2013.

If ever a move gave a player wings, it was Gareth. Any thought the size of the fee would weigh heavily on his shoulders was disproved over and over. Any thought that he'd be unable to perform in the company of the latest clutch of Galacticos from the Bernabeu was swiftly dispelled. He stood alongside the likes of Cristiano Ronaldo. He belonged. By the end of his first season he not only helped Real lift the European Cup, but he netted in the final. And let us not forget Luka Modric, another recent Lilywhite who helped Bale and Real to that European Cup triumph. He was the linkman central to Harry Redknapp's Champions League campaign with his quick feet, quick brain and technical skills.

Lots of teams, players and managers have been associated with Spurs since my day. And they have achieved glory in cups, if not the leagues, and deserved credit rather than comparison to my one.

But if I were to pick individuals to make up the greatest ever Spurs team the entire 11 would come from the one which won the Double, with substitutes including Jimmy Greaves, Ron Burgess, Glenn Hoddle, Gazza, Pat Jennings, Ossie Ardiles, Jurgen Klinsmann, David Ginola, Gary Lineker, Eddie Baily and Gareth Bale. I could go on and on.

And the greatest manager? You've guessed it – Bill Nick. There have been many decades of players and managers at Spurs since he resigned in

1974 after 16 years in charge. There were many before he took over. He remains top of the pile. Although he never suffered fools gladly, he had a romantic view of how the game should be played and for him, apart from our 1961 FA Cup Final performance, our team generally epitomised it.

But the game was changing in the 1970s and I don't think he liked the direction. Teams were setting themselves up with the priority of ensuring victory at the expense of entertaining the fans – something he always insisted was of paramount importance.

Also, he considered wage demands from players too high and certainly couldn't have handled them as they are today. You see, he considered it an honour to play for Spurs and you should play for them for nothing. He was honest and made the club what they are.

Bill was Mr Tottenham. He was involved in everything. Even ground maintenance. It's been suggested he would know if a lightbulb needed replacing in the toilets. I heard he regretted missing seeing his daughters grow up because of the amount of time he spent at Spurs. And he gave his life to the club while remaining in the same modest house close to the stadium.

He might have resigned as manager but I felt the board treated him badly. Faceless wonders, that lot. Just one or two to make the decisions and the rest were just a bunch of 'yes' men.

They could have offered him another role at the club or even an immediate testimonial after all he had done for Tottenham. I heard he even had to sign on the dole. What a disgrace! He went to West Ham to help their manager John Lyall out but Tottenham was in his blood and he used to sit and watch the Hammers and say to whoever was next to him, 'John White would have done that', 'Dave Mackay wouldn't have done that' and 'Bobby Smith would have been challenging there.' He couldn't help himself from comparing because he thought so much of the Glory Glory players.

I was delighted when they got Bill back as a consultant at the insistence of Keith Burkinshaw, a fellow Yorkshireman who took over from Bill's successor, Terry Neill.

Bill was an unbelievable man and an unbelievable manager. There was a campaign to make him a knight of the realm. All his players and fans supported it, but it never came to pass. Although to all of us who supported the bid he will forever be Sir Bill. They named the lane which leads up to the stadium Bill Nicholson Way.

But what he helped achieve in the Double season alone should have ensured that knighthood.

28
Modern Football

I F ONLY Spurs could have hung on to Gareth Bale and Luka Modric one wonders where we'd be today, but there's no point crying over spilt milk.

Tottenham, with Andre Villas-Boas as manager, used up the world record £85.3m fee they got for Gareth Bale from Real Madrid to buy a lot of new players for big money like Paulinho, Roberto Soldado, Erik Lamela, Christian Eriksen, Etienne Capoue, Vlad Chiriches and Nacer Chadli. They actually cost a combined £110m.

And the jury was still out on how good they could be as Mauricio Pochettino came in for the 2014/15 season following an unsettling campaign under Villas-Boas and then Tim Sherwood in which perhaps Eriksen was the only one of the new arrivals who looked a decent purchase.

It does make you wonder just who selects and buys the players. How much of a say do managers have in bringing them in? When Bill Nick managed Spurs there was no question he made the decisions on which players came and went.

These days the power of the manager has been diluted with directors of football, chief executives, chairmen and agents part of the process. It must drive old-school managers like Harry Redknapp and Neil Warnock up the wall, but it is something they have to accept.

And they don't seem to last long. Tim Sherwood seemed to do a decent job after taking over from Villas-Boas midway through the 2013/14 term and getting an 18-month contract. But when there was a lot of speculation about who Spurs were lining up to replace him in the summer of 2014 he told the board, 'You've got to make a decision about it.' That was a daft comment by him. You can't say that to people in power. They do what they like – and they did. They sacked him.

It's something that happens at all clubs. No one is fireproof. The person who gives these guys a job would not sack themselves should things go pear-shaped. And you can't dump an entire squad of players on the dole at the same time so a scapegoat has to be found. Step forward the manager.

International managers tend to have a longer shelf-life and will often fall on their swords if things don't work out at the big tournaments. Although Fabio Capello didn't when his England squad flopped in the 2010 World Cup in South Africa, with the FA knowing it would cost a king's ransom to sack him.

And Roy Hodgson – winner of the race to replace Capello, who finally quit in 2012 – remained in charge as our country failed to make it beyond the group stage in Brazil in 2014. Hodgson's squad ended up bottom of it with just a point, gleaned from a goalless draw against Costa Rica. But Roy was reckoned to be a Steady Eddie with heaps of international experience, a diplomat, a likeable bloke and an individual able to bring out the best in a few promising youngsters such as Raheem Sterling by the kingmakers at the FA.

It is no easy job managing England these days. When I played almost 100 per cent of players in the Football League were British, with a very high percentage of them English. Now the percentage of English players is a lot smaller due to the foreign invasion.

It really is exciting to have some of these global stars wandering around England each week showing their skills, but it has come at a price.

There have been, unsurprisingly, a lot of changes in English football in the past half-century.

Tactics now differ hugely to my day. We had five forwards. FIVE. Ossie Ardiles gave that a go at Spurs in the 1990s but that approach didn't last long. The reason? It was considered cavalier and didn't bring the success demanded. More significantly, it didn't avoid defeat enough. The more you get beaten the greater the risk of relegation and in turn a drop in income.

The modern game is built on fear of losing matches, and of losing money or missing out on extra money. That's why there is so much emphasis on Premier League clubs getting into the Champions League. 'Let's finish fourth and then we'll get in it,' is the mantra. It means more guaranteed money coming in, but there's no title for ending up fourth.

Money should be a priority for regular businesses in the City of London, for instance. And, yes, running a football club is business. But my sport is a peculiar business. It is also about winning silverware and providing unforgettable moments players, staff and supporters can share in.

There's no victory parade down the high road for finishing fourth. But those obsessed with balance sheets rub their hands in glee and supporters are told – and many are convinced – that being in the Champions League is what matters. And, to me, the competition's name is a misnomer. When Spurs took on Gornik, Dukla Prague and Benfica, it was an accurate description. The fact whoever finishes fourth in the Premier League gets in tells you that is no longer. What a load of rubbish.

And that, by the way, sums up the Europa League, the competition Spurs have qualified for in recent years. I don't like it. It's a bit of a Mickey Mouse competition with Spurs playing many teams nobody has ever heard of. One mark against it is matches have been played on Thursday nights which has affected Spurs' ability to perform at their peak in the league at weekends.

What about the gap between the haves and have-nots in today's football? The money-rich clubs, who rake it in through the Champions League revenue, billionaire owners, and the rest who lack the financial muscle to close it.

The money swishing around at the top of our game in England still continues to attract the foreign stars. Many might claim they are tempted by the prospect of playing for top clubs or winning silverware. But when English clubs offer £200,000 a week for the services of these superstars no one can deny wages must have been a huge pull for the likes of Radamel Falcao, Angel di Maria, Sergio Aguero and Diego Costa.

And yet you get the impression so many of today's Premier League players who kiss the club badges on their shirts, implying undying devotion for it, would be off if someone waved a few extra pound notes under their noses.

I STILL love football, keeping in touch via television and radio. Kay likes watching and listening to it too. And the Premier League can be hugely entertaining and throws up a few characters.

Jose Mourinho is a bit of a flash so-and-so but he's quite a showman and is a good motivator. And he gets results, as he has proved with Chelsea.

The Blues, Manchester City and United, Liverpool and Arsenal have their personalities, good managers and provide skilled, up-tempo, enjoyable football. As do Spurs, occasionally.

The future for Spurs, it seems, for better or worse, is tied up with the development of a new White Hart Lane Stadium with a bigger capacity that will increase revenue to enable Spurs to compete with the best in the Premier and Europe.

In the meantime, perhaps if Spurs could provide me with a car park space I might go down to the White Hart Lane I know on a matchday to savour the live experience first hand more regularly than I have done in recent years. Hopefully it could be as a hospitality host, which I did once against Manchester United around three or four years ago, thoroughly enjoyed and would love to do again. And once there I might again sense the ghosts of our Double team playing once more on our field of dreams.

29
Eighty Not Out

I PASSED my 80th birthday on 29 November 2014 and am still enjoying life, a simple life.

Kay and I had moved from Kenton in Middlesex out to Stevenage in Hertfordshire the previous year for a better quality of life, one less frenetic and crowded.

It wasn't to a gated mansion like so many of the top footballers of today. Or perhaps a home akin to my adopted town's sporting icon, two-time Formula One world champion Lewis Hamilton.

Our choice had to be more modest given that my professional career kicking a ball around did not afford us such extravagances. As you have discovered, the money I earned out of the game was minimal. The figures in my wage packets did not add up to telephone numbers. And commercial opportunities to bump up earnings weren't about.

We upped roots from a modest semi-detached in an area we'd lived in since 1968 to another in a quiet cul-de-sac in the first English 'new town'.

And we are perfectly happy. We have a light and airy house which we've made our own by putting up pictures of the family and my glory days with Spurs along the walls, a lovely little garden with a small fish pond, and wonderful neighbours.

Kay likes to spend time on the computer e-mailing friends and family, while I still pop down the local bookies for a small flutter.

We do most things together, paying visits to friends. And we revel in being racehorse owners. Neil and Barry have joined us in buying shares in one through Malton trainer Richard Fahey's assistant Robin O'Ryan. We were going to call her Lilywhite after the Spurs nickname but settled on Miss Van Gogh because she was out of Dutch Art. Yet she runs in Tottenham colours – white and navy blue – with Neil having sorted the design.

Family and friends were all there to see her first win at the sixth attempt at Leicester in October 2014. I got a similar rush to the one I got when

222

scoring a goal. I got tearful when I saw her hit the front in the sprint she was in. It also took me back to when I watched my dad race. It was so brilliant. I can't overstate how happy I was. We all were.

We wrote to Richard and champion jockey Paul Hanagan who rode her, thanking them for a magic day, and they both told us our words were a reminder as to why they were in their game.

OUR LIVES, though, largely revolve around the grandchildren these days. So you will have to indulge me a bit as I waffle on about them for a while.

Each Thursday after picking them up from school, Kay and I take a couple of of them, Ben and Jessica, out. When the weather's nice, for instance, we'll take them to play crazy golf over at the local sports park. We have a lot of fun imagining we're playing for trophies.

During half-term we usually take them to the cinema. We all love films. There's a lot of banter flying around and we'll have a sing-song, like singing the song 'Happy' from *Despicable Me 2*. I was, as you know, in a choir back in the day but I don't think Kay thinks much of my voice these days! We also treat them to a McDonald's. It's the highlight of the week for Kay and I.

And it seems several of our grandkids have the family's sporting gene. Our eldest son Neil has a daughter called Katie, who was born in January 1997. Like her dad, she is keen on tennis. She's had a few injuries on the senior circuit over here but is climbing up the rankings. She also works part-time with Hollisters clothing at Brent Cross in north London and occasionally has to wear their latest fashions around the store.

Barry's Conner, born in March 2004, is a keen junior golfer and can already hit the ball a long way. Conner's sister Lauren (born in December 1993), by the way, is very bright and a hard-working student at Winchester University.

The only footballers among the grandchildren are Mark's two. Ben (born in December 2000) loves the game. He's been with his junior club, Parkfield, since he was seven. And he has started collecting trophies before I did with plenty from the 2013/14 season.

He is a bit of an all-rounder, though. Ben plays cricket for a regional side, and his local club, and hockey for Harrow. He plays basketball, cricket and tennis for his school, and swims like a fish!

Mark's daughter Jessica (born in October 2004) plays football for Garston Ladies – and is very quick on her feet. She is also versatile, loves gymnastics – always seeming to be the wrong way up when Kay and I watch her! – and plays hockey. Another 'fish', she can already swim half a mile. She has done a charity swim for Aspire – who support people with spinal cord problems – with brother Ben. She is also keen on drama and played a part in *Annie* with Potters Bar Theatre Company in November 2014.

My brother John's son Simon is currently the family's highest-profile sportsperson. Born in December 1977, Simon was a promising footballer and it looked as though he might follow me into the pro game from Scarborough when he was a teenager. He was also on the books of York City, the team I'd watched as a kid. But his brother Nick, a keen golfer who played off scratch by the time he was 16, talked Simon into giving golf a go.

Simon found he was pretty good at it and in 1999 was runner-up in the English Amateur Championship and part of the British and Irish team which won the Walker Cup, the amateur equivalent of the Ryder Cup, and went pro in the September.

He started collecting titles in Asia and broke through in Europe to become the only golfer apart from the late legend Seve Ballesteros and Bernhard Langer to win the KLM Open in the Netherlands three times. Simon also took Ryder Cup star Justin Rose to a sudden-death play-off for the Volvo Masters title at Valderrama. And he's qualified for all the majors. I'm a proud uncle.

THE YOUNGER generation in the family do get involved with my footballing past on occasion. There was the first time the family sat down in our living room to watch an entire re-run of my European Cup Winners' Cup Final.

Ben, my third of five grandkids, was shocked, stunned, shaken and not a little stirred as we sat alongside each other on the comfy sofa.

Our focus had been the television screen in the far corner. Mark had managed to get the DVD working – something beyond my expertise – to enable us to see it. The picture was in black and white and grainy. There was my Spurs team in all-white playing Atletico Madrid wearing dark-and-white striped shirts and dark shorts. We had built up our 4-1 lead when this small figure thumped home a fifth and I screamed 'get in' to make Ben, who had been totally captivated by the action, jump.

I was the figure and viewing the goal spun me out of control. I was back in the moment. Dr Who's Tardis had transported me in my mind. It was my second goal in the game of my life.

I'd only ever seen the match in its entirety once as I helped prepare the DVD for public consumption a month or two earlier. It was in a recording studio with Cliffy Jones and I provided reflections and insights to a voice-over from TV sports commentator Jon Champion, a fellow Yorkshireman.

They hadn't long found the entire match on film – I'd only ever seen it on a highlights video. It was better 50 years late than never.

The commentary was by Kenneth Wolstenholme, of 'they think it's all over' fame, his line as Geoff Hurst completed the hat-trick which secured England the World Cup.

There was one camera going up and down the field and one microphone placed near the dugouts. It was all quite primitive in comparison to how they do things today with tons of cameras, other digital technology and more pundits than you can shake a stick at.

I apologised to Ben but he and the family indulged me, perhaps because I've never thrust what I did as a footballer down their throats.

Not long after there was a promotion for the DVD that Cliff and I attended. Cliff's son Steve helped put that together. It was in the 100 Club in Oxford Street in London's West End. It's normally a legendary music venue. I have been told the Rolling Stones, the Sex Pistols and quite a few others back in the day, like Glenn Miller, Benny Goodman and Louis Armstrong, have played there.

There were no musical heroes there but a few footballing ones. A few other former Spurs players like Ricky Villa, the 1981 FA Cup hero, and John Pratt. Cliffy and I were top of the bill and we did a double act, recalling memories and exchanging banter.

THE SPURS jubilees keep coming round. There was a dinner to celebrate the 40th anniversary of the Double at the Marriott Hotel in London in 2001 with the other members of the side still around.

Kay couldn't go so she gave her ticket to our youngest, Mark. And he sat with all the wives. Mark tells me they were brilliant with him. Dave Mackay's wife Isobel told Kay later, 'It was lovely meeting your wonderful son.' They took him under their wing. Mark also says he got emotional when I was called up first, saying, 'When I saw you on stage the realisation of what you've achieved hit home.' That was nice. I was as pleased as punch to be part of the first Hall of Fame night Spurs put on. The Double team were reunited as its members and manager became the club's first inductees at a swanky dinner at White Hart Lane on 11 March 2004.

It really was a special occasion with legendary TV football commentator John Motson the master of ceremonies. They, quite rightly, made a big fuss of Bill Nick. No person deserved the recognition more than him. He might not have got the knighthood he deserved but at least he got the honour of being the first inductee into a Hall of Fame set up by the club that was his life. And I was grateful he lived to receive it, because he passed on seven months later.

Our goalkeeper Bill Brown couldn't come over from where he lived in Canada but the eight remaining survivors were there. Besides myself, Peter, Ron, Maurice, Dave, Cliff, Bobby and Les, Tony Marchi, Mel Hopkins and Terry Medwin were also representing the 1960/61 playing squad. We were all presented with an engraved crystal glass decanter by chairman Daniel Levy.

It was a touching moment when John Motson revealed Danny and John would be inducted posthumously. The fans there gave us a great reception. I think they appreciated our generation really cared about them. And, of course, we cared about Bill.

Bill's memorial service had all the remaining Double team there as well as players from every following era. It was so moving. Every club sent someone down for it. As the service went on I just thought back to what Bill was like, that the club meant everything to him, and my relationship with him. The church was so packed. We were all invited back to White Hart Lane and the club opened up the ground for supporters to attend and pay their respects.

Cliff and Jimmy from my team said a few words. Cliffy remembered Bill's no-nonsense attitude mixed with humour, telling those present that his manager had told him, 'Remember that a pat on the back is only a couple of feet away from being a kick up the arse.'

Jimmy recalled Bill telling the team, 'Whatever you're feeling now, remember you are going to run out now in front of people that pay your wages. Their expectancy is high, their value of you is high, their opinion of you is high. Do not let them down. Entertain and you can only do that by being honest with yourself, respect your team-mates, your opponents and as a team play as one.' That was Bill's philosophy. Cliff and Jimmy had got it right.

Steve Perryman, who played in a later team for Bill, quoted one of his old boss's adages, 'If one ball goes back, the next goes through and forward. Play the ball the way you are facing. If you are not in possession, get in position. When the game dies, make sure you are alive.' I remembered all of them, of course! Glenn Hoddle, Gary Mabbutt and Martin Chivers were others to speak with touching tributes.

And the organisers released 100 doves in Bill's honour. The memories kept flooding back to me, like when he always insisted we called him 'Bill' not 'boss'. Just take the way he signed off a letter he sent to me following one reunion:

> Dear Terry,
> At last I have been able to enclose the photographs we had taken at the re-union of the 61-62 team last August.
>
> They are not as good as I was hoping for but I do hope they will be a good reminder to you of a very nice evening together and of course many good times in the past.
>
> Thanks very much for coming along and I do hope you really enjoyed the opportunity to discuss and possibly compare the old times in the game with the new.

Every good wish,
Yours sincerely,
Bill
William Nicholson

There was Tottenham's 125th anniversary match against Aston Villa in October 2007. The idea was for a lot of Spurs legends to bring on trophies they had helped win at half-time. Mark came with me and wondered where I'd got to as the likes of Glenn Hoddle and Gary Mabbutt came out of the tunnel holding on to silverware to parade. There must have been about 30 players.

But then I emerged last of all carrying the European Cup Winners' Cup – which was very heavy I remember – and got a fantastic reception. It was wonderful for me and a special moment for my youngest son.

It's humbling the team I played for continues to be remembered.

30
The Survival Game

NOT SO long ago I was in a spare room on the ground floor of a block of flats in Enfield, north London. I was there for a picture signing session involving surviving members of Spurs' Double-winning side, the results of which would be sold in shops and on the internet. There seems to be a market for that sort of thing.

Cliff Jones was there with Tony Marchi, our outstanding stand-in, and Peter Baker, our right-back, who happened to live upstairs with his wife Linda.

Maurice Norman, our centre-half, was due but had to care for his wife Jacqueline, who was poorly. Les Allen couldn't make it, having had to take things easier since a triple heart bypass operation.

There were absences due to progressive diseases which damage the brain. Dave Mackay had been struggling with Alzheimer's – the most common cause of dementia – and Parkinson's disease.

Dave was the player who turned us into winners, the driving force. He is a good friend I used to spend a lot of time with while we were together at Spurs. It had been – and remains – so tough to see how his ailments have affected him. Dave was the player who turned us into winners, the driving force. He is a good friend I used to spend a lot of time with while we were together at Spurs. It had been – and remains – so tough to see how his ailments have affected him.

Peter also has Alzheimer's, although he takes medication which helps him deal with it.

Several are no longer with us. Bobby Smith, who passed on in September 2010 aged 77, had suffered physically from being our battering ram and had too many injections to mask injuries.

But he had been in good form when we attended the night to celebrate Jimmy Greaves's 70th birthday at the 02 Arena in London seven months earlier.

We lost our goalkeeper Bill Brown, who had suffered a heart attack and prostate cancer, aged 73 six years before, the same year our manager Bill Nicholson departed following a long illness aged 85.

Alzheimer's and Parkinson's helped claim our perfect captain Danny Blanchflower at the age of 67 in 1993.

And John White, generally rated, and rightly so, along with Danny and Dave, as an integral part of the team, was tragically killed by that lightning strike at Crews Hill Golf Club in 1964. He was only 27.

I joined Cliff, Les and Peter from the Double team as well as Pat Jennings – who had just joined Spurs when John died – and John's son Rob at the unveiling of a plaque on the first hole at the club a couple of years ago. It brought back all the fond memories. It was an emotional, poignant occasion with a few tears.

So was the 50th anniversary with Pipe Major Willie Cochrane – who served the King's Own Scottish Borderers regiment with John – playing bagpipes. I told the Spurs website how it was such a shock to us all. It still upsets me now to think about it.

Two days after Christmas in 2014, tragically, my old Army pal Ron Henry was taken from us aged 80, another to suffer Alzheimer's.

He had been in a home and didn't seem to know anybody. His condition had got worse following the death of his wife Edna. His grandson Ronnie, who had a spell at Spurs under Glenn Hoddle around 2002 and has gone on with Stevenage to become the first captain to lift a trophy at the new Wembley, told us, 'Granddad is not well.'

Cliff rang me on the day Ron died to give me the news and Kay and I attended his funeral. I'm so sad he's gone. He was someone I'd known for such a long time. He was a good person and my heart goes out to his family. I can only offer my condolences, although in some respects it was probably a relief he passed given his quality of life.

Ron was given a minute's heartfelt applause by a packed house at White Hart Lane before Spurs took on Manchester United in a goalless draw the day after his passing.

Ron was, with myself and Peter, reckoned to be an unsung hero of our team so it was only right he got due recognition as a bona fide club legend. After all Ron was among only four players, with Danny, John and Les, to play in EVERY game of our Double-winning season.

Grandson Ronnie watched the moving moments on television before going out and helping Stevenage defeat Cambridge United just up the road from our home, telling the *Hertfordshire Mercury*, 'It was difficult for me, but my grandfather was a big inspiration to me and I know that he would have wanted me to go out there and play. That was what he was like as a footballer. He wanted the best for me.'

It was appropriate that the tribute for Ron should be prior to our old club taking on Manchester United as they were the opposition when Ron scored his only goal for Spurs in a 1-0 win at the Lane in February 1965. Ron, along with myself, Maurice Norman and Cliff, were the only remaining members of the Double team that day against the eventual champions – playing in front of nearly 59,000!

I feel proud to have played a part in getting Ron into Spurs from our Army days together. We shared so many wonderful memories.

Kay wonders whether the progressive mental diseases so many of my team-mates have suffered – and in a couple of cases, still suffer – was the result of heading the heavy leather balls that were about in our day; that soaked up the rain and became heavier. So do quite a few people. I will leave it for others to judge.

All this is so hard to think about and write as it is. It is heartbreaking to consider so many of the individuals who made up what a lot of people consider one of the greatest – if not the greatest club side – are either no longer with us or suffering mentally and physically.

As we never earned fortunes in our day, it has often been difficult financially over the years for us. That's why I am more than happy to help support the Tottenham Tribute Trust which backs players who have fallen on hard times.

There was a recent fundraiser, a special big screening of Julie Welch's *Those Glory Glory Days* at the Bernie Grant Arts Centre next to the Tottenham Town Hall.

The film is about three girls who were Tottenham supporters and wanted a ticket for the 1961 FA Cup Final. It was superb, funny and touching. I enjoyed it. I liked the bit where the girls found some chewing gum Bobby Smith had chewed and treated it like a holy relic! Danny appears in it.

It was a great night. Peter was there and John White's son Rob with his wife and daughters. So was Gary Mabbutt, a great Spurs captain who skippered his team to the FA Cup in 1991.

I spoke to Julie and her husband Ron, a nice fellow and a top journalist. I asked Julie how long it had taken her to write the screenplay and she said a year. An unbelievable woman, a Tottenham fan – and the first female Fleet Street football reporter.

The actor who played the main role, Zoe Nathenson, spoke. And MC Paul Coyte asked Cliffy and I – doing a double act – questions about the days the film referred to. It was lovely to be appreciated.

It is clear my Spurs team remain in the hearts and minds of all true Spurs fans. I know that first hand from when I go back to White Hart Lane.

I'm talking about the reverence the supporters have for that team. That's reflected when we have our reunions – and at the book promotions I've done with Cliffy for *Spurs Greatest Games* by my ghost-writer Mike Donovan (and also published by Pitch) and *1961 The Spurs Double*.

We had the big get-together at the NEC in Birmingham in the 21st century with the then-surviving members of the Double team, although we had to share the limelight with a few old Chelsea legends and some from the acting world like the late Roger Lloyd Pack, who played Trigger in *Only Fools and Horses* and was a Spurs fan.

The actress Shirley Eaton, painted in gold for the James Bond film *Goldfinger*, was there, with Richard Kiel, who played the villain Jaws in the movies *Moonraker* and *The Spy Who Loved Me*.

The supporters also turn out in force when I do tours of White Hart Lane. I've done a couple with Cliff. It does seem to be the two us a lot – which I enjoy because he is the member of the team I am most in touch with. We don't live too far from each other just north of London, enjoy each other's company and care about each other's families.

I love meeting all the fans. I always have done going back to the days under Bill Nicholson who, as you know by now, always insisted they were the most important people at the club. Cliff is of the same opinion. The supporters know their stuff and I'm delighted to share memories and give my opinions.

There was one I remember which was no exception. We stood behind the three replica trophies which epitomised the Glory Glory Years. The Football League First Division trophy, the FA Cup and the European Cup Winners' Cup were lined up on a table against a backdrop depicting a packed West Stand with the legend 'the game is about glory', that phrase coined by Danny.

The silverware glittered in the room used by families on matchday. I sat to the left, closest to the continental trophy, with Cliff at the other end. Facing us were our audience and inquisitors. The windowless room – also adorned with framed pictures of Jimmy Greaves and Bill Nicholson – was packed out, from adults too young to remember my day to men and women who had supported the club almost from when I first arrived in the mid-1950s.

It was the first Spurs Legends Stadium Tour to feature two players. John Jackson, a smashing bloke who was in charge, told me he wanted the Dyson–Jones double act to symbolise the Double team.

Cliff was on good form, teasing me about how I always milked the success I had in the final of the European competition, telling his audience, 'Terry's always saying to anyone who will listen "remember Rotterdam".' But he did add that I'd had the performance of my life.

I felt proud sitting there right next to the trophy and describing the night. In fact I felt proud all the way round the tour that people recognised my part in the lifting of those trophies.

Cliff and I had begun the tour in the media room. We told those who had joined us a few stories from our playing days. Some were light-hearted while others were tinged with sadness as we spoke of the ill health some of our surviving team-mates were enduring.

We wandered up into the directors' box and spoke of our Spurs debuts among much else with the pitch behind us. We moved in to the Bill Nicholson Suite where the very ball I'd scored with to win the cup and seal the Double was on display. And we told the assembled of our love and respect for Bill Nicholson.

We found our way to the pitch out of the old corner entrance from which we trotted out on matchdays to the refrain of McNamara's Band.

Next stop was the dressing rooms. That old inner sanctum. The memories flooded back as I remembered opening fan mail which had been placed on a long table, now replaced by a rather sleeker version. Cliff gave me a light, jokey kneeing on my left leg when insisting he scored more goals than me in the Double team. And that's when we moved on to see those glittering prizes.

One fan on the tour, Peter Sugden, remembered me from when I played for the reserves. Peter reckons he wasn't sure about me at first but said I soon won him and the rest of the fans over. We still managed to play great football even when the pitches were muddy and covered in sand.

I loved those days – and I love my life. The only real dark cloud, for me, has been concern about my eyes with the unfortunate development of cataracts, something I discovered through a visit to my optician who referred me to a hospital. The eyes clearly weren't quite as sharp as when I saw Bobby Smith float over that cross in the 1961 FA Cup Final and headed the ball past Gordon Banks!

My sons spoke to me about the problem. They laid out what might happen if I didn't do something about it. If left untreated my vision would get so bad I wouldn't be able to do much at all. I don't like surgeries, but thought I'd better do something about it.

I went to a specialist eye doctor who assessed my eyes to see what strength of artificial lens I would need to replace my natural lens, also checking on my general health.

It was a straightforward procedure which only took about 45 minutes under local anaesthetic and Kay drove me home a few hours later. All that showed was a patch over my eye. They advised someone kept a close 'eye' on me for 24 hours, if you'll pardon the pun, and then it settled down.

I want to be able to still do things and be able to see people around me. It would be awful if I was unable to do all that.

I appreciate Kay as well as my sons for giving me the shove to get it sorted. My quality of life is good. Joining Spurs was a positive life-changer, but losing proper sight would have been a negative. I can see more clearly now – and hopefully way into the future.

DAVE MACKAY passed away as this book was being published. He was a key player, a winner, an inspiration and a big, big friend. We shared so many good times. I'll miss him. I feel sorry for his wife.

Q & A With Terry Dyson

GREATEST NON-SPURS TEAM OF MY ERA?

Gordon Banks: There were a lot of goalkeepers in my time but he was the best.

Right-back: Don Howe. He was West Brom and Arsenal's right-back and I found him very difficult to play against. A good full-back. Good tackler. Marked you well, didn't give you a lot of room. Quite quick. Jimmy Armfield of Blackpool was good as well. He used to get himself forward more than Don.

Left-back: Tommy Banks. The Bolton Wanderers defender was hard but I didn't mind playing against him, especially at home. Eddie McCreadie of Chelsea was another good full-back, good defensively; a good tackler, marked very well.

Right-half: Bobby Robson. Excellent wing-half. He used to get himself forward, a good passer. And he helped stop us getting the First Division points record in 1961 when he got the winner for West Brom at White Hart Lane on the day we received the trophy.

Centre-half: Brian Labone (Everton) or **Ron Yeats** (Liverpool). Both good in the air and brave and tackled well.

Left-half: Duncan Edwards. A key player for Manchester United's Busby Babes. I only played against him once. So strong. Could defend, make goals and score big ones. It was a tragedy he didn't live long enough to fulfil his potential. Bobby Charlton said Duncan had the lot – in terms of ability and what he brought to any side he played in – and he was right. I remember meeting him in a Manchester hotel once. We were there for a match against Bolton while United were relaxing before a home game. We asked each other how the other was. A few months later the Munich air disaster happened and he died along with so many of that great team.

Right wing: Stanley Matthews. A wonderful footballer. As I've said, he was a tall lad who always used to feint by me when I defended. He used to lean so far one way and then he was gone in the other direction before I could move as I stood there.

Inside right: Bobby Charlton. Two good feet. Had everything. Nice lad. Nothing flash about him.

Centre forward: John Charles. Great player. He was idolised in Italy. He scored against Spurs in a friendly against us for Juventus in Turin.

Inside left: Jimmy McIlroy. A clever schemer. Good on set plays. Big pal of Danny's.

Left wing: Tom Finney. One of the greatest of legends with his versatility enabling him to play on both wings and at centre-forward. A gentleman.

HIGH POINT?
Scoring in the 1961 FA Cup Final.

LOWEST?
When I had cartilage trouble which put me out for about six weeks.

WHAT MAKES YOU HAPPY?
Watching horse racing, backing a couple of winners and most sports.

WHAT MAKES YOU ANGRY?
People not being polite, not saying their please and thank yous. In sport, it is conning refs by diving. Refs should be able to see video replays immediately so as to give the appropriate punishment.

WHAT DO YOU THINK OF THE TELEVISION COVERAGE OF FOOTBALL?
When I was playing there was only the FA Cup Final, although *Match of the Day* and *The Big Match* eventually screened highlights. But these days the coverage is excellent. Sky in particular do a great job, although it is a shame some just cannot afford to pay the extra cash to watch the live games they broadcast.

VIDEO TECHNOLOGY?
The powers-that-be have dragged their feet over introducing it during games. They finally brought in goal line technology in the English Premier League for the 2014/15 season. But there's a lot more they can do. Besides sorting out diving, if there's a doubt over an offender who might warrant a red card, referees should be able to double check on screen. I remember ref Andre Marriner sending off the wrong Arsenal player at Chelsea in March 2014, giving Keiran Gibbs his marching orders when it should have been Alex Oxlade-Chamberlain. Everyone can make a mistake. Checking a monitor first would avoid any potential embarrassment for the ref. Lots of sports have embraced technology pretty much completely like tennis,

cricket and rugby, so why not football? The trouble is, though, that clubs outside the Premier League might not be able to afford to install the new technology.

MODERN-DAY REFEREES?
Sometimes they don't help themselves. I see them give a free kick when it is an opponent's skill that has brought the foul. Far too many cards early doors. There are some good refs, like Howard Webb. Our referees aren't too bad overall but get too big for their boots at times.

HOW DO REFS COMPARE TO MY DAY?
We got away with a lot more than players do today. Didn't send so many off. There wasn't really backchat. Can't remember any. The Premier League is high profile and there is a lot of focus on the referee. But I don't feel too sorry for them now – they get well paid. In my day, they were part-time and holding down another job during the week. We had some good ones, like Jack Taylor, who refereed the 1974 World Cup Final – and gave a penalty in the first minute!

MATCH FIXING?
There was an infamous betting scandal involving two of the Sheffield Wednesday team we beat to seal the 1961 title, Peter Swan and Tony Kay, along with team-mate David 'Bronco' Layne. They all ended up in jail and deservedly so. But it ruined their football lives and it will always leave a stigma. It's harder to fix football matches as it is part of a team sport. There were match-fixing allegations involving a few players in 2013. Any player found guilty of such things should be banned. If they are caught and the case is proved they should be finished.

WHAT DO YOU THINK OF RACISM IN FOOTBALL?
You always get a few idiots shouting something if they've had a few drinks. There was the Dani Alves incident. Some idiot threw a banana at him as he played for Barcelona against Villarreal in Spain. Dani took the heat out of the situation by picking it up and eating it. Generally I don't think you get too much racism in the game.

FIRST FINAL YOU REMEMBER?
The one dubbed The Matthews Final of 1953, so-called because Sir Stanley won it at the third attempt. I was in the Army and all us soldiers crowded round the radio listening to it in the barracks. It was a big occasion. Massive. Everyone wanted to be there. It was the biggest domestic game in the world.

MOST MEMORABLE MATCH WITNESSED?
The Matthews Final.

FIRST WORLD CUP FINAL SEEN?
It was in 1958 in Sweden. Brazil beat the host country 5-2. It was the game that established Pele. He was only 17 but magic. He proved even at that young age that no one could compare to him. I still think he is the best player that has ever lived. He could do everything. That Brazilian team had other great players like Garrincha and they've had many more down the years, although the 2014 team weren't up to the standard of the great sides they have had in the World Cup finals hosted by their country. What also made the final special was the fact not much football was shown on TV at the time. Danny Blanchflower (Northern Ireland) and Wales pair Cliff Jones and Terry Medwin helped their countries to the quarter-finals in Sweden, while Spurs team-mates Maurice Norman and Bobby Smith were on the bench as England failed to get past the group stages. Sound familiar?

CHILDHOOD SPORTING HERO?
He wasn't really a hero, but I liked Alf Bottom, the centre-forward for York City that myself and my friend used to cheer as he came out of the tunnel in the afternoon after we'd played in the morning. We were there when he got his 100th goal.

WORST TRAINER?
Greavsie (Jimmy Greaves). Great in the five-a-sides but not on the runs.

BEST TRAINER?
Jimmy Conway at Fulham. An unbelievable runner. And John White, a natural runner.

BEST TEAM-MATE?
Dave Mackay.

WORST DEFEAT?
The Spurs loss at Sheffield Wednesday which ended our unbeaten run in the 1960/61 season. A body blow.

WORST HOME RESULT?
The 1-1 draw with Manchester City on 10 October 1960 which ended our record 11-win start to the season. It was the only point we dropped in the first 15 games!

BEST PERSONAL HOME PERFORMANCE?
My history-making hat-trick against Arsenal on 26 August 1961.

BEST PERSONAL AWAY PERFORMANCE?
The 1963 European Cup Winners' Cup Final. And the 1962 European Cup tie against Dukla Prague in which I got the winner.

WORST INJURY?
I had a bone in my back displaced against Blackburn, but wasn't out too long. I was lucky with injuries.

WHAT WOULD PEOPLE BE SURPRISED TO LEARN ABOUT YOU?
I was a darts champion at Kenton Tennis Club! I also helped the club achieve promotion to the Middlesex Premier – playing tennis.

ROMANTIC?
I'm inclined to forget dates.

SCRAPBOOK?
Brother John kept one.

FAVOURITE FILMS?
Shane, a 'cowboy' starring Alan Ladd, *The Godfather* with Marlon Brando, *Taken* with Liam Neeson and *Beaches* with Bette Midler, plus the *Bourne* series with Matt Damon.

FAVOURITE ACTORS?
Michael Crawford, James Cagney, Liam Neeson, Michael Douglas, Kevin Costner, Matt Damon, Bette Midler.

LAST FILM SEEN?
Avatar, science fiction epic I saw re-run on the television.

FAVOURITE TELEVISION PROGRAMME?
Only Fools and Horses, the comedy with David Jason.

POLITICS?
I follow my parents and vote Conservative.

RELIGION?
Church of England. Don't go to church very often but I believe.

Q & A WITH TERRY DYSON

CURRENT AFFAIRS?
Don't think this country is firm enough on immigration.

STATE OF THE COUNTRY?
Depends on what paper you read and who you believe.

WHAT OR WHO MAKES YOU LAUGH?
Comedian Peter Kay, Morecambe and Wise and Tommy Cooper.

WHAT WOULD YOU HAVE BEEN HAD YOU NOT BEEN A PROFESSIONAL FOOTBALLER?
A jockey.

WORST TRAVELLING EXPERIENCE?
To and from South Africa. Couldn't put my feet up. Coming back I thought, 'I'm not having that again' and laid down in the aisle.

FAVOURITE MANAGER?
Have a guess? Yes, you are right – Bill Nicholson. He was so dedicated.

FAVOURITE PLAYER?
Pele.

FAVOURITE MODERN-DAY MANAGER?
Sir Alex Ferguson was until he retired. Jose Mourinho, he has produced plenty of winning teams.

FAVOURITE MODERN-DAY PLAYER?
One of Sergio Aguero and Luis Suarez. So skilled and exciting.

FAVOURITE MODERN-DAY TEAM TO WATCH RATHER THAN SUPPORT?
Don't shout – I like to watch Arsenal.

MUSIC?
The Beatles, the Stones, Dave Clark Five, Il Divo, Take That and Westlife. I saw Westlife at the 02 Arena in London. They were brilliant.

HOBBIES?
Tennis – had to stop playing in 2010 as my knees packed up, golf and horse racing.

FOOD?
Fish and chips down by the seaside.

DRINK?
Vodka and tonic, half a pint of lager.

CAR?
Anything that gets me from A to B.

FAVOURITE SPORTS PERSON OTHER THAN FOOTBALLER?
Golfers Phil Mickelson and Tom Watson. Phil for his ability to hit an unbelievable shot from a bad position. Tom for maintaining a high level at an advanced age. Athlete Mo Farah, sensational in the 2012 Olympics in the 5,000 and 10,000m and followed those efforts up with two more golds at the same distances in the World Championships. I love people who excel.

Terry Dyson
Career Statistics

TOTTENHAM HOTSPUR

1954/55
First Division
19 March: v Sheffield United (h) won 5-0

1955/56
First Division
22 October: v Sunderland (h) lost 2-3
4 February: Newcastle Utd (a) drew 2-2
11 February: Birmingham City (h) lost 0-1

1956/57
First Division
26 December: Everton (a) drew 1-1
29 December: Bolton Wanderers (h) won 4-0 (1)
12 January: Wolverhampton Wanderers (a) lost 0-3
19 January: Aston Villa (h) won 3-0
3 April: Manchester United (a) drew 0-0
13 April: Birmingham City (h) won 5-1 (1)
19 April: Charlton Athletic (away) drew 1-1
20 April: Cardiff City (a) won 3-0 (1)

FA Cup
Third round
5 January: Leicester City (h) won 2-0

1957/58
First Division
14 September: Preston North End (a) lost 1-3
18 September: Birmingham City (h) won 7-1 (1)
21 September: Sheffield Wednesday (h) won 4-2 (1)
28 September: Manchester City (a) lost 1-5
14 December: Blackpool (a) won 2-0
21 December: Chelsea (a) won 4-2
26 December: Wolverhampton Wanderers (h) won 1-0
28 December: Newcastle United (a) drew 3-3
11 January: Burnley (a) lost 0-2
18 January: Preston North End (h) drew 3-3
1 February: Sheffield Wednesday (a) lost 0-2

FA Cup
Third round
4 January: Leicester City (h) won 4-0
Fourth round
25 January: Sheffield United (h) lost 0-3

1958/59
First Division
23 August: Blackpool (h) lost 2-3
27 August: Chelsea (a) lost 2-4
30 August: Blackburn Rovers (a) lost 0-5
6 September: Newcastle United (h) lost 1-3
25 October: Leeds United (h) lost 2-3
1 November: Manchester City (a) lost 1-5
30 March: Aston Villa (a) drew 1-1

1959/60
First Division
14 September: West Ham United (h) drew 2-2
17 October: Sheffield Wednesday (a) lost 1-2
18 April: Chelsea (h) lost 0-1
23 April: Wolverhampton Wanderers (a) won 3-1
30 April: Blackpool (h) won 4-1

CAREER STATISTICS

1960/61

First Division

20 August: Everton (h) won 2-0

22 August: Blackpool (a) won 3-1 (2)

27 August: Blackburn Rovers (a) won 4-1 (1)

31 August: Blackpool (h) won 3-1

3 September: Manchester United (h) won 4-1

7 September: Bolton Wanderers (a) won 2-1

10 September: Arsenal (a) won 3-2 (1)

14 September: Bolton Wanderers (h) won 3-1

17 September: Leicester City (a) won 2-1

24 September: Aston Villa (h) won 6-2 (1)

1 October: Wolverhampton Wanderers (a) won 4-0 (1)

10 October: Manchester City (h) drew 1-1

15 October: Nottingham Forest (a) won 4-0

29 October: Newcastle United (a) won 4-3

2 November: Cardiff City (h) won 3-2 (1)

5 November: Fulham (h) won 5-1

12 November: Sheffield Wednesday (a) lost 1-2

19 November: Birmingham City (h) won 6-0 (2)

26 November: West Bromwich Albion (a) won 3-1

3 December: Burnley (h) drew 4-4

10 December: Preston North End (a) won 1-0

17 December: Everton (a) won 3-1

24 December: West Ham United (h) won 2-0 (1)

26 December: West Ham United (a) won 3-0

31 December: Blackburn Rovers (h) won 5-2

16 January: Manchester United (a) lost 0-2

21 January: Arsenal (h) won 4-2

4 February: Leicester City (h) lost 2-3

11 February: Aston Villa (a) won 2-1 (1)

22 February: Wolverhampton Wanderers (h) drew 1-1

25 February: Manchester City (a) won 1-0

11 March: Cardiff City (a) lost 2-3 (1)

22 March: Newcastle United (h) lost 1-2

25 March: Fulham (a) drew 0-0

31 March: Chelsea (h) won 4-2

8 April: Birmingham City (a) won 3-2

17 April: Sheffield Wednesday (h) won 2-1

22 April: Burnley (a) lost 2-4

26 April: Nottingham Forest (h) won 1-0

29 April: West Bromwich Albion (h) lost 1-2

FA Cup
Third round
7 January: Charlton Athletic (h) won 2-0 (1)
Fourth round
28 January: Crewe Alexandra (h) won 5-1 (1)
Fifth round
18 February: Aston Villa (a) won 2-0
Sixth round
4 March: Sunderland (a) drew 1-1
Sixth round replay
8 March: Sunderland (h) won 5-0 (2)
Semi-final
18 March: Burnley (Villa Park) won 3-0
Final
6 May: Leicester City (Wembley) won 2-0 (1)

1961/62
First Division
19 August: Blackpool (a) won 2-1
23 August: West Ham United (h) drew 2-2 (2)
26 August: Arsenal (h) won 4-3 (3)
28 August: West Ham United (a) lost 1-2
2 September: Cardiff City (h) won 3-2
4 September: Sheffield United (a) drew 1-1
9 September: Manchester United (a) lost 0-1
16 September: Wolverhampton Wanderers (h) won 1-0
23 September: Nottingham Forest (a) lost 0-2
30 September: Aston Villa (h) won 1-0 (1)
9 October: Bolton Wanderers (a) won 2-1
14 October: Manchester City (h) won 2-0
21 October: Ipswich Town (a) lost 2-3
28 October: Burnley (h) won 4-2
4 November: Everton (a) lost 0-3
11 November: Fulham (h) won 4-2
18 November: Sheffield Wednesday (a) drew 0-0
25 November: Leicester City (h) lost 1-2
20 January: Manchester United (h) drew 2-2
21 February: Aston Villa (a) drew 0-0
24 February: Bolton Wanderers (h) drew 2-2
30 April: Leicester City (a) won 3-2

European Cup
Preliminary round
First leg
13 September: Gornik Zabrze (a) lost 2-4 (1)
Second leg
20 September: Gornik Zabrze (h) won 8-1 (1)
First round
First leg
1 November: Feyenoord (a) won 3-1 (1)
Second leg
15 November: Feyenoord (h) drew 1-1 (1)

1962/63
First Division
15 September: Blackburn Rovers (h) won 4-1
19 September: Wolverhampton Wanderers (a) drew 2-2
3 November: Leicester City (h) won 4-0
17 November: Sheffield Wednesday (h) drew 1-1
12 April: Liverpool (a) lost 2-3 (1)
13 April: Fulham (h) drew 1-1
15 April: Liverpool (h) won 7-2
20 April: Everton (a) lost 0-1
27 April: Bolton Wanderers (h) won 4-1
4 May: Sheffield United (h) won 4-2 (1)
11 May: Manchester City (a) lost 0-1
18 May: Nottingham Forest (a) drew 1-1
20 May: Blackburn Rovers (a) lost 0-3

FA Cup
Third round
16 January: Burnley (h) lost 0-3

European Cup Winners' Cup
Semi-final
First leg
24 April: OFK Belgrade (a) won 2-1 (1)
Second leg
1 May: OFK Belgrade (h) won 3-1
Final
15 May: Atletico Madrid (Rotterdam) won 5-1 (2)

1963/64

First Division

24 August: Stoke City (a) lost 1-2

28 August: Wolverhampton Wanderers (a) won 4-1

31 August: Nottingham Forest (h) won 4-1

4 September: Wolverhampton Wanderers (h) won 4-3 (2)

7 September: Blackburn Rovers (a) lost 2-7

14 September: Blackpool (h) won 6-1

16 September: Aston Villa (a) won 4-2 (1)

21 September: Chelsea (a) won 3-0

28 September: West Ham United (h) won 3-0

2 October: Birmingham City (h) won 6-1 (1)

5 October: Sheffield United (a) drew 3-3 (1)

15 October: Arsenal (a) drew 4-4

19 October: Leicester City (h) drew 1-1

26 October: Everton (a) lost 0-1

2 November: Fulham (h) won 1-0

9 November: Manchester United (a) lost 1-4

16 November: Burnley (h) won 3-2

23 November: Ipswich Town (a) won 3-2 (2)

30 November: Sheffield Wednesday (h) drew 1-1

7 December: Bolton Wanderers (a) won 3-1 (1)

14 December: Stoke City (home) won 2-1

21 December: Nottingham Forest (a) won 2-1

26 December: West Bromwich Albion (a) drew 4-4

28 December: West Bromwich Albion (h) lost 0-2

11 January: Blackburn Rovers (h) won 4-1 (1)

18 January: Blackpool (a) won 2-0

25 January: Aston Villa (h) won 3-1 (1)

1 February: Chelsea (h) lost 1-2

4 February: West Ham United (a) lost 0-4

15 February: Sheffield United (h) drew 0-0

22 February: Arsenal (h) won 3-1

29 February: Birmingham City (a) won 2-1

7 March: Everton (h) lost 2-4 (1)

21 March: Manchester United (h) lost 2-3

27 March: Liverpool (h) lost 1-3

28 March: Fulham (a) drew 1-1

18 April: Bolton Wanderers (h) won 1-0

21 April: Burnley (a) lost 2-7

25 April: Leicester City (a) won 1-0

FA Cup
Third round
4 January: Chelsea (h) drew 1-1 (1)
Third round replay
8 January: Chelsea (a) lost 0-2

European Cup Winners' Cup
First round
First leg
3 December: Manchester United (h) won 2-0 (1)
Second leg
10 December: Manchester United (a) lost 1-4

1964/65
First Division
22 August: Sheffield United (h) won 2-0
25 August: Burnley (a) drew 2-2
29 August: Everton (a) lost 1-4
2 September: Burnley (h) won 3-1 (1)
5 September: Birmingham City (h) won 4-1 (1)
9 September: Stoke City (a) lost 0-2
12 September: West Ham United (a) lost 2-3
16 September: Stoke City (h) won 2-1
19 September: West Bromwich Albion (h) won 1-0
26 September: Manchester United (a) lost 1-4
28 September: Blackpool (a) drew 1-1
5 October: Fulham (h) won 3-0
10 October: Arsenal (h) won 3-1
17 October: Leeds United (a) lost 1-3
24 October: Chelsea (h) drew 1-1
31 October: Leicester City (a) lost 2-4
7 November: Sunderland (h) won 3-0
21 November: Aston Villa (h) won 4-0 (1)
28 November: Liverpool (a) drew 1-1
5 December: Sheffield Wednesday (h) won 3-2
12 December: Sheffield United (a) drew 3-3
19 December: Everton (h) drew 2-2
26 December: Nottingham Forest (a) won 2-1
28 December: Nottingham Forest (h) won 4-0
2 January: Birmingham City (a) lost 0-1
16 January: West Ham United (h) won 3-2 (1)
23 January: West Bromwich Albion (a) lost 0-2

6 February: Manchester United (h) won 1-0
13 February: Fulham (a) lost 1-4
10 March: Chelsea (a) lost 1-3
13 March: Blackpool (h) won 4-1
20 March: Sunderland (a) lost 1-2

FA Cup
Third round
9 January: Torquay United (a) drew 3-3
Third round replay
18 January: Torquay United (h) won 5-1
Fourth round
30 January: Ipswich Town (h) won 5-0

FULHAM

1965/66
First Division
21 August: Blackpool (a) drew 2-2
25 August: Blackburn Rovers (h) won 5-2
28 August: Chelsea (h) lost 0-3
1 September: Blackburn Rovers (a) lost 2-3
4 September: Tottenham Hotspur (h) lost 0-2
8 September: Sheffield United (h) drew 0-0
11 September: Liverpool (a) lost 1-2
15 September: Sheffield United (a) lost 0-2
18 September: Aston Villa (h) lost 3-6
25 September: Sunderland (a) drew 2-2
2 October: West Ham United (h) won 3-0
9 October: Arsenal (a) lost 1-2 (1)
16 October: Everton (h) won 3-2 (1)
23 October: Manchester United (a) lost 1-4
30 October: Newcastle United (h) won 2-0
6 November: West Bromwich Albion (a) lost 2-6
13 November: Nottingham Forest (h) drew 1-1
20 November: Sheffield Wednesday (a) lost 0-1
27 November: Northampton Town (a) lost 1-4 *
18 December: Everton (a) lost 0-2
28 December: Leicester City (a) lost 0-1
25 January: Burnley (a) lost 0-1

FA Cup
Third round
22 January: Sheffield United (a) lost 1-3

League Cup
Second round
22 September: Wrexham (a) won 2-1 (1)
Third round
13 October: Northampton Town (h) won 5-0 (2)
Fourth round
3 November: Aston Villa (h) drew 1-1
Fourth round replay
8 November: Aston Villa (a) lost 0-2

1966/67
First Division
19 November: Arsenal (a) lost 0-1 **
8 April: Aston Villa (a) drew 1-1 **
19 April: Arsenal (h) drew 0-0 *
22 April: Manchester City (a) lost 0-0 **

1967/68
First Division
16 December: Wolverhampton Wanderers (a) lost 2-3 **

COLCHESTER UNITED

1968/69
Fourth Division
24 August: Chester (a) lost 1-5
26 August: Scunthorpe United (h) lost 0-4 *
31 August: Doncaster Rovers (h) lost 1-2
14 September: Bradford City (a) drew 1-1
16 September: Chesterfield (a) won 2-0
20 September: Port Vale (h) won 1-0
28 September: Exeter City (a) drew 1-1
4 October: Grimsby Town (h) won 2-1
8 October: Scunthorpe United (a) won 3-2
12 October: Newport County (a) lost 0-1
19 October: Darlington (h) drew 0-0
26 October: Lincoln City (a) won 3-0
2 November: Wrexham (h) won 2-1
4 November: Workington (h) won 3-0
9 November: Bradford Park Avenue (a) lost 1-2
23 November: Swansea Town (a) lost 0-2
29 November: Southend United (h) won 4-0 (1 pen)
14 December: Newport County (h) won 2-1
26 December: Grimsby Town (a) won 4-2
11 January: Wrexham (a) won 3-0
18 January: Bradford Park Avenue (h) won 3-0 (1 pen)
24 January: Workington (a) won 1-0
1 February: Aldershot Town (a) won 2-1 (1)
14 February: Southend United (a) lost 1-3
22 February: Notts Co (h) drew 1-1
28 February: Brentford (h) won 2-1
4 March: Halifax Town (a) lost 1-2
8 March: Rochdale (a) lost 0-4
10 March: Aldershot (h) won 2-0
14 March: Chester City (h) drew 1-1
22 March: Doncaster Rovers (a) lost 0-1
29 March: York City (a) lost 0-2
4 April: Chesterfield (h) won 1-0
5 April: Exeter City (h) won 1-0
8 April: Peterborough United (a) won 1-0
12 April: Port Vale (a) drew 0-0
14 April: Peterborough United (h) drew 2-2
18 April: Bradford City (h) drew 1-1
25 April: Swansea Town (h) lost 0-1

28 April: Darlington (a) drew 1-1
2 May: Notts Co (a) lost 0-2

FA Cup
First round
16 November: Chesham United (h) won 5-0
Second round
7 December: Exeter City (h) lost 1-2

1969/70
Fourth Division
11 October: Bradford Park Avenue (h) won 2-1 *
18 October: York City (a) lost 2-4
1 November: Aldershot Town (a) drew 1-1
8 November: Southend United (h) lost 0-2 *
22 November: Grimsby Town (h) won 3-2
25 November: Northampton Town (a) drew 1-1
13 December: Crewe Alexandra (a) won 1-0
20 December: Darlington (h) won 2-1
26 December: Notts Co (h) won 2-1
10 January: Hartlepool (h) drew 1-1
27 March: Aldershot (h) won 3-1
28 March: Exeter City (h) won 2-1
1 April: Chester City (a) lost 0-1
25 April: Port Vale (a) drew 1-1 (1)
28 April: Grimsby Town (a) lost 3-5

* Played as substitute ** Unused substitute ( ) Goals scored

Appearance And Goals Breakdown

Tottenham Hotspur

1954/55

	Appearances	Goals
First Division	1	0
FA Cup	0	0
Total	1	0

1955/56

	Appearances	Goals
First Division	3	0
FA Cup	0	0
Total	3	0

1956/57

	Appearances	Goals
First Division	8	3
FA Cup	1	0
Total	9	3

1957/58

	Appearances	Goals
First Division	12	2
FA Cup	2	0
Total	14	2

1958/59

	Appearances	Goals
First Division	7	0
FA Cup	0	0
Total	7	0

SPURS' UNSUNG HERO

1959/60

	Appearances	Goals
First Division	6	0
FA Cup	0	0
Total	6	0

1960/61

	Appearances	Goals
First Division	40	12
FA Cup	7	5
Total	47	17

1961/62

	Appearances	Goals
First Division	23	6
FA Cup	0	0
European Cup	4	4
Total	27	10

1962/63

	Appearances	Goals
First Division	13	2
FA Cup	1	0
European CWC	3	3
Total	17	5

1963/64

	Appearances	Goals
First Division	39	11
FA Cup	2	1
European CWC	2	2
Total	43	14

1964/65

	Appearances	Goals
First Division	32	5
FA Cup	3	0
Total	35	5

Total for Spurs

	Appearances	Goals
First Division	184	41
FA Cup	16	6
Europe	9	8
Others	35	13
Total	244	68

Fulham

1965/66

	Appearances	Goals
First Division	22	2
FA Cup	1	0
League Cup	4	3
Total	27	5

1966/67

	Appearances	Goals
First Division	1	0
FA Cup	0	0
League Cup	0	0
Total	1	0

Total for Fulham

	Appearances	Goals
First Division	23	2
FA Cup	1	0
League Cup	4	3
Total	28	5

Colchester United

1968/69

	Appearances	Goals
Fourth Division	41	3
FA Cup	2	0
League Cup	0	0
Total	43	3

1969/70

	Appearances	Goals
Fourth Division	15	1
FA Cup	0	0
League Cup	0	0
Total	15	1

Total for Colchester

	Appearances	Goals
Fourth Division	56	4
FA Cup	2	0
League Cup	0	0
Total	58	4

CAREER TOTAL

Appearances	Goals
330	77

Terry also appeared in non-league for Guildford City, Wealdstone and Dagenham.

Compiled by Bill Pierce